In the Memory of the Map

sightline books

The Iowa Series in Literary Nonfiction

Patricia Hampl & Carl H. Klaus, series editors

Christopher Norment
In the Memory of the Map

A Cartographic Memoir

University of Iowa Press, Iowa City

University of Iowa Press, Iowa City 52242
Copyright © 2012 by Christopher Norment
www.uiowapress.org
Printed in the United States of America
Text design by Richard Hendel

The University of Iowa Press is a member of
Green Press Initiative and is committed to
preserving natural resources.
Printed on acid-free paper

Library of Congress
Cataloging-in-Publication Data
Norment, Christopher.
In the memory of the map: a cartographic memoir /
by Christopher Norment.
    p.   cm.—(Sightline Books: The Iowa series in
literary nonfiction)
Includes bibliographical references.
ISBN-13: 978-1-60938-077-9 (pbk.)
ISBN-10: 1-60938-077-0 (pbk.)
ISBN-13: 978-1-60938-096-0 (ebook)
ISBN-10: 1-60938-096-7 (ebook)
1. Cartography—Philosophy.   2. Cartography—
Methodology.   3. Map reading.   4. Maps—
Symbols.   I. Title.
GA102.3.N67 2011   2011035853
526—dc23

"You write it down, because/stories and maps are the same."
RALPH BLACK, "21st Century Lecture"

Contents

Introduction

Late March in western New York: currents of snow drift from a gray sky, eddy around the edge of Lennon Hall, drift across the soggy, salt-edged campus lawns. A hard wind spills out of the west, throws the hesitant spring into open retreat. The first flowers of the year — a coltsfoot at the edge of the local woodlot, a dwarf alpine mustard in my garden — seem like lost souls. The wind and snow push me, too, deeper into winter and the academic year. I am restless and find it difficult to focus on the papers that I should be grading. After reading the same incoherent sentence three times, and finding little meaning in the student's words, I drop my pen and walk down the hall to my lab. I open a cabinet drawer, search through the alphabetized "California" file, and pull out a 15-minute topographic map of Mount Whitney, California. I unfold the map on the lab bench, note the thick blue scatter of crystalline lakes, the deep, scimitar-shaped bowls of alpine cirques, the passes and peaks of promise, the names that drew me deep into the high country so many years ago, as they still do today: Lake South America, Crabtree Meadow, Milestone Basin, Chagoopa Plateau, Bubbs Creek, Milly's Foot Pass. The names flow on and on, like the mountains themselves, and all of those names, all of that promise, all of those mountains, come drifting back to me, and once again it is spring. But the map has an edge. The contour lines, streams, and trails run their course and then disappear into the frame of the map. They vanish into blankness as the world of information abruptly gives way to *terra incognita*. Beyond knowledge there is uncertainty, even if the antidote to this uncertainty may be held by adjacent maps. Or perhaps the map's border is not the edge of the known world; instead it is the matte upon which the map is mounted, the canvas against which I read and imagine it. Perhaps the wash of white that surrounds the map also serves as the setting for my desire; this potent mix of history and inclination, possibility and promise, action and reaction, is the context for my love of maps, and what they represent for me.

With its own spare aesthetic and utilitarian purpose the Mount Whitney map is, to my eye, beautiful — not, as the aviatrix Beryl Markham wrote about maps, "cold . . . humourless and dull." It depicts space with the sinuous flow of contour lines, an amalgam of signs representing lake and stream, peak and valley, road and trail, and anchors this geography to lines of latitude and longitude. The map also is a potent symbol — not in the sense of those postmodernist geographers who view maps as "texts" to be deconstructed, but as triggers of memory, representations of a life spent exploring the wild lands of the West and North. But there is more to it than this. I understand enough about my life to believe that while maps have promised me access to a world of wonders, to the burnt and hardscrabble desert ranges of the Mojave Desert, the clean and empty alpine cirques of the Sierra — to situations and experiences that were, in the fullness of the word's meaning, good — there sometimes was an edge to this promise, a hint of other, more complicated agendas. For maps also may represent a way out of one's current situation, a currency that involves the exchange of one life, with its failures and undertones of anguish and anxiety, for the seductive possibilities of another, more transient and distracting existence. Maps, and the movement they promise, may take you toward someplace that pleases and heals, while simultaneously spiriting you away from family and those who need you, and perhaps from the fears you need to face. Of course, when we trace some imagined and tempting route on the map before us, and then fall into movement, we also may become, briefly, less burdened and more open to the world. It may be as Richard Hugo has it: "when we drove down that hill / and flared out on that empty prairie, home seemed / less ashamed of us" — or perhaps, we of home.

I turn toward my bookshelf, note the titles: *A Map of the World, The Insufficiency of Maps, Disappearances: A Map, Maps of the Imagination, Without a Map, The Power of Maps, Fathering the Map.* The books are a hodgepodge of fiction and nonfiction, prose and poetry, scholarly and creative works, much like the ideas that have found their way into this book. What I am aiming for is an examination of the role of maps in my life, and by extension, in the lives of others. *In the Memory of the*

Map is a "cartographical psychology," a combination of personal history, the scholarship of others, and mythology — a dialogue with desire and the maps of my life, an exploration of their pleasures, utilitarian purposes, benefits, and character. Memoir is the matrix in which I embed an exploration of how maps function in our lives. Hopefully, it is not the other way around: maps are the matrix, and I am the focus of the analysis. What's most important is the map, and by making my analysis personal, I hope to draw readers more fully into their aesthetics, mystery, function, power, and shortcomings, and into a consideration of the role that maps play in their lives.

In the Memory of the Map is arranged as a series of triptychs — three sections of three chapters each. "First Maps" investigates experiences related to the maps I discovered between the ages of eight and eighteen, when I was growing up in the Santa Clara Valley and Santa Cruz Mountains of California. "Middle Maps" explores the maps I encountered during my undergraduate years and into my early thirties, by which time I was married and had finished my master's degree in zoology at Washington State University. The final section describes maps and experiences extending from my early years as a parent until the recent past. Each chapter is built around a map, one which I used extensively and epitomizes the main theme of the chapter. The book ends with a chapter describing a "trip without a map" that I took with a friend in July 2007. This thirteen-day backpacking trip in Washington's Pasayten Wilderness was an experiment and exploration, a cost-benefit analysis of the ways in which maps may both bind and blind us to the world, expand the compass of our experience as well as dampen the swing of its needle. In the Pasayten I sought an adventure as much emotional and intellectual as physical, a counterpoint to the mapped journeys that I usually take — although such a mapless journey, taken in my middle age, may also be seen as metaphor, and may have possessed a subconscious logic and dynamic that at the time were not apparent to me.

Maps are solid things. They depict particular pieces of geography, suggest where to travel, position us in space. But they may also tell us much more — sometimes with a deafening shout, sometimes with the softest of whispers. Maps may induce in us the kind of feeling that I had when I saw an exhibit of Craig Barber's black-and-white photographs of Vietnam's landscape and villages. His sixteen-inch by twenty-four-inch platinum prints, many displayed as diptychs or triptychs, were as large and luminous as any Ansel Adams photograph, yet all of them were taken with a large-format pinhole camera that lacked a viewfinder and lens. Because the negatives had such long exposures—a few seconds to several minutes or more—Barber's photographs possessed none of the knife-sharp detail of the f/64 school; most of the images were slightly out of focus and seemed almost as far away from Adams's aesthetic as Saigon is from Yosemite Valley. Each had the brown tones and melancholy softness of a nineteenth-century photograph. There was an ethereal quality to the rice paddies, village lanes, temples and bamboo groves, which seemed to float, suspended, in humid heat and tropical light. The photographs were almost devoid of people—or if any were present, their features were blurred and indistinct, a function, too, of long exposure times. A curious and powerful effect was that although there were no people in most of the photographs, they were *everywhere*—ghosts hidden behind a brick wall or in that copse of trees, or gazing out at Barber from the stained darkness of a hut. Most often, though, it was as if the observers were standing just beyond the edge of the image, watching as he set up his tripod and camera—or more precisely, as if they were Marine riflemen on patrol, moving with him through the desultory heat and strangely empty villages, fear and tension thick in their mouths, M-16s with safeties off, the crackle of static on a military radio. Barber served as a combat soldier in Vietnam, and I had the distinct sense that, while looking at the photographs, I was gazing directly into his memory. Its details, edges and junctures were rendered slightly indistinct by the passage of time, yet still possessed of a potent and demanding immediacy. But what touched me as much as the images themselves were their titles: "We Were Each Questioning," "Some Days It Just Felt Relentless," "The Past Will Haunt Us Forever," "Slowly the Future Comes into Focus," "Peace Is Forever Fragile."

And so the maps of my life are much like Barber's photographs: they are conduits to, and expressions of, memory. They may lack the fuzzy, slightly out-of-focus quality of his platinum prints, but in the same way they draw me deeply into the past. When I look at a Chevron road map of California, circa 1966, or a 15-minute topographic map of Cedar Mesa, Utah, I am pulled into another time and place.

I can sense the excitement of a fragile, fourteen-year-old boy as he crossed the smog-laden San Joaquin Valley, headed for his first hike in the Sierra or, thirty years later, feel the warm grit of sandstone beneath my sunburned leg as I sprawled on an outcrop of rough rock somewhere deep in the slickrock country, the Bear's Ears standing on the horizon, etching that wonderful sweep of distance. And so I have borrowed from Craig Barber, and given a title to the map that accompanies each chapter—maps which rise out of my past like the fault-block ranges that thrust from the great basins of the Intermountain West, maps which carry their own, solid presence as well as the enigmas of the past, maps which "point us toward a world we might know," as well as toward another world, the one we once knew.

I believe—desire to believe—that the air is full of maps, the very earth alive with them. I sense their presence everywhere, in the wash of my own history, in the lives of others. I hear them in the thin songs of migrating blackpoll warblers that drift through the late May maples, songs given out on some glorious morning by birds on their way north from Central America to their boreal breeding grounds. I touch them when I run my hand over a piece of water-smoothed Redwall Limestone somewhere deep in the Grand Canyon and feel the faint impression of a three-hundred-and-forty-million-year-old nautiloid, suspended in the deepest well of time. I smell them in the rich and acrid odor of buckbrush and laurel, chinquapin and manzanita, which rise from the sun-pounded California chaparral, and in the memory of how the scent of baby shampoo lingered in the hair of my young son and daughter after their evening baths. I taste them in a spoonful of curried rice and lentils, taken somewhere deep within the Barren Lands of northern Canada, at the edge of some arctic lake, wind-driven surf slapping against the shore. I see them in the forty-eight-year-old scar that slices across the veins on the back of my right hand, a relic of an intersection between a young boy and a shovel along a sycamore-lined creek in the Santa Clara Valley. These maps are with me always. They trace the path of my days, point toward possible futures, carry me out of the past and into the present. They are as much a matter of neuron and neurotransmitter as ink and paper. And so I unfold the maps of my life and plot my meandering course: a cartography of memory and intellect, dream and desire. It's what I have, this way through the world.

First Maps

The Past Is Always with Me

As a small boy, living in Saratoga, California, with my mother, stepfather, and younger sister, I spent as much time outside as possible and even now, more than four decades later, my memories of the landscape are vivid, in contrast to what little I recall of my home's interior. The layout of the house's rooms, its furniture and ambience, mostly remain a mystery. I must have shut most of these memories away, for that house is where I was first molested by my stepfather — a wrenching, tectonic event that led me to seek refuge in the comforting world that surrounded my home. We lived in the midst of a plum orchard in the Santa Clara Valley, which in 1960 was an agricultural paradise being quickly and inexorably inundated by a tsunami of urban and suburban sprawl. The plum and apricot orchards and truck gardens were metamorphosing into tract homes and shopping centers, but at the time the land still offered up a world of possibilities, one where kids could roam freely in what I now recall, undoubtedly falsely, as an endless succession of mild days. And so I wandered. I kept my distance from the white stucco house with its red tile roof, and turned toward the waiting world. And as I wandered I encountered my first map — not one of paper and ink, but one that I constructed myself, a cartography of taste and touch and smell, a mental representation of the physical world in which I sought my home, my place — what developmental psychologists and cultural geographers call a cognitive map.

Although I belonged to that class of preadolescent children who exhibit maximal ranging habits — fourth- and fifth-grade boys with bicycles and parental permission to roam freely ("Just be home by six for dinner.") — most of my time outside was spent in a relatively small area, centered on the plum orchard and bounded by the two

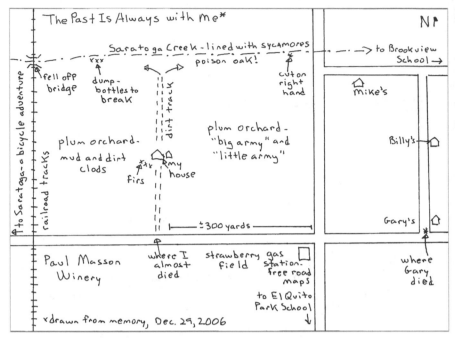

The Past Is Always with me*

Saratoga Creek - lined with sycamores

← to Saratoga - a bicycle adventure

railroad tracks

fell off bridge

dump - bottles to break

poison oak!

cut on right hand

plum orchard.

mud and dirt clods

Firs

my house

plum orchard - "big army" and "little army"

—— ±300 yards ——

Paul Masson Winery

where I almost died

strawberry field

gas station-free road maps

to El Quito Park School ↓

Mike's

Billy's

Gary's

where Gary died

—. —.→ to Brookview School →

N↑

*drawn from memory, Dec. 29, 2006

Chris's memory map of Saratoga, circa 1960.

lanes of Saratoga Avenue to the southeast, railroad tracks to the southwest, Saratoga Creek to the northwest, and the first few blocks of a subdivision to the northeast, where my friends Mike, Billy and Gary lived. Except for trips to and from school—in second and third grades El Quito Park Elementary, in fourth and fifth grades the newly constructed Brookview School, about three quarters of a mile to the northeast—I spent most of my nonschool waking hours within this home range, which my memory estimates as being no more than three hundred yards by eight hundred yards in size. Within this space, and even beyond its informal boundaries, we wandered freely, with little direct supervision, our parents being of a generation less burdened by fears for their children's safety than are many parents today—less concerned about physical danger, sexual predators (the irony here is obvious), kidnappers, and children who disappear into the void.

The world my friends and I inhabited was what Rachel and Stephen Kaplan call "nearby nature," and its locus was the cobbled necklace of sand and rock that traced Saratoga Creek. There, in the gray gravel, we built an endless succession of dams and watched caddis fly

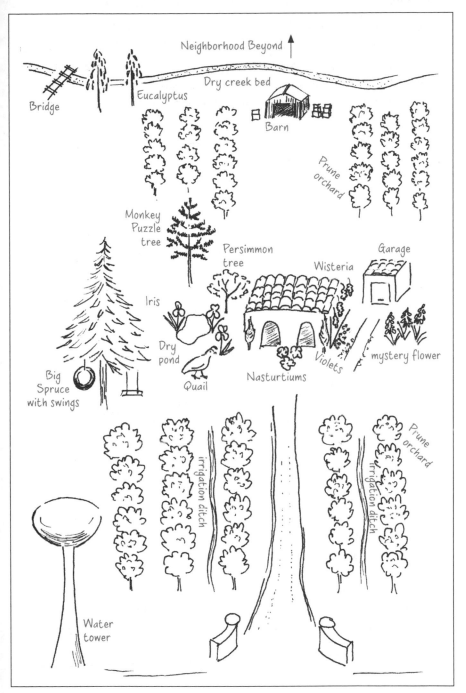

Lisa's memory map of Saratoga, circa 1960.

larvae haul their debris-encrusted shelters across the bottom of the intermittent pools that lined the streambed. Along the creek's banks were stands of willow, cottonwood and California sycamore, riparian refugees from the surrounding, semi-arid landscape. The sycamores, in particular, offered a wealth of amusement for my friends and me. We climbed and scrambled amongst their tangled trunks, built ramshackle shelters beneath their branches, picked apart the mottled plates of the picture-puzzle bark, and tossed the prickly, spherical fruiting heads at each other. Among the sycamores were thickets of poison oak, which turned from bright green to brilliant red during the course of the year. We all had been warned to assiduously avoid the stuff, but of course we didn't always do so, and my friends often wore pink, crusty badges of calamine lotion on their arms and faces. Thankfully, I didn't react to poison oak. I paid no penalty for my trespasses and instead took false pride in my immunity, perhaps my first flirtation with hubris. And scattered among the sycamores and patches of poison oak, along the steeply sloped margins of the creek, were small dumps where we salvaged old Gallo wine bottles for target practice with BB guns, rocks and dirt clods, an expression of our young males' fascination with breaking things.

Surrounding the house was the orchard of Italian plum trees, with their egg-shaped, bluish-purple fruits, which when dried were transformed into the prunes that my friends and I detested. But any plums that escaped the migrant workers' hands were great for fights once they ripened sufficiently, although by then they also drew the bees and wasps that we feared with irrational fervor. Each knobby plum tree was ringed with a garland of a yellow-flowered herb we called "sourgrass"—most likely the exotic *Oxalis pes-caprae*, sometimes known as Bermuda buttercup—that we picked by the handfuls and chewed for the tart flavor, thereby receiving our minimum daily requirements of oxalic acid (I wonder if any of my friends are plagued with kidney stones in their middle age) and the pesticide *du jour*. Amongst the trees was the glorious dirt, which under the proper moisture conditions was transformed either into viscous mud, grand for filthy wallowing, or into chunks with just the right heft for tossing at each other whenever impending testosterone poisoning induced the urge for a good dirt-clod fight. And immediately behind the house was a persimmon tree, which produced inedible fruits—at least as far as I was concerned—and in the fall, more weapons for further battles.

It seemed, then, that we were always moving, always fighting—not in anger, but in the generally good-natured way in which little boys usually tussle, yet also with the incipient spirit of aggression that in eight to ten years would help lead many young men of my generation into the rice paddies and jungles of southeast Asia. We roamed the orchard, streambed, nearby suburban streets, and railroad right-of-way, digging in the dirt, breaking bottles, and constructing forts of various sizes, which were suitable for either "little army," which we played with small, olive-drab plastic toy soldiers, or "big army," in which we became the olive-drab soldiers, outfitted with plastic submachine guns, canteens, and helmets, again in the manner of young boys practicing for bigger and far more serious things. Still, we were mostly outside, away from television and parents, certain enough in our navigation and orientation, dodging amongst the plum trees or on our hands and knees next to a creek-water pool, the distant sound of traffic from Saratoga Avenue drifting through the brilliant air of the occasional rain-washed, vernal day or the smoky, smog-ridden autumnal light that dominated the sky before the first winter storms blew in off the Pacific Ocean.

And scattered across the surface of my cognitive map was a profusion of landmarks: the nearby strawberry field, across Saratoga Avenue, where there always seemed to be several Japanese-American workers bent over their crop; the thick copse of trees along the creek, where we would build our forts; the low railroad bridge, where I once (accidentally) threw myself into the creekbed as I tossed a rock at the opposing abutment, spraining my ankle and foreshadowing my abysmal high school athletic career; the pool below a road bridge to the east of my house, where Mike split open the back of my hand with a rusty shovel while we dug in the gravel. And in the nearby subdivision, Mike's backyard, with its tree fort and its sandbox full of the bright-yellow Tonka trucks that I lusted after because my parents could not afford them. Billy's house was around the corner from Mike's; his parents often fought, but my friends and I were awed by the sporty turquoise Thunderbird sheltered in the garage. A bit farther down the same street was Gary's house, with a thick grove of bamboo in the backyard, ideal for games of "big army" and hide-and-seek. And just beyond the front yard was the corner where, in his tenth year, Gary was hit and killed by a truck. (The inarticulate, yawning blackness and blankness flushed through me when the news came and I stood silently holding the phone.) Finally, the school bus stop at the end of our driveway on Saratoga Avenue, where in my ninth year I came within a second and foot or two of foreshadowing Gary's fate when I disobeyed the school bus driver and sprinted into the path of an approaching car—almost instantaneously aware of my mistake and shutting my eyes as my world collapsed into a loud screech of tires as I veered away from the impending impact and felt the car's grille come to rest, ever so gently, against my outstretched hand. And afterward, having so recently touched the edge of annihilation, my tears, nausea and shaking body as the bus driver screamed at me for my stupidity, as well she should have. But whatever the joys and terrors of our physical world, my friends and I understood our space and navigated confidently through it.

Psychologists and geographers interested in children's use of space and development of cognitive mapping abilities have, in the manner of academics, divided themselves into competing schools. There are the "constructivists," intellectual descendants of Jean Piaget, who view children's spatial awareness as progressing through a series of rather distinct stages until they reach a "formal operational stage" at ages twelve and beyond, in which complex spatial relationships between objects, as defined by proximity, order, separation, and enclosure, are fully developed. According to the constructivists, until children reach this stage they are not fully capable of using spatial images (maps) that entail what the landscape theorist John Jackle has referred to as "unreal transformations." Opposed to the constructivists are the "incrementalists," who argue that an innate and relatively sophisticated ability to comprehend spatial relationships exists even in young children, and that cognitive mapping ability "opens up" with experience rather than following a strict pattern of sequential development. If my memory is correct—and I have an innate suspicion of long-term memory—my eight- to ten-year-old friends and I were fairly sophisticated in our use and understanding of space. Young incrementalists that we were, we learned about and used the local geography in rich and complex ways. Within our world we knew where we were and where we were going, and if some researcher had asked us to map our surroundings, we would have obliged him or her with a detailed drawing of our home range.

In *Topophilia*, the cultural geographer Yi-Fu Tuan writes,

"Landscape" is not a meaningful word to a young child. To see the landscape requires, first of all, the ability to make the sharp distinction between self and others. . . . Then, to see the landscape and evaluate it aesthetically one needs to be able to identify an unbounded segment of nature and to be aware of its spatial characteristics. . . . Though the landscape escapes the young child, he is intensely aware of its separate components: a tree stump, large boulder, bubbling water in a section of a stream. As the child grows older his awareness of spatial relations gains at the expense of the quiddity of the objects that define them. . . . The young child's world, then, is animated and consists of vivid, sharply delineated objects in a weakly structured space.

When I first read the above passage, I wondered if the 1960s-era landscape of Saratoga did "escape" my friends and me. Although by "young child" Tuan meant a six- or seven-year-old, and he was concerned with the development of an aesthetic concept of landscape, which he defined as "a prospect seen from a specific standpoint," my eight- to ten-year-old friends and I did have a detailed and accurate understanding of our space. Through our endless and often aimless wanderings, we created sensory and cognitive maps, constructed from the intricate details of our experiences. We were young cartographers, directly engaged with the elements of our world and mapping their structure and arrangement. Perhaps the landscape of our youth was closer to the definition proposed by the British geographer Denis Cosgrove—"the external world mediated through subjective human experience"—but what most distinguished the landscape of my childhood from Tuan's concept was its spatial scale. I don't believe that our landscape was "weakly structured," but it was almost entirely local. For example, my house was only about two miles northeast of the center of Saratoga. Just beyond the town were the oak- and chaparral-clad hills of the Santa Cruz Mountains, which rise more than twenty-five hundred feet above the valley, and about twenty miles to the east were the higher, more distant peaks of the Coast Range. Both ranges must have been visible from my house, at least on those days when the smog wasn't thick, yet I have absolutely no memory of this; it was as if I lived on a wide swath of prairie, not in a broad valley cradled by mountains.

Our focus on the local environment was a function of both the dimensions of our habitual range and the tendency of children to concentrate on their immediate surroundings and ignore the more distant world. Gary Paul Nabhan has remarked on this behavior in his children, who explored the natural world "on their hands and knees, engaged in what was immediately before them," while adults were "scanning the land for picturesque panoramas and scenic overlooks." For the most part my friends and I restricted our daily movements and explorations to an area of less than one square mile. My lone long-distance bicycle excursion, a two-mile pedal to the center of Saratoga with a friend, was an exotic and grand adventure into what seemed like *terra incognita*, even though our parents drove us there often and the route was an uncomplicated ride down Saratoga Avenue. After eating lunch in the center of the village we quickly returned home, feeling just about as adventurous as I would during my first explorations of the Sierra Nevada wilderness five years later.

Forty-five years after we moved away from the orchard in Saratoga, I began thinking seriously about the ideas that would find their way into this book, including what Gary Paul Nabhan and Stephen Trimble call the "Geography of Childhood." As an exercise, I drew a map of my orchard-centered world as I recalled it, which I had not seen for over forty years. I wanted to test my recollections — artifacts of my childhood cognitive map, circa 1960, transformed, to some unknown extent, by the winnowing effect of memory — against spatial reality. This seemed problematic because the world as I once knew it had vanished beneath an avalanche of McMansions, golf courses, strip malls, shopping centers and expressways, and I did not know our street address on Saratoga Avenue. But if I could locate the spot where we had once lived and thus anchor my memories in space, Google Earth would provide the necessary frame of reference.

It turned out that the distinctive nature of the orchard's boundaries — railroad tracks, Saratoga Avenue, Saratoga Creek, plus a road to the northeast — along with the small stucco house and curved pillars that marked the entrance to our driveway, which still existed, allowed me to identify where I had lived. Although the orchard had vanished, replaced mostly by tract homes and an office park, and there was an expressway running parallel to the railroad tracks, I was able to "geo-reference" my map, which turned out to be surprisingly accurate, given that I had not seen the area since the mid-1960s. Its orientation was reasonably correct, although I showed Saratoga Avenue as running east-west, rather than in its true northeast-southwest direction. I also had thought in classic geometric shapes as I drew my map, and depicted my home range as a perfect rectangle, when in reality it was an irregular polygon, narrower to the southwest and broader to the northeast. However, I did recall, precisely, the spatial relationships between our house, the railroad tracks, Saratoga Creek, the surrounding roads, my friends' neighborhood, and Brookview School. I was even fairly accurate in my map's scale; I judged the distance from our driveway to the nearest intersection to the northeast to be 300 yards, when in reality it was about 340 yards. Not bad for forty-five-year-old memories.

Although I was pleased by the accuracy of my spatial memories, I was stunned by how well my sister, Lisa, did when I asked her to repeat my map-making exercise. She was just six when we moved away from Saratoga and had never returned, yet her map portrayed the correct position of Saratoga Creek, Saratoga Avenue, and the railroad bridge. Her drawing was larger-scaled than mine, and focused entirely on the area bounded by the orchard, an outcome of her more restricted home range. Impressively, her map depicted more detail than mine about the immediate vicinity of the house, including many plants in our gardens — violets, iris, wisteria, nasturtium, persimmon, monkey puzzle tree, and what she labeled the "mystery flower," a stalked inflorescence of orange-red, tubular flowers which must have been torch lily, an introduced ornamental from South Africa. Her map also showed several features that I omitted from my drawing: a water tower near the Paul Masson winery, directly across Saratoga Avenue; irrigation ditches; a small pond near the house; and a barn used to store fruit crates and equipment for the orchard. Of these, I recall the irrigation ditches, water tower and the pond, but not the barn, although our mother tells us that there was one on the property.

The extraordinary particularities and accuracy of my sister's map make me question, even more than my own childhood cognitive map, the "constructivist" view of the spatial learning abilities of young children. M. H. Matthews, a British geographer who studied the environmental cognition of young children, found that "by carefully documenting children's views of their everyday worlds . . . a richness and variety emerges. . . . The way in which children learn about and depict space cannot be described by a simple linear progression, instead a complex developmental patterning is evident." Other researchers have discovered that six-year-olds "can use simple maps to plan and execute complex routes in large spaces," which they take as evidence of "fairly sophisticated spatial cognition." Lisa was just five and six years old when she roamed parts of the orchard nearest to our house, playing in the gardens and muddy irrigation ditches, wandering among the plum trees—sometimes with me, when I couldn't find friends to play with, but often on her own. In the language of cognitive psychology, her mental map—much richer in detail of the area immediately surrounding the house than her older brother's—displayed an impressive "object location memory." I doubt that I would have done nearly so well at mapping the home range surrounding the house where I lived in Missouri when I was five or six years old, and although I am loath to build any argument based on a sample size of two, I wonder if the vivid detail of Lisa's early spatial memory might have something to do with her gender. One British study of children's cognitive mapping abilities found that although young boys between the ages of six and nine possessed increased knowledge of paths (roads, alleys, and footpaths), girls of the same age displayed "greater awareness of spatial elements." Another study indicated that adult females possess "more detailed imagery of their immediate surroundings" than males, perhaps due to the cumulative effects of gender-related differences in home ranges and activity patterns, with girls and women historically being more restricted in their movements than males of the same age. Controlled experimental studies also suggest that adult females may have superior object location memory relative to adult males, especially when the memory tasks involve "ecologically valid stimuli" such as plants—a pattern that evolutionary psychologists suggest results from an adaptation to the hypothesized role of females as gatherers and foragers in our evolutionary past. This "Gathering Hypothesis," and even the existence of a female advantage in object location memory, or male advantage in other kinds of spatial ability, is controversial, as indicated by the title of a section of one scholarly paper comparing the map-use skills of males and females: "The Polemics of Spatial Ability." Yet as a biologist, I like to imagine that the ways in which Lisa formulated her early cognitive map were influenced by the faint whisper of genetic memories retained across thousands of generations, as well as by her early, direct experiences of the natural world—in much the same way that the area in Saratoga where we once lived, as impacted as it has been by Silicon Valley, must still harbor some vague memory of sycamores and bee-loud orchards blossoming in the spring sun.

My sister and I were absorbed by "nearby nature"; we knew our landscape intimately and were enmeshed, nourished, and molded by networks of sight, sound, scent, taste and feel. The plum orchard and sycamore-lined stream, the cobbles of gray stone and thickets of poison oak, the rain-washed winter days and smog-laden summer afternoons: these things were the locus of our lives, and held us, gently and firmly, to the world. We ranged widely and perhaps more freely than we should have, but in doing so we drew our maps well, maps that we would carry through the cascade of our years, from adolescence on into middle age. Neither of us would stay in California or often return to the Bay Area, but we would remain deeply attached to the natural world. We would find much of our pleasure, passion, and comfort there. The warp and weft of neurons and experience developed as they did, and eventually we understood how our lives had been shaped by the viscid scent of oaks on a hot summer's day, the tongue-curling taste of sourgrass plucked from beneath a plum tree, the drowsy trickle of water through shaded pools, or the solid heft of a dirt clod snatched from the edge of an irrigation ditch. These were the contours and coordinates of our childhoods, engraved in memory, and binding us to this earth.

What I Desired Most Was Escape

id-August in the plum orchard, the afternoon air thick and lazy with smoggy heat. I rouse myself from lethargy, hop on my bicycle and pedal down the dirt driveway, cross Saratoga Avenue and turn left toward the gas station at the corner. I am very careful about traffic and frequently glance over my left shoulder; ever since my near miss at the school bus stop, I have been paranoid about cars. At the station I drop my bike in the shade, pull a dime out of my dusty jeans, and buy a soda. But it's not the ride that's drawn me to the station, or boredom, or even the cold drink—it's the lure of road maps of California, Nevada, Oregon, Utah, and Colorado. The maps are held in a dusty gray metal rack and blessedly free for the asking, although the owner of the gas station usually lets me snatch only one or two at a time. After finishing my soda I pedal home, retreat into my bedroom, and open up a fresh map. Perhaps it's Nevada. I trace U.S. Highway 50 as it crosses the Sierra at Echo Summit, descends to Lake Tahoe and Carson City, then tracks east past Fallon and into the Great Basin. How many miles across Nevada? What is Austin Summit like? Ely? The sprawl of distance, the allure of Toiyabe National Forest, the promise of the Ruby Mountains, north of U.S. 50. And what lies beyond Nevada, where the highway disappears into the Utah desert? I plot my adventures, the routes that I hope to travel. My view expands outward, away from my house, away from my particular corner of the Santa Clara Valley and into the larger world. In am only nine years old, but already I have latched onto maps. I am seduced by distance and the unknown, pulled toward country more enticing and perhaps safer than my home ground: a route of passage into the wide and wonderful world, but also a way out, as some day I would understand.

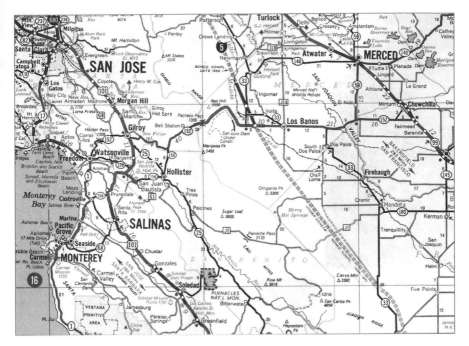

From a 1966 Chevron road map of California.

The free road maps that I collected from the gas station were most likely published by the H. M. Goushá Company, which had one of its plants in San Jose, only a few miles from my house. These maps, such as the 1960 Chevron Colorado "Points of Interest and Touring Map" now spread before me, were published near the end of the post-World War II period of road-map design that focused on the natural beauty of the American landscape. According to Douglas Yorke, Jr. and John Margolies in *Hitting the Road: The Art of the American Road Map*, Chevron maps such as the 1960 Colorado edition, with a cover featuring a painted, moonlit view of a Rocky Mountain lake, "took the concept [of scenic maps] to magnificent heights." I collected many of these maps and I am certain that their cover artwork, with their romantic views of the West's stunning landscapes, whether of the Grand Canyon or a mountain meadow on Mount Rainier, helped stoke my childhood desire for travel. And inside the 1960 Chevron map was a fascinating, red network of mostly two-lane highways crisscrossing the state, which were linked by a tangle of blue secondary roads. The roads were identified by numbers placed within clear shields

(U.S. highways), or circles or ellipses (state highways). Although there was a smattering of limited-access, "dual" highways (yellowish green) and undivided four-lane highways (yellow) surrounding Denver, Colorado Springs, and Pueblo, the dominant road color was red, while the blue Interstate Highway shields were mostly absent from the Intermountain West. At the time, the Interstate Highway System, begun in 1955 by the Eisenhower administration, was still primarily restricted to the West and East Coasts, and most long-distance driving was done on two-lane highways.

The highways were alluring, but what attracted me most were the blotches of color that identified U.S. National Parks and Monuments: green for parks (Rocky Mountain and Mesa Verde), orange for monuments (Dinosaur, Great Sand Dunes, Black Canyon of the Gunnison). And then there were the U.S. National Forests, which covered most of the western part of the state—Arapaho, White River, Rio Grande, San Juan, Routt, Uncompahgre—with their endless, exotic collection of mountains, passes, and rivers. I wanted to see Rabbit Ears Pass, Trail Ridge, Pikes Peak, the Continental Divide—and soon—although I did not have any specific ideas about what I might do once I arrived in one of those fiercely imagined places. Still, I yearned for the mountains and for the highways that might take me to them. By the time I was nine I had made two long automobile trips—the first when I was four, the second when I was seven—on either end of a three-year stay near Kansas City, Missouri, where my stepfather was in ministerial school. Contrary to Piaget and the constructivists, I believe that these trips, combined with explorations of my local world along Saratoga Creek and some innate proclivity, gave me an accurate sense of the spatial and temporal issues involved with automobile travel from California to the Rocky Mountains and beyond. I was ahead of the developmental curve, however unpredictable its trajectory, and already was capable of understanding maps, those images that required John Jackle's "unreal transformations." These transformations involved a mental leap from an eighteen-inch by twenty-eight-inch piece of paper—with its abstract symbols for roads, towns, parks, rivers—into a complex understanding of the spatial relations and structure of an unknown world. By nine or ten years of age my focus was moving beyond my immediate, familiar environment, with a radius of less than one mile, toward a world scaled on the order of thousands, or even tens of thousands, of square miles. I was falling in love with space and movement. I was entranced by places I had never seen, yet through the agency of maps, desired with all of the passion of a young boy's soul and intellect. And on any auto trip longer than a few miles I traveled with my head buried in a map, and dreamed.

At nine years of age I lacked the means to undertake independent journeys beyond the boundaries of a world made accessible by my rattletrap one-speed bicycle, but my cache of road maps was a catalyst for my imagination. The maps provided an opportunity for unlimited mental exploration, and it was as the geographer Denis Wood writes: "This is the very point of a map, to present us not with the world we can *see*, but to point toward a world we might *know*." And the world that I might know was far removed from the Saratoga orchard where I lived. Although the reasons for my obsession with maps and automobile travel were no doubt complex, created out of a particular chemistry of personal experience and innate tendency, I suspect that some of my motivation lay in the possibility of escaping from my childhood home. Subconsciously I desired distance from what, or who, threatened my safety and made me unhappy—a motivation that I became much more aware of in my adolescence, when the tension, misery, and convulsions in my family escalated.

In *The Lure of the Local*, Lucy Lippard sees place as "the locus of desire," with place being

> a portion of land/town/cityscape seen from the inside, the resonance of a specific location that is known and familiar. . . . Place is latitudinal and longitudinal within the map of a person's life. It is temporal and spatial, personal and political. A layered location replete with human histories and memories, place has width as well as depth. It is about connection, what surrounds it, what formed it, what happened there, what will happen there.

As I moved toward preadolescence my youthful imagination, aided by those H. M. Goushá road maps and a third road trip to Missouri, ranged across the mountains and highways of the American West, but for four years it had no intense focus, no "locus of desire." There was resonance in the California sycamores and quiet pools of water that lined the intermittent creek behind my house, but the possibility of developing a prolonged, intense, and intimate childhood connection with a specific place was disrupted by my family's frequent moves. When I was ten we moved again, this time from the Saratoga plum orchard to a small house in a subdivision near my stepfather's church in San Jose, our sixth residence in less than six years. The succession of houses and neighborhoods in which I lived interfered with my ability to develop the emotional coordinates that would have anchored me firmly in the present and to the locale.

And then, when I was thirteen, my parents sprung my sister and me from school and took us to Yosemite Valley. It was May, the waterfalls were booming, the meadows and granite cliffs were alive with light, the California black oaks and cottonwoods had leafed out, burning to green. We stayed in a tent cabin at Camp Curry, walked to the base of Bridal Veil Falls and a short way up the John Muir Trail to Vernal Falls, and explored Mirror Lake; it was there, in that valley of light and water and stone, that I first fell passionately in love with a place, and with an idea — that of hiking in the mountains. During the short hike around Mirror Lake on the valley floor, I encountered the first trail sign of my life (*Snow Creek 3.7 miles, Tuolumne Meadows 21.4 miles*), which led to the less-than-brilliant conclusion that footpaths traversed the roadless Sierra. I am unclear as to exactly what motivated me on that luminous day, although I imagine it was a potent combination of personal history and innate inclination, incubated in the scent of warm pines, the sight of booming waterfalls and the monolithic face of Half Dome, and a prepubescent rise in blood testosterone levels. Whatever the stimuli, during that hour or two near the shores of Mirror Lake I experienced a transformative epiphany: *this place, this world.* Thoreau would have appreciated that this moment of realization came at Mirror Lake, its calm surface a transcendental reflection that revealed the inner workings of my teenaged soul — and at that moment I knew I had to hike in the Sierra, as soon as I could assemble the necessary equipment, locate some hiking companions, and convince my parents that such an endeavor was a perfectly reasonable ambition for an inexperienced and callow thirteen-year-old boy.

The following winter I discovered that one of my schoolmates had done some hiking with the Boy Scouts, and I eagerly agreed to go along when he suggested a two-week backpacking trip of one hundred miles — eastward on the High Sierra Trail from Crescent Meadow in Sequoia National Park to Mount Whitney, north along the John Muir Trail to Vidette Meadows, and then down Bubbs Creek to the trailhead at Cedar Grove in Kings Canyon National Park. And so it was in August 1966, on that first drive to Sequoia National Park with my friend's parents, and during subsequent approaches to trailheads in Yosemite, Kings Canyon, and Sequoia National Parks over the next three years, that I became even more addicted to the romance of road maps and the highway travel that they represented.

From San Jose our approach to the Crescent Meadow trailhead carried us south through the Santa Clara Valley to Gilroy, then east across the Coast Range at Pacheco Pass and into the San Joaquin Valley. We then turned south to Fresno and finally eastward into the Sierra Nevada and Sequoia National Park. The interior of the 1966 Chevron road map on which I may well have traced our progress was similar to the 1960 version of the same map, although the symbols for controlled access highways and other divided highways were more prominent — an indication of the rapid spread of the Interstate Highway System and multilane highways. The front and back covers were different, too; gone was the state-specific landscape painting, replaced by a series of generic scenic photographs, at least two of which clearly were not Californian landscapes. Another significant difference was the increased prominence given to marketing the Chevron National Credit Card. On the 1960 map the ad for John A. Jones's card was relegated to a tiny area at the bottom of the back cover and promised only the "convenience of charging gasoline, oil, and other car needs at stations in all 50 States and Canada." But the 1966 map devoted the entire back cover to an advertisement for J. Q. Modern's Chevron National Credit Card which promised: "This card will let you charge **more** things, at **more** stations, throughout the West, than **any** other credit card." (Mr. Jones, whose spending habits were not contemporary enough, had been replaced by the gender-neutral J. Q. Modern.) The increased prominence of the solicitation, the advertising copy, and the boldface type are indicative of changing American attitudes toward consumer debt. While BankAmericard (later Visa) had launched its credit card operation in 1958, not until 1966 did it, along with the Interbank Card Association (which metamorphosed into Master Charge and eventually MasterCard), become national credit card systems. However, by decade's end the credit card industry, with its now all-too-familiar world of revolving credit, had undergone a major expansion; between 1960 and 1968 Bank of America's cardholder base increased from 234,000 to over one million, while the volume of its credit card sales increased nearly sevenfold, from $59 million to $400 million.

Issues of road-map design and America's developing addiction to credit aside, those early approaches to the mountains were magical, leavened as they were by my excited anticipation of adventure and encounters with the landscapes of my longing. These landscapes were known to me mostly through the agency of other maps, such as Triple Divide Peak, the 15-minute U.S. Geological Survey topographic map that covered the first miles of my baptismal hike, and also the small-scale map that accompanied *Starr's Guide*, the Sierra Club's guidebook to the region from northern Yosemite south to the Kern River drainage. But before I reached the trailhead, hoisted my pack onto my back, and followed the dashed lines representing trails into the mountains, there was that wondrous, five- or six-hour drive, which I always tracked with a road map spread across my lap.

We stow our heavy packs in the trunk, when the subdivision is asleep and the slam of a car door assaults the predawn suburban stillness, then slip out of the Santa Clara Valley before traffic builds to its morning crescendo: south on a divided highway, U.S. 101, to Gilroy, where the agricultural fields drowse in dawn light and the mild and humid air is laden with the rich odor of garlic. Too excited to sleep, my body is tensed and tingling as we turn east and climb into the Coast Range on two-lane California 152, the first rays of the sun breaking across the parched, tawny grasslands, burnt to tinder by August's heat, brittle as a locust's rasp, dark green oaks tracing dry gray creekbeds. At Pacheco Pass we gaze eastward into the thick gauze of smog that blankets the San Joaquin Valley, but from the pass there is no magnificent view of the Sierra to welcome us, such as the one that confronted John Muir when he first crossed the divide one April in the late 1860s: "the Central Valley, but little trampled or plowed yet, was one furred, rich sheet of golden compositæ, and the luminous wall of the mountains shone in all its glory." Breakfast in Los Banos: as we step from the car, the faint smell of moisture and irrigated fields in the air, their humid scent not yet burned from the morning. Then on through the Central Valley, across that vast agricultural garden that in 1966 was still four decades shy of its methamphetamine- and drought-laden dreams. North-south side roads tracing the boundaries of orchards and agricultural fields; endless rows of crops, each a thin, perfect vector marching toward the hazy, shrouded horizon; an endless litany of ramshackle fruit stands, farm homes, and packing-houses. We head south on U.S. 99, its margins lined with dusty ole-anders and eucalyptus, its four concrete lanes choked with the first heavy traffic of the day, semis pounding toward Fresno as tires thump across the seams that separate the highway's concrete panels from one another. Restless now, we abandon Highway 99 and turn east again, this time onto California 180, through Fresno as the day blossoms into heat. Give me those shining mountains, give me those pines and cool air. Then, blessedly, the road begins to weave and climb through the foothills. Live oaks, blue oaks, and scraggly gray-green pines ap-pear, the last of the orchards left to the smog and gathering heat. Out of the lowlands and into higher forests of ponderosa pine, Douglas fir, and white fir as we cross the boundary of Sierra National For-est. Closer now—let me out of this car!—my body quivering like a Jack Russell terrier. Then the General Grant Grove section of Se-quoia National Park and finally Giant Forest and the first, magical trail sign at Crescent Meadow: *Bearpaw Meadow, Hamilton Lakes, Mount Whitney.* Yes. During those approaches to the High Sierra, it was as Christopher Koch wrote in *Highways to a War.* "Highways have always brought me joy; highways on which we move at speed, and which go out across flatness to some edge that's beyond the possible. . . . Only out there, on that edge to which we were speeding, was I promised all the answers I never seem to find: out there, where the world could at last change."

Now, forty years or more down the many roads that radiated out-ward from those first approaches to the mountains, I understand more about the complex reasons that have driven my continued fascination with those Colorado and California road maps, circa 1960. It's partly a matter of nostalgia, which I assume impels many members of the Road Map Collectors Association: the yearning for what seems, per-haps mistakenly, like a less complicated era, one in which there were no perceived limits to growth, no awareness that oil supplies might be limited, and no sense that indiscriminate use of an automobile might be a luxury rather than a God-given American right. In 1960 gas con-tained lead additives and cost roughly thirty-one cents a gallon, unless there was a gas war on, when prices might plummet to twenty-three cents per gallon. Catalytic converters were a thing of the future, and a look under the hood of a 1960 Chevy Suburban Carryall revealed a small-block V-8 (283 cubic inch displacement), with a carburetor and distributor — equipment that you could actually understand and work on, rather than the confused, computerized maze of tangled tubes and wires that powers a contemporary Suburban. It was a time before the Interstate System had metastasized into the tangled 46,726-mile network that it is today, when most transcontinental driving was still done on two-lane roads, such as U.S. Highways 50 ("The Loneliest Highway in America") and 66 ("The Mother Road"), prior to the rise of the franchised fast-food restaurants and motels that have done so much to homogenize the country, when the road-weary traveler might buy a meal in a local café along Main Street, rather than by the interchange on the edge of town, or find a bed in some mom-and-pop, neon-signed motel, rather than a Motel 6 or Day's Inn.

The first free oil-company road maps were developed by the Gulf Oil Company in Pittsburgh, Pennsylvania in 1913 and during the next seventy-three years, eight billion were distributed to American motorists. Although the last maps were given away at Exxon's New York City travel bureau in 1986, by 1966 the era of the free oil-company road map was drawing to a close. According to Yorke and Margolies, three events during the 1970s presaged the death of the free road map: rapidly escalating costs of map production, the oil embargo arising out of the 1973 Yom Kippur War, and the maturation of the Interstate Highway System. The embargo suddenly transformed oil from a cheap, plentiful commodity into a scarce resource, which removed the need for promotional incentives and made the spiraling costs of map production less attractive to oil companies. Yorke and Margolies also believe that the approaching completion of the Interstate Highway System transformed Americans' automotive habits from exploratory to destination travel, and "reduced long-distance travel to a purposeful, passive, almost hypnotic affair" that helped destroy the "motoring fantasies" and wanderlust inspired by the 1940s to 1960s era of free road maps.

Child of the 1950s and 60s though, I carried my motoring fantasies, adolescent obsession with maps, and love of motion — especially if its vector took me toward the wilderness — into my twenties. Impelled by personal history, the ethos of the times, and student poverty, I began hitchhiking across the West and Midwest. Restless wandering would take me from the California Bay Area to Nebraska in two days, Arizona to Kansas City in three days, New Mexico to Oregon in forty hours. I read the seventeenth-century Japanese poet Bashō and recognized myself: "So—when was it—I, drawn like blown cloud, couldn't stop dreaming of roaming, roving the coast up and down." And later, from the early 1980s onward, as my improving economic fortunes gave me access to a vehicle and enough money to fill it with gasoline, and work took me eastward and away from the West, I began an extended series of transcontinental drives, both solo and with my family, which at last count had reached thirty-three. Connecticut to Spokane, Washington in three-and-one-half days and Rochester, New York to Missoula, Montana in two and one half days: peregrinations of the body and soul across countless meridians, ecotones of desire, the miles of asphalt unraveling like flocks of snow geese flowing north above the black-earth Illinois prairie on a March morning, wings flashing black and white, a primal undulation across an azure spring sky. Like the birds, perhaps, I was following an internal compass, although unlike them, I did not have such a clear sense as to my destination. Perhaps, through those long drives and miles and miles of hitchhiking across the continental latticework of highways, I was (and still am) searching for some kind of solace—attempting, as Tom Wingfield said in his closing soliloquy from *The Glass Menagerie*, "to find in motion what was lost in space."

"Out there where the world could at last change." Yes. Out there, somewhere in a new and imagined world, one promised to me by road maps, light years away from where I lived, and the fear and insecurity that sometimes pursued me. There: trace the yellow, red and blue lines that lead beyond the endless subdivisions and tangled freeways of the Santa Clara Valley, across the desiccated summer slopes of the Coast Range and smog-shrouded fields of the San Joaquin Valley, toward those lovely mountain meadows. Highways of my longing, illumined by maps. When I opened those folded sheets and spread them across my lap, I beheld seductive stories, stories that would transport me into the future, toward the trails and wildlands of my desire, and as far as I could get into the waiting world. The stuff of dreams and longing, and of safety.

It Was Impossible Not to Wonder . . . .

n 1966 we moved yet again, this time to a new house high in the Santa Cruz Mountains, twelve miles south of Los Gatos, and almost an equal distance from the Pacific Ocean at Santa Cruz. But even before we abandoned our tract home in San Jose, I purchased two large-scale topographic maps of the area from the United States Geological Survey. The 7.5-minute Laurel and Loma Prieta quadrangles each covered about nine miles by seven miles of steep, mountainous terrain. Our house was the farthest out along Highland Way, a narrow paved road leading to Summit Road, California Highway 17, and eventually Los Gatos, where I was to attend high school. The mountainsides and valleys immediately surrounding our new home were undeveloped, and a glance at my "topo" maps promised adventure — if not on the scale that I would find in the High Sierra, at least in a grander and wilder fashion than what was available in the subdivision where I had lived for the previous four years. I recall opening the cardboard mailing tube when it arrived from the USGS and excitedly unrolling the enclosed maps, as yet unblemished by creases and dirty thumbprints, or indelibly marked by memory. The maps were beautifully smooth and washed with green, a symbol of the thick chaparral and oak forests that clothed the Santa Cruz Mountains, and I spent hours scanning them and imagining the trips that I would soon take: working my way into the gorge of Soquel Creek, some nine hundred feet below our house, or hiking the seven miles and nineteen hundred feet of elevation gain to the summit of Loma Prieta — the highest point rising above the surrounding landscape of "Beautiful Earth."

My initiation into the sensory and aesthetic details of this mapped landscape began during my daily walks from the nearest school bus stop, which was three miles northwest of my home. On most days I hitchhiked the first two miles, but the last mile was always on foot,

Starr's Guide *map of the High Sierra.*

along Highland Way as it traversed the steep, southwest-facing slopes above Soquel Creek. The road cut through thick stands of live oak, madrone and bay laurel, then broke into open slopes of shrubby chaparral as it approached our house. Along the way were several shaded gullies that ran heavy with runoff during the spring—and just beyond the house, a permanent stream that supported a small stand of redwoods. I loved the contrast between the arid environment of the chaparral-covered hillsides, with their thick stands of six- to twelve-foot tall shrubs, and the somnolent patches of deep shade in the side canyons, where in the right season I found Pacific tree frogs and California newts. Although I often gravitated toward the water, it is the viscid, sweet smell of chaparral that has stuck with me most strongly across all the years. And so I think of olfaction-driven recognitions, of history recorded in the reaction of my brain to the aromatic ecology of the Santa Cruz Mountains and to the nearby Ventana Wilderness, where I would first hike as a fifteen-year-old, walking west on a bright spring day with two friends, from a trailhead to our first camp in Pine Valley, where a stream meandered among lush green meadows and beige monoliths of eroded sandstone. The next day we climbed over Pine Ridge, then dropped through thick chaparral to Redwood Camp, where there was a vibrant little creek and a small, hidden glen of redwoods set amidst the scrub-covered hillsides, before finally walking out in one long day to Big Sur State Park, hiking quickly and steadily above the Big Sur River, stopping only to fix a blister and for a quick lunch.

As I write, thousands of miles and forty-four years removed from the Santa Cruz Mountains and Big Sur, the visual images of that country are immediate and direct. I can picture the cut of the road as it approached my house, the dappled shade beneath the live oaks, and the trail's arc into Redwood Camp, the way it dropped from Pine Ridge, and even the particular shape of the rectangular, rusted metal stoves that many camps in the Ventana Wilderness had at the time. But what remains most strongly embedded in my memory is the acrid, pungently sweet smell of chaparral on a warm day, or the rich, damp smell of a shaded redwood glade. I imagine the neural templates forming as I grew through adolescence and inhaled the volatile chemicals given off by the thick sclerophyllous leaves of oak, manzanita, chamise, and chinquapin—the developing dendritic connections forever encoding the scent of chaparral in my brain, its neurons primed to fire whenever I encounter the familiar odors. Immersion in the local creates a template of recognition from molecules of protein and lipid, as the external physical world is transformed into a chemical catalog of experience and desire. Memories of my time in the Santa Cruz Mountains blossom on those rare occasions when I travel to the California coast and am exposed to its olfactory cues, but I've noticed (or imagined?) that the faint scent of chaparral also rises from my 7.5-minute Laurel and Loma Prieta quadrangles. It's as if those volatile molecules somehow had been encoded in the meandering contours and myriad symbols of the forty-four-year-old maps.

"Beautiful Earth" those mountains may have been, but they were no place for a house—or at least our small bit of property wasn't. It was impossible to ignore the ominous, block-letter vector that on the Laurel quadrangle lay only one inch to the northwest of our home: SAN ANDREAS RIFT ZONE. Those four words suggested a potential collision—of Norment family history with implacable geological forces—and our house often shuddered with tremors generated by the restless fault, although we were never subjected to anything approaching the 7.1 magnitude Loma Prieta earthquake that struck the Bay Area on October 17, 1989. The earthquake, with its epicenter only four miles from our former house, occurred when crustal rocks of the Pacific and North American Plates suddenly shifted by as much as seven feet, killing sixty-seven people and causing seven billion dollars of damage. Although we escaped a catastrophic shift of tectonic plates, plenty of slippage was occurring along family fault lines—enough to more than compensate for the relatively quiescent natural world. The geological term for the forces that accumulate and eventually cause movement along a fault line is "shear," and during the 1960s my stepfather generated enough emotional shear to tear apart a dozen families. As he worked his way through the 1960s his debilitating and destructive behavior escalated. He had several affairs, drank heavily, spent irresponsibly, neglected his ministry, and by the time that we moved to the Santa Cruz Mountains, was behaving in increasingly erratic and unpredictable ways. By 1969 the centrifugal forces of familial disintegration scattered me to college in Arizona, and my mother and sister to Missouri, where my mother would enter ministerial school and within a year divorce my stepfather. During the same period my stepfather resigned from his church, one step ahead of being fired by the board, and headed off to failed ministries in Trinidad and Minneapolis before leaving the ministry altogether in the early 1970s.

Given the tension, arguments, anger, and unpredictability of family life in the Santa Cruz Mountains, I focused my energies on the mountains, an environment far removed from the domestic battle zone where I was trapped. Although my stepfather ceased molesting me when I was fifteen—the last time he attempted it, revulsion pushed me to gather enough courage to refuse his advances—I still wanted, desperately, to float free of my home. Between 1966 and 1968 I had come to passionately love my wilderness refuges, mostly by way of long hiking trips into the High Sierra, John Muir's "Range of Light." There, among the immaculate and barren glacial cirques and stunted whitebark pine, flower-studded alpine meadows and backlit granite ranges sliding into dark, were the mountains of my dreams. As a passage in *On the Loose*, a book popular in the 1960s, stated, "Got to move on, got to travel, walk away my blues." And so I would, and did—into a pain-free and peaceful world, one promised to me by experience but also by the maps of the High Sierra that I poured over incessantly whenever I could seal myself away, behind my bedroom door.

According to Arthur Robinson and Barbara Petchenik, authors of *The Nature of Maps*, one of the first scholarly works to propose a theory of maps and mapping, maps have five primary, partly overlapping functions. These are to perceive and understand geographical data, store spatially anchored data, recover information, ornament, and serve as allegory. The maps that I obsessed over fulfilled all five of these functions. The first three were obviously necessary to plan my fantasy hikes. Jean de Boudrillard has written that "it is the map that precedes the territory," and I used a variety of maps to envision my wanderings, from the 1:340,000 scale map that accompanied *Starr's Guide to the John Muir Trail and High Sierra Region* to the 1:62,500, 15-minute USGS topographic quadrangles. With the aid of my well-worn copy of *Starr's Guide* I would choose a trailhead and route, then switch to the USGS quads to calculate distances and elevation changes, and locate campsites. I'd use the brown undulations of contour lines to determine if a cross-country route would "go," and identify the most spectacular terrain, especially those alpine valleys where the gathered contour lines formed a thick-sided, elongated "U," depicting a ladder of lakes ascending to a glacial cirque and massive headwall—visions of some timberline tarn cupped in a gray granite basin, a garland of deep green sedge meadows around the margin, water lapping against

the shore, with steep, snow-filled couloirs and knife-edged arêtes arcing to a broken ridgeline. The next day, then, over pizza or fish sticks
in the high school lunchroom, I'd unveil my proposed route to the
small clique of hikers and climbers that constituted my primary circle
of friends: "How about hiking east from Crescent Meadow to Bearpaw Meadow, then heading north on the Elizabeth Pass Trail? From
about two miles north of the pass, we could cut cross-country, past
Big Bird Lake, then hop an easy divide into the Tablelands and pick
up the trail at Pear Lake." Someone would counter with a route in
the Evolution region of Kings Canyon National Park, and we would
launch into a passionate debate about the two routes, in much the
same manner that we argued about the relative merits of braided nylon and kernmantle ropes, or white gas and butane-cartridge stoves.

The maps and the magical names they held (Thousand Island Lake,
Evolution Basin, Enchanted Gorge, Golden Trout Creek, Sky Parlor
Meadow, Scylla and Charybdis, Hell-for-Sure Pass, Mount Darwin)
suggested a world that I might know. It was a world that I desired
with all the enthusiasm and passion of my adolescent soul, one symbolized by the 1:125,000 topographic maps of Yosemite, and Sequoia
and Kings Canyon, National Parks, which I tacked to my bedroom
walls. These maps fulfilled Robinson and Petchenik's fourth map
function, that of ornamentation, and provided the only decoration
for my sparsely furnished room. I was particularly entranced by the
thirty-nine-inch by thirty-one-inch map of Sequoia and Kings Canyon, upon which I traced a spiderweb of the routes I'd completed.
The map was based on surveys made between 1901 and 1937, and I
loved the sense of antiquity generated by its features, which harkened
back to a more adventurous era—the italicized print used for lakes
and rivers; the concentric, blue lines that filled lakes; and the unpaved
roads that led to many of the trailheads. Even the map's primary
color, brown, added to its historical aura, as the more recent Yosemite
map had a green overlay symbolizing forest cover. When I thought of
1901, I imagined a time when one of my folk heroes, John Muir, was
alive and mapping was done by men who used pack animals to haul
brutally heavy camping and surveying equipment through the Sierra,
across streams swollen with spring meltwater and up steep passes and,
when the terrain grew too difficult for stock, carried plane tables and
transits on their backs to the summits of unclimbed mountains.

I loved that map of Sequoia and Kings Canyon National Parks, but of all the High Sierra maps that I studied, my favorite was the foldout map that nestled in a sleeve on the inside back cover of *Starr's Guide*. The scale of the map was too small for developing a detailed sense of the lay of the land, and I could not determine elevations because it used hachuring—parallel lines drawn in the direction of the slope to represent topographic relief—instead of contour lines. As compensation it showed the entire, grand sweep of the High Sierra, from Emigrant Basin north of Yosemite National Park, south to Mount Whitney and the Cottonwood Pass country. Aligned along both sides of the Sierra crest was a broken blue necklace of glacial lakes, with irregular blue lines flowing west, down each of the main drainage systems: the Tuolumne, Merced, San Joaquin, Kings, and Kern Rivers. Along the western and eastern approaches were roads, and radiating from these thick black continuous lines were the black, dashed lines of myriad trails and the dotted lines of the occasional cross-country route. And snaking through the center of this wonderful world, from Yosemite Valley south to Mount Whitney, was the meandering red line that marked the John Muir Trail—all 211.9 miles of it, a route that I would walk with a friend during three weeks in 1967, when I was fifteen.

The *Starr's Guide* map lacked the detail of the larger-scale 15-minute topographic quadrangles that we carried on our hikes, but this also was one of its chief virtues. For that map, and the high mountain terrain it represented, was the primary theater for my teenaged soul, and its small scale left sufficient room for my imagination to wander and wonder. I didn't need the cartographic details. I would fill them in later with 15-minute maps, and then through experience. I desired a world of possibilities and adventure, leavened by an imprecise hint of the known. For, as Peter Turchi has observed, maps are a common feature of children's and adventure books, such as *Winnie-the-Pooh, Treasure Island,* and *Lord of the Rings,* and it was the quest that I craved, the experiences that would take me deep into another country. I wanted *terra incognita*, not *terra cognita*. Turchi describes the map in *Treasure Island* as creating "a space precisely the size of a boy's imagination," and in me this space was filled by maps of the High Sierra. I began my adventures with preexisting maps, and then constructed my own depictions of the world through experience: a cartography and topography of body and soul.

The *Starr's Guide* map was the perfect stylistic companion to the spare language of the guidebook, which covered the major trails and cross-country routes from Yosemite to Kings Canyon and Sequoia National Parks in only 122 pages. Many of the descriptions must have dated from the first edition, written by Walter A. "Pete" Starr, Jr. and published by the Sierra Club in 1934. The guide hurries along the trails in the same way that Pete Starr raced through the Sierra backcountry; on one solo scouting trip over a long Labor Day weekend in 1930, he walked 143 miles in about ninety hours. Pete Starr disappeared in 1933 while climbing south of Yosemite National Park, but his laconic language lives on. In *Starr's Guide*, four miles of trail might be described in a single sentence: "Our trail follows down the deep, beautiful canyon of Mono Creek on the north side to the *Muir Trail* (8,300 — 4.0)." Such brief descriptions made the country more alluring than the painfully detailed accounts in so many modern guidebooks, in much the same way that the best writing about sex is short on graphic images and reveals only the sensual edges of erotic experience, leaving the reader's imagination to supply the intimate details. I wonder if the elaborate descriptions that grace many modern guidebooks indicate something about the collective psyche of America—the need for certainty and security, for expediency and efficiency. We seek predictability, a world without surprises and wrong turns, one in which expectations accurately predict future experience. We want the details in advance. We insist upon a world precisely described by the surfeit of information at our disposal, stored and then revealed to us by the World Wide Web and GPS devices—perhaps because so many events, from urban violence to global change, collapsing twin towers, and a manic-depressive stock market, seem unpredictable and beyond our control. Many of us profess that we desire adventure, but if so we want it in "mountains with handrails." We seek certainty in a natural world that is, at its core, uncertain. Mountains shift, storms blow up, seemingly out of nowhere, and bears move in unpredictable ways that directly confront our own interests. We might quote Thoreau's dictum, "in wildness is the preservation of the world," but most of us are loath to confront such wildness in our lives, and so we seek assurance by knowing as much about the route as we can. Consider the contrast between the following descriptions of a trail in Kings Canyon National Park, climbing from the South Fork of the Kings River to Granite Basin. The first passage, from the 1964 edition of *Starr's Guide*, describes the route from north to south; the second, from the 2006 edition of *Sierra South*, covers the same ground, although in the opposite direction.

Granite Basin (10,000 — 1.0) (camping and grazing) from where we descend to the head of Copper Creek. At Tent Meadow (3.0) a trail (rough and difficult to follow) branches east to Paradise Valley on the South Fork of the Kings via Goat Mountain (fine view). We follow down the west side of Copper Creek on the long zigzag descent to the floor of
Kings River Canyon (5,035 — 9.0)

Starr's Guide uses about sixty words to provide essential information: a trail descends the north side of the Kings River Canyon; in the nine miles from Granite Basin it loses 5,000 feet of elevation, about 550 feet per mile, with a "long zigzag descent" along the way. In contrast, the passage in *Sierra South*, with boldfaced and italicized warnings, uses more than eight times as many words:

HEADS UP! *Because the canyon walls are so steep, the Copper Creek Trail climbs out of the canyon very quickly—5000 feet in a mere 6 miles. This ferocious ascent, often exposed to blazing sunlight, is suitable only for the backpacker in top shape. With a starting elevation just barely over 5000 feet, you should plan on a very early start to try and beat the heat.*
Day 1 (Copper Creek Trailhead to Lower Tent Meadow, 4.5 miles): The Copper Creek Trail begins on the north side of the parking loop (5036) under the tall pines, but all too soon it leaves the shady pines behind on a hot climb up the north wall of Kings Canyon. Canyon live oaks provide insufficient shade for the first 1.25 miles of ascent to the first stream. The granite walls reflect much sunlight, and on a typically hot summer's day, hiking up this trail produces the sensation of being baked in a glaring furnace. Despite the heat, this route has been well used for centuries. . . . The first set of switchbacks gains 1400 feet and then the trail swings into Copper Creek's canyon, where the

path is partially shaded under Jeffrey pines, sugar pines, incense-cedars, and white pines . . .

The trail crosses several previously burned slopes with a healthy covering of manzanita. So intense is the heat radiating from the sandy trail across these slopes, that imagining the forest floor is still smoldering is quite easy. Soon, the trail reaches a large, aspen- and brush-covered clearing harboring a small campsite. Hop over a couple of rivulets in this well-watered clearing and then reenter forests on the way to the next creek crossing. Just after the crossing, the path arrives at Lower Tent Meadow Camp (7825; 11S 359057 4077125), with five designated campsites and a bear box. Be forewarned, Lower Tent Meadow is the only decent place to camp from here to Granite Basin.

Day 2 (Lower Tent Meadow to Granite Lake, 7 miles): Continuing a northward, now moderate climb, the trail passes through an area burned in 1980. After two long switchbacks, the path nears the creek in a wide avalanche swath where only low-lying shrubs and a profusion of wildflowers are allowed to grow. The trail switchbacks again and nears the creek for the last time (9100); fill your water bottles here.

Enter the shady red fir forest and begin a long series of switchbacks that angle northwest as the trail climbs 1300 feet up a moraine dividing Copper and Granite creeks. En route, cross a belt of western white pines and then lodgepole pines along the ridgetop. From here, you see two prominent peaks to the east, Mt. Clarence King, on the left, and Mt. Gardiner.

A short, winding descent leads through a drift fence and down toward Granite Basin filled with delightful tarns and irregular-shaped meadows. The trail avoids the floor of the basin in favor of an undulating traverse across a lodgepole-shaded hillside above. Parties interested in camping at locations within the basin other than Granite Lake must leave the trail and go cross-country.

Too much information and, curmudgeon that I am, the paragraph beginning with "**HEADS UP!**" irritates me. It reminds me of the warnings that plaster every consumer product, alerting us to the obvious, like the label on the butane lighter I use to ignite my camp stove, which admonishes me to keep the open flame away from my face and not chuck the lighter into a fire. In a similar way, the passage in *Sierra South* states what should be obvious — that a trail beginning at five thousand feet and ascending a steep, south-facing slope may be a brutal bugger on an August afternoon. If I were contemplating hiking into Granite Basin I'd ignore the rococo of *Sierra South* in favor of *Starr's Guide*'s minimalism and leave more to my imagination. I'd settle for Pete Starr's best Phillip Glass imitation and get most of my information from the 15-minute USGS Marion Peak quadrangle, which shows a trail beginning at 5,035 feet and switchbacking steeply up the south side of the Kings River Canyon for over a mile with an elevation gain of 1350 feet, through scrubby vegetation (shown by stippled green on the map). The trail then makes a traversing ascent along the west side of the Copper Creek drainage, mostly in forest (solid light-green overlay), crossing two small streams before reaching Lower Tent Meadow. From Lower Tent Meadow, the trail climbs, generally steeply, past Upper Tent Meadow (the "meadow" is perched on a steep hillside and probably would make for a poor campsite) to a divide at 10,347 feet, before gradually descending into the open, most likely meadowy, expanse of Granite Basin. The steepness of the trail, its south-facing exposure, the initial climb through an area with little shade, and the paucity of water (three stream crossings during the 5,300-foot climb to the divide above Granite Basin) suggest a tough climb, an early-season trip or pre-dawn start, and a pack made heavier with two one-liter water bottles.

The Marion Peak quadrangle gives the discerning map-user more information than in the brief *Starr's Guide* description. So why prefer the map to the verbose passage from *Sierra South*? I think because the map's information is represented visually rather than verbally. This visual symbolism provides essential information, yet leaves much more to the map-reader's imagination than does the written description. He or she may understand the basic lay of the land from a map, while knowing relatively little about its essence and flavor. Although the map is a form of knowing, it also retains a certain mystery, and in this mystery lies much of the wonder and seduction of a map. According to Denis Wood, the map is an abstraction whose meaning unfolds "through *a cycle of interpretation* in which it is continually torn down and rebuilt; and to be truthful, this is not really the map's work but that of its user, who creates a wealth of meaning by selecting and subdividing, combing and recombining its terms in an effort to comprehend and understand." This strikes me as a postmodernist view of the map, which in recent years has become another kind of "text" that demands interpretation. Although the excesses of postmodernism seem silly, I'll agree partially with Wood and admit that when I look at the Marion Peak quad, I see not only contour lines and features such as lakes, streams, canyons and mountains, and names and elevations—but by "selecting and subdividing, combing and recombining," I also sense something of a sensual world, imagined and waiting for me beyond the trailhead.

So, what is that tough pig of a climb from Kings Canyon to Granite Basin like? You'll find out someday, but for now you envision what you will come to know amidst the sweet and sticky scent of chaparral and broken granite (there, in the thick contours and stippled green just beyond the trailhead), along the conifer-scented, dusty trail (there, as the trail cuts across the contour lines and makes a rising traverse above Copper Creek, through green shaded overlay), or the small expanse of scrub willow, wildflower, and blessed mountain water (there, where three small branches of Copper Creek merge, in the small, cool, refreshing basin of Lower Tent Meadow). Or perhaps the best thing will be the view from the divide above Granite Basin, where the trail tops out at 10,347 feet, when you throw down that forty pound (or is it sixty-pound?) pack, strip off your sweat-stained T-shirt and drape it on a warm boulder, then take a long pull from your water bottle. You imagine sitting down to rest those weary legs, wobbly and muscle-fatigued after too many damned months spent in civilization, and taking a look around: the long view down Copper Creek into the hazy lowlands of the Kings River Canyon, your eyes tracing the steep, hot, and desiccated way that you have come, under your own power. You'll scan the magnificent sweep of the gray granite high country, with its tough, frost-shattered peaks, and recall the promise of freezing mountain lakes cupped gently in steep-sided basins, and sweet, lovely green sedge meadows dotted with the carmine-colored paintbrush, bright flashes of lemon-yellow cinquefoil. There will be the delightful breath of wind on your face, drying your sweat, as you pull out the Marion Peak quad and plot the route ahead, much as you did last winter, when you imagined being somewhere other than where you were, desired it above all other things: an escape from what ailed and pursued you but also an escape *to* something, to a world of wonder, one that kept you going and gave you hope.

For me, maps of the High Sierra were also allegorical, fulfilling the last of Robinson's and Petchenik's five cartographic functions, although it is one associated more with the period between the fifteenth and nineteenth centuries than with the twentieth century. Allegorical maps were not merely maps of the physical world, decorated on the margins with dragons, sea serpents, hippogriffs, and other imaginary creatures. Instead they portrayed regions of the mind, moral lessons, social attitudes, and manifestations of cultural identity. One of the earliest examples of the genre is the 1499 woodcut illustration of the imaginary island of Cithera, which accompanies Francesco Colonna's *Hypnerotomachia Poliphili* (The Strife of Love in a Dream). The woodcut depicts Cithera as a perfect circle, divided into twenty sectors by rays radiating from the center of the circle. The rays represent the paths taken by lovers as they travel toward the sacred fountain of Venus.

Allegorical maps were popular in seventeenth-century France, such as *Carte du chemin d'amour* (Map of the path of love) and *Carte du Royaume des Cieux avec le chemin pour y aller* (Map of the Kingdom of Heaven, with the way thereunto). Following the French example, allegorical maps flourished in Britain during the eighteenth century, depicting features encountered by those in matrimonial bliss ("The Road of Love," "The Land of Desire," and "Felicity Harbour" from *A Map or Chart of the Road of Love, and Harbour of Marriage*) or distress ("Province of the Jealous" and "Province of the Ill-matched" from *Map of the Island of Marriage*). And in the United States, advocates of Prohibition navigated through the perils of temptation with help from the *Gospel Temperance Railroad Map*, as they traveled from "Decisionville" in the "State of Accountability," along the "Way That Seemeth Right," having fortunately avoided the "Great Destructive Way Route," which undoubtedly was littered with broken whiskey bottles and empty beer kegs.

Although the Marion Peak and *Starr's Guide* maps had their utilitarian purposes, and bore no toponyms such as "Peaceful Meadow," "Mount Toughness," or "Lake of Strength," for me they were every bit as allegorical as *Carte du chemin d'amour*. If I considered my Sierra hikes in geographical terms—this many miles in this many days, across these passes, with this much elevation change—I also yearned to escape from the "Slough of Despond" by crossing "Arduous Pass," and ascending "Mount Identity." I was entranced by adventure and the beauty of the natural world, but I also craved self-worth and a sense of identity at a time when I desperately needed them, when they were mostly unavailable in my life's main theaters: home and school.

If I yearned for escape from my home environment, my attitude toward high school was more ambivalent. Although I often felt safer at Los Gatos High than at home, my position in the school's social hierarchy was tenuous. I was not particularly awkward or socially inept, nor did I bear any of the marks of Cain that rendered me a target for testosterone- (or estrogen-) induced adolescent scorn and bullying, such as a face scarred by acne, a wardrobe five years out of date, or a physique that tended toward either the Pillsbury Doughboy or Ninety-eight-Pound-Weakling extremes, although at the start of my sophomore year I was only five-foot-three inches tall. I was moderately active and did not play the role of an Invisible Boy who did nothing besides attending classes before retreating to an after-school job or home. I was on several athletic teams, although my achievements were less than stellar, doomed as I was by my small stature and the lack of physical coordination that had propelled me off that railroad bridge in Saratoga seven years earlier. As a freestyler and backstroker on the "C" swim team (one level below junior varsity), I never placed higher than third in a race, handicapped as I was by the lack of a training venue outside of the swim season and my poor kick turn. As a second-string varsity soccer player, I was incapable of dribbling properly with my left foot—a major inconvenience because my coach seemed to always place me at left wing. I had roles in both the junior and senior plays, was active in the Key Club and National Forensic League, and successful in the academic realm, graduating with high honors. I even won a regional B'nai B'rith Anti-defamation League essay contest, for my earnestly liberal essay entitled "Has Racial Violence Changed Our Basic Commitment to Social Justice?" Yet none of these accomplishments resonated much with me, for I traveled with the bright kids, most of whom also did not belong to the social elite. The late 1960s were in the waning years of the "ability group" era, a legacy of John Dewey's education reforms. Members of my ability group received the "H" label and were placed together in a series of honors classes, where we were often taught by the better teachers and got away with more mildly disruptive behavior than our less academically talented peers. This scholastic apartheid meant that "H" kids migrated as a small herd through their years at Los Gatos High, partially isolated from their supposedly less-intelligent "X" or "Y" brothers and sisters (shades of the alpha, beta, gamma, delta and epsilon castes of Aldous Huxley's *Brave New World*), whom I imagine looked upon us with some mixture of envy and contempt, if they considered us at all.

Whatever the case, my academic success provided little social capital. I saw myself as completely unremarkable, with no notable talents or achievements other than an ability to score well on standardized tests. And even my academic exploits were suspect, not only in the wider high school culture but also to myself, because my self-image was poor. I was traveling in disguise, masquerading as a competent student when in reality I was good only at fooling my teachers. In my mind I was a very ordinary guy with an inconvenient physical handicap—my small stature. Under no circumstances would I ever acknowledge my other disability—the emotional fault line created by my stepfather's behavior, which generated so much self-inflicted angst and prevented me from fully accepting my successes or positive qualities.

It didn't help my self-image, or satisfy my adolescent yearnings for excitement and status, that I had absolutely no success with girls. Patricia Nelson Limerick, an historian at the University of Colorado, quotes one academic as saying, "We must remember that professors are the ones nobody wanted to dance with in high school." I was that kind of a guy—too shy and insecure to make the first move, and neither attractive nor interesting enough to earn the attention of girls who were less inhibited and insecure than I. My adolescent dating career is perfectly summarized by my experience with the annual Sadie Hawkins Dance. I must have been the only boy at Los Gatos High who was asked to the dance, then dumped before the event. Yet I took the girl anyway—it was too late for her to find a more suitable partner—then my "date" and I quickly separated and I spent the evening alone in an Eeyore-like state of misery. And my romantic opportunities were not helped by my culturally conditioned attraction to unattainable girls. Fool that I was, I secretly lusted after the cheerleader types, the classically pretty and often wealthy girls who had all of the status and all of the boyfriends, and for whom I must have been invisible—while I ignored the more interesting girls, the ones who were, like me, not particularly cool, but with whom I might have shared some common ground. And so at every dance I remained among the gaggle of nervous boys that collected in the corners of the gym, trying to act nonchalant. There, in the awkward security of a sexually segregated flock, I furtively watched my more fortunate and confident classmates gyrate to Iron Butterfly's "In-a-gadda-da-vida." As the plodding drum and bass lines, and transcendent lyrics ("In-a-gadda-da-vida, honey / Don't you know that I love you?") flooded the cavernous gloom and the light show spat out pulsating, amoeba-like splotches of color in a queasy imitation of Jackson Pollock on a bad day, I imagined shedding my inhibited skin and transforming myself into someone other than the poor sod that I was.

As much as I hated my home situation and uncertain social status at Los Gatos High, I did not voice many complaints about my life, unlike some of my friends, nor did I gravitate toward the late-1960s rebelliousness articulated by many of my peers—at least until my senior year, and then only in mild ways. There were no drugs or alcohol, no sexual escapades; I never yearned for the former, although I bemoaned the absence of the latter. I made few trips to the exotic and forbidden worlds of Telegraph Avenue in Berkeley, where aspiring young capitalists were eager to sell you the drug of choice, or to the Fillmore West and a Grateful Dead or Jefferson Airplane concert, where aspiring young capitalists also were eager to sell you the drug of choice. My basic problem was that I was not cool. I lacked physical attractiveness, athletic ability, wealth and social ease, artistic or musical skills—attributes that carried some social currency and would have marked me as someone other than ordinary.

Thus my desire for an identity that would set me apart from my classmates, something physically challenging that would compensate for my lack of status and demonstrate that I wasn't as scrawny and weak as I felt. And so the mountains beckoned, bathed as they were in the light of grace and adventure, where I might test my physical mettle in an environment as remote from the lives of the popular kids as I was from their privileged world. Backpacking and rock climbing had not yet achieved the popularity that they soon would, and they provided a crucial sense of self-worth, purpose, and individuality at a time when I desperately needed them. I also enjoyed the temporary and moderate notoriety that sometimes was mine when I recounted my adventures — such as the secret flush of pride I felt when a non-hiking friend, after listening to stories (only slightly embellished) of my first Sierra hike, responded, "Two weeks hiking, carrying all of your stuff and sleeping on the ground? Norment, you're crazy!"

Unable to gain entrance to the world of the socially privileged and uninterested in most of the alternative cliques at Los Gatos High, I joined the tiny cadre of hikers and climbers, exclusively male and mostly "H" students, who took pride in their independence and disdained the Boy Scouts as a paramilitary organization. We identified ourselves by adopting a uniform that included canvas Millet rucksacks, heavy mountain boots (perfectly suited to the steep and snowy trails of a suburban California high school), and, as soon as the school's dress code began to crumble under the assault of 1960s culture, shorts — especially during the winter. Like all fanatics, we were proud of our obsessions. We talked incessantly of weekend climbing trips to Pinnacles National Monument, spring hikes in the Big Sur country, and summer adventures in the Sierra. We idolized John Muir, engaged in protracted, impassioned debates over the merits of different kinds of equipment, and fantasized about finding girlfriends who hiked and climbed. In all of this we were a bit self-conscious, but we were adolescents out to establish our identities, while being buffeted by hormonal storms, chafing under the increasingly irritating demands of adults, and confronting the swirling tumult of the Vietnam War, the 1968 Democratic Convention in Chicago, and the assassinations of Bobby Kennedy and Martin Luther King.

In our most insubordinate moments we would lie to our parents, as during one week in May of my senior year when a friend and I cut classes and hitchhiked to Yosemite, where we spent several days hiking up the John Muir Trail until we were stopped by deep snow. Disciplinary actions even sent several of us to the principal's office — unusual events for the usually well-behaved, tractable "H" kids. Once, two of us were admonished for practicing our rock-climbing moves during the brilliant, first ladderless ascent of the high school library. On another occasion, four of us, including a kid who was a pilot, forsook the officially sanctioned senior sneak day. Instead we flew in a single-engine plane to Lake Tahoe, where we rented motorcycles and rode down to the water, and had a picnic that couldn't be beat, spiced as it was by our incendiary behavior. Mild stuff, which we paid for by enduring a tongue-lashing from the vice-principal, who called us "a bunch of puds" for going AWOL when the rest of the senior class was at the beach. Our cultivated insouciance and petty rebelliousness were partly a product of an innate adolescent disdain for authority and the political and social upheavals of the late 1960s, but an equally important influence was the time that we spent in the wilderness. In the mountains we were free to ramble as we pleased. We could howl at the moon, succeed or screw up on own—a pot full of mucilaginous, burnt macaroni, a tent pitched so that rainwater pooled beneath our sleeping bags, a cross-country route more dangerous than anticipated. There were no adults to warn us or to admonish us for our mistakes, only the gloriously neutral land itself. We learned to accept the consequences of our actions and responsibility for our safety and comfort, and so we chafed under authority. Flyweight anarchists that we were, we cultivated a healthy suspicion of power, and we would have identified with the sentiments expressed by Ed Abbey:

> We cannot have freedom without wilderness, we cannot have freedom without leagues of open space beyond the cities, where boys and girls, men and women, can live at least part of their lives under no control but their own desires and abilities, free from any and all direct administration by their fellow men. "A world without wilderness is a cage," as David Brower says.

And so I was obsessed by the mountains and by my place in them. Like the novitiate whose training for the priesthood leads him to read and reread Biblical passages, I endlessly studied my wilderness maps. On those winter nights when my stepfather was at his worst, and the Sierra seemed as far removed from my life as were the Himalayas, I would retreat to my bedroom. There I would dress in my outdoor gear, fill my pack with equipment, and picture the transformation that would occur once I was on the trail, like some medieval page donning his chivalric armor and imagining the jousts and quests to come. And on those Sundays when I was obligated to attend worship services, I mentally traveled as far as I could from my stepfather's church. I refused to sing hymns or listen to his sermons and prayers, both as a form of passive resistance and because the tenets of his brand of "new-thought" Protestantism, which resembled lo-cal Christian Science, irritated me. "Unity," as it was called, did not completely eschew medical doctors, as did Christian Science, but it still held that people create their life experiences through their attitudes. The implications of this belief were infuriating, given my childhood history. My worldview also was antithetical to Unity's, which was basically Neoplatonic at its core and discounted the physical world in favor of the spiritual. Because my incipient spiritual life was so strongly rooted in the physical realm of the mountains, I saw myself as a heretic pantheist and so, in my own quiet way, I rebelled. I silently rejected the doctrines that I was being force-fed and, while held captive in the pews, created a private liturgy by retracing, in great detail, the routes that I'd hiked—mile by mile, campsite by campsite, pass by pass.

This process of mental recapitulation, repeated Sunday after Sunday, created a series of rich and enduring mental maps of my High Sierra experiences, many of which are with me more than forty years later: the particular grove of foxtail pine along Tyndall Creek, where in 1966 we camped before crossing Forester Pass and my ineptitude in backpack cookery led me to ruin a highly coveted meal by adding two tablespoons of salt to the mix of instant mashed potatoes, water, and gravy—which caused us to forsake our hunger, abandon camp, and hike three miles north to a high bivouac and a cold dinner of dried milk and muesli. Or the pitch of the trail on the Bubbs Creek side of Glen Pass, where it cut through a steep cliff and descended to a small lake, which we hurried down one bright morning in early August 1967, on the third-to-last day of our John Muir Trail hike, eighteen days gone from Yosemite Valley—the still mountain air, the rough feel of chipped granite underfoot, and the unhappy young couple that we passed, hiking north, the man toiling under a huge pack laden with two sleeping bags and pads, and decorated with a dangling cooking pot and assorted clothes, while the woman was following about fifty feet behind, wearing a clean white long-sleeved button-down shirt, arms folded and scowling, not even carrying a day pack, but burdened down nevertheless. And finally, next morning's ecstasy as I raced up Forester Pass without stopping—six miles of trail and three thousand feet of elevation gain—leaving my companion far behind as the trail climbed past a high alpine lake and switchbacked up to the 13,200-foot divide. I was breathing easily, feeling the animal strength after almost three weeks in the mountains, pulled south toward Mount Whitney by visions of that final summit, by a sense of achievement and, yes, validation and wholeness. And at the pass, while the Sierra did their brilliant best as John Muir's "Range of Light," I pulled out the 15-minute Mount Whitney quadrangle and looked south toward the final two days of our trip, into the Kern-Kaweah country, and scanned the distant peaks, rivers, ridges, and lakes that I had to visit someday, chanting their names quietly, looking into a magical terrain, a world of endless possibilities where I could hope and dream, and claim some sense of wholeness. *Out there*, where it was impossible not to wonder.

Middle Maps

The Silence Was Like No Other

washed ashore in Mankato, Minnesota, in the autumn of 1972, three years after finishing high school and escaping to Prescott College, an "experimental" school in Arizona. There I'd fallen into ecology, drawn partly by a vague interest in the science and its implied aesthetic, but mostly by the pleasing prospect of getting paid to work outside. My first field job came after my freshman year, on a project studying bird communities along the Verde River. I liked the work — wandering into a gallery of cottonwoods at dawn, the world a cacophony of birdsong, the brilliant, startling flash of a vermilion flycatcher in the rich riparian air. We would work the lowland forests through morning's coolness and into the gathering heat, then seek some mountain refuge: the shady delight of Douglas fir and big-toothed maple sheltering within a north-facing gully, far above the heat-soaked valleys; an arc of cold springwater spilling from a galvanized pipe; mountain chickadees and Audubon's warblers claiming the trees from the black-capped chickadees and Lucy's warblers we'd left behind. The work held my passion, but academics did not. I lasted two-and-one-half years before Prescott College's entropic decay and my restlessness, catalyzed by the collapse of my first love affair, threw me into a fit of wandering: a month on a winter mountaineering course in Colorado; several weeks hiking in the Grand Canyon; a trip into the slickrock country of southeastern Utah; another three months of ornithological fieldwork in Arizona; a two-week backpacking trip in the High Sierra, a walk with my sister in the Oregon Cascades. It was a syncopated life of wilderness trips, hitchhiking, and sporadic work, with no melodic line. Finally there'd been a two-week canoe trip in the Boundary Waters of northern Minnesota, where the Indian summer sweetness was diluted by rain, financial worries, concern about my aimless wandering, and a vague but chronic angst—the detritus of my youth—lying like a belligerent dog in restless sleep, turning in its bed, never quite still. My condition during the canoe trip could be described as one of emotional disorientation; although I could situate myself easily amidst the sprawl of Canadian Shield lakes, I had no internal sense of direction. I wanted wilderness, but little more. My maps were mostly blank, and my compass needle sought no loadstone.

Mankato was less a destination than a hesitant afterthought. After the canoe trip, I stopped there to visit friends who had transferred from Prescott to the local state college. I had ten dollars in my pocket and no plans, other than to stave off starvation and save money for a trip to Nepal. One of my friends said that I could share his apartment, and a visit to the state employment office yielded a job as a laborer on a construction project outside of town. And so, for a few months, I was set. I would rise before dawn, walk two miles to work, past cornfields fading into fall, earn my three dollars per hour, and then trudge back to the apartment. I liked having money in my wallet, but it was a lonely and unsatisfying life. My friends had their own concerns: coursework, romantic involvements, families in the area. I was a refugee from the West, adrift in a heartland landscape of woodlots and agricultural fields. I was the "college kid" at the job site, the unskilled cipher lost among a small group of older men who'd worked construction most of their lives and were good at what they did. I, on the other hand, was not. I knew nothing about construction, although I did understand physical exertion and was happy enough to haul lumber and dig ditches for eight hours a day, as a way to fill my time. There was a deaf mute on the crew, a skilled carpenter whose entire vocabulary apparently consisted of the word "coffee." His verbal isolation mirrored the cocoon of loneliness that enveloped me. I could find no purchase in the desultory conversations during our breaks, on Friday afternoons, when I prodded my reluctant self into drinking beer at a local bar with my coworkers.

As much as I'd wanted to leave Prescott College, I missed the structure and mental stimulation of academic life, and yearned for the West. I tried to claim some familiar ground by taking a continuing education course on Roderick Nash's classic work of environmental history, *Wilderness and the American Mind.* When I saw the course announcement, I'd felt a small flush of excitement—the opportunity

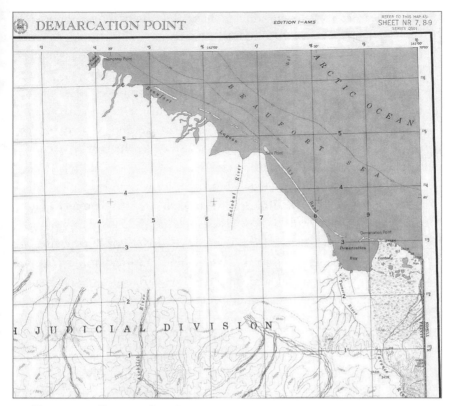

Demarcation Point quadrangle map.

to meet folks who shared my passions, plus the promise of intellectual sustenance. My enthusiasm vanished, though, when I walked into the classroom and confronted row after row of empty seats. Besides the professor, there were only three of us, and rather than embrace our uniqueness—a small band of kindred spirits seeking inspiration among the cornfields—we allowed our mutual disappointment to dictate the atmosphere of the class. It was as if Mankato's lack of interest in Nash's book was an offhand, critical comment on us, which fed our collective lassitude. The instructor sagged, and we approached *Wilderness and the American Mind* with as much enthusiasm as a vegetarian confronting a can of Libby's potted-meat food product.

I was restless and displaced. To calm down I took a weekend course on Transcendental Meditation, and sought serenity in a personalized mantra and forty minutes per day of focused breathing. Not a bad idea, but I did not have the patience to cultivate patience; I had not yet learned to welcome stillness. Instead, I sought refuge in books such as *Alaska Wilderness*, Bob Marshall's account of his Brooks Range explorations. Marshall's writing took me deep into that glorious country, made me yearn for the spirit captured by a photograph, taken in August 1939, at what literally would be his last camp — for less than three months later, at only thirty-eight, Marshall would die of heart failure. Marshall stands on a cobble bar, arms around his two companions: Jesse Allen, a barefooted, one-armed prospector, and Nutirwik, whom Marshall described as a five-foot-tall "Kobuk Eskimo." Marshall and Allen sport scraggly beards, Nutirwik smokes a pipe. All are bedraggled, filthy, and grinning. Marshall's face is illumined. He looks to be in his prime and in his element, in the most basic sense of the word, which comes from the Latin *elementum*, or "first cause." Marshall's smile, and those of his companions, beamed at me across thirty-three years and pulled me into the Brooks Range. I craved Marshall's wilderness, the camaraderie and adventures described in his narrative. And as is my habit, I wanted to place Marshall's explorations on a map. In search of nothing more than a good atlas, I wandered into the college library's map room, where I stumbled upon a rich collection of North American topographic maps, covering all fifty states. I located the index map for the 1:250,000 Alaskan maps, published by the Army Map Service, identified several that covered the Brooks Range, and pulled open the large, gray metal tray where they lay. I sorted through the stack, selected a sheet, and then felt my heart stutter. There was a tiny flutter of recognition as my longing locked onto the external world, a momentary symmetry of desire and experience: for that twenty-nine-inch by eighteen-inch sheet was part cartographer's standard fare, part proverbial "blank spot" on a map, where the familiar symbols for lakes and rivers, peaks and valleys, their blues and browns, disappeared into a solitude of white. Contours arced across the map, then vanished at the long and lonesome boundary between the known and the unknown, the demarcation as sharp as a backlit prairie horizon, the glorious expanse of white broken only by a few hesitant, dotted lines, marking the hypothetical paths of rivers. As I gazed at the map, I confronted the spirit of Marshall's explorations, and Aldo Leopold's question: "Of what avail are forty freedoms without a blank spot on the map?" For a few minutes I held to the belief that there still were unmapped places "out there" — even though I knew that I was looking at a purely historical phenomenon. The topographic sheet before me was a relic, obsolete and twenty years or more out of date, undoubtedly superseded by maps that transformed the sea of white into color, and the known world. Aerial photography, supplemented by hard work on the ground, would have done the job long before I walked into the Mankato map room. Yet the story remained, as history and metaphor, as a promise and reminder: there is more to the world than we can ever know. There are vast regions of life that remain open and undiscovered, and which carry all the promise of the cumulonimbus that rears up over the Arizona mountains on a hot July day, four months after the last rains. The sky goes electric as clouds climb thirty thousand feet or more above the parched ground and blossom into anvils. The first hints of moisture drift downwind, and you know that the Earth, after months of drought, shall bloom green.

At some point in college I read *Heart of Darkness* and stumbled across these lines:

> Now when I was a little chap I had a passion for maps. I would look for hours at South America, or Africa, or Australia, and lose myself in all the glories of exploration. At that time there were many blank spaces on the earth, and when I saw one that looked particularly inviting on a map (but they all look that) I would put my finger on it and say, 'When I grow up I will go there.'

Almost forty years after reading *Heart of Darkness*, as I considered the notion of blankness and what that Brooks Range map represented to me, I encountered three interpretations of Conrad's quotation: first, in the introduction to *Arctic Wilderness*, written in 1956 by Bob Marshall's brother, George; later in Peter Turchi's *Maps of the Imagination: The Writer as Cartographer*; and then in J. B. Harley's *The New Nature of Maps*. Of the three, Marshall's vision is the most traditional, with maps seen primarily as a catalyst for the imagination. Although Marshall mentions how Conrad's "blank space of delightful mystery" was transformed into "a place of darkness," he does not pursue this idea, instead focusing on how his brother's joy was magnified by the unmapped vastness of the Brooks Range. Harley, writing almost forty years later, finds something sinister in the above passage, and argues that "Conrad's delight in the blank spaces on maps—like that of other writers—is a symptom of a deeply ingrained colonial mentality. . . . In this view the world is full of empty spaces that are ready for the taking." Turchi, whose *Maps of the Imagination* was published in 2004, claims the middle ground. He views writing as an analog of geographical exploration, with the blank map operating as a positive metaphor, one central to the creative process, as it offers a "world of possibility." Yet he also acknowledges that blank spaces sometimes were a product of the imperialist mindset, with its "call for colonialism and conquest," which saw unmapped regions of the world as uninhabited, at least by anyone with legitimate title to the land.

The perspectives of Harley and Turchi represent postmodern, postcolonial views, far different from the traditional interpretation of cartographic blankness, which mostly seems a straightforward insistence on accuracy, an expression of humility in the face of our ignorance. Early European maps, such as Mercator's 1569 world map, filled the interiors of continents and unexplored reaches of oceans with narrative descriptions of nature, ethnography, and history; other contemporary maps added graphic and pictorial information. These additions, while not eliminating blankness, deemphasized it, and co-opted it for cosmographic and overtly symbolic purposes. Maps became increasingly complex and ornate, perhaps an expression of the seventeenth-century Baroque aesthetic. However, by the late 1700s the Enlightenment ideal of disciplined scientific accuracy had banished the cornucopia of icons, cosmographic symbols and illustrations, and speculative elements from maps' blank spaces. Among the most influential cartographic reformers of the time was Jean Baptiste Bourguignon d'Anville, who sought to exclude from maps all inadequately supported information. Maps became more austere and blankness blossomed, at least temporarily. What remained in the empty spaces was an admission of geographical ignorance, a challenge, and an implied assertion: we will know the Earth, and every last corner of it will be mapped.

Inspiration, joy, and curiosity, or else proprietary rights, power, and imperialism—the map's blankness as seen from a traditional perspective, or from the mist-shrouded heights of postmodernism. Although my reaction to the Brooks Range map was innocent—no postcolonial implications for Chris Norment, circa 1972—I'll side with Harley and Turchi and admit that blank spots on a map may represent more than unmapped terrain. The notion of cartographic "blankness" is more complex and confusing than it first appears; it operates at many levels, has cultural and political implications, as well as metaphorical ones, and speaks to both public and private issues. As I struggle with the idea of cartographic blankness, both in the abstract and in the context of my own life (why is it that I am drawn so intensely to mapped representations of the world yet also to what at first glance appears to be a polar opposite, the blank spot on the map?), I am struck by a passage from *The New Nature of Maps*: "I am deliberately insisting on the term *silences* in the context of maps, rather than the somewhat negative *blank spaces* of the older maps." It is here, nestled in the word "*silences,*" that I find my hook, my passage into allegory, a way in which I might understand blankness and my passion for that Brooks Range quadrangle, a passion that came to me so suddenly as I drifted, a bit lost and alone, through that Minnesota fall of 1972.

In *The Tuning of the World*, Murray Schafer distinguishes between "negative silence," which we fear, and "positive silence," which nourishes us. Schafer discusses silence in the context of our acoustic environment, but his distinction between negative and positive silence is useful to consider in relation to Harley's map "silences," which involve control and selective expression of cartographic knowledge in the service of economic, military, and political power. The sketch maps and drawings from Sir Francis Drake's voyage around the world were state secrets, the Soviet Union systematically falsified cartographic information, early maps of colonial New England often failed to show the region's native inhabitants, and a 1980 map of the Love Canal area in Niagara Falls gave no indication of the hazardous waste contamination that sickened residents in the 1970s. However, maps hold other silences, some of which are necessary. There is a utilitarian silence embraced by maps, one more generalized, profound and necessary than the silences meant to deceive or control, or those based upon a lack of geographic information—for while maps depict many aspects of the world, they necessarily omit more than they represent. Information must be abandoned, whether details of the terrain between adjacent contour lines on a topographic map, contour lines on a road map, roads on a map depicting the breeding and wintering range of the American robin, or the distribution of American robins on almost any map. As Denis Wood writes in *The Power of Maps*, "No map can show everything. Could it, it would . . . *no more than reproduce the* world, which, without the map . . . *we already have.* It is only selection from the world's overwhelming richness that justifies the map." All maps, then, are in some ways silent, because the cartographer must choose what to include in a map, based on its purpose. This process of "content generalization promotes clarity of purpose or meaning by filtering out details irrelevant to the map's function or theme."

And if, as the epigraph to this book suggests, "all maps are stories," then silence—that necessary and compelling cartographic blankness—is an integral part of every map's story, just as every written "story contains, and is surrounded by blank spaces." Silence is woven into all maps; the trick of the telling is to find the silence most appropriate to the map's story, for as Turchi observes, "The most accurate map, and the most detailed map [the one with the fewest silences], is not necessarily the best map." Music and poetry, too, are defined as much by silence as they are by sound. What would iambic pentameter be without the cadence of stressed and unstressed syllables, the short pauses between sounds? What would Dylan Thomas's "Poem on His Birthday" be without the ebb and flow of sound?

> Oh, let me midlife mourn by the shrined
> And druid herons' vows
> The voyage to ruin I must run,
> Dawn ships clouted aground

What would any melody be without the rests? Murray Schafer, in *The Tuning of the World*, mentions the "value of silence" in the music of Anton Webern. I would speak instead of the "necessity of silence" to all music. Without silence, Puccini's beautiful "Nessun Dorma," the tenor aria from *Turandot*, would vanish. Without silence, Richard Thompson's aching guitar solo in his live version of "Hard on Me" would sour into a solitary, tonal note of noise. Without silence, the canyon wren would forever lose its lovely, tumbling waterfall of notes amidst the cliffs and canyons of the American West. As the Japanese poet Ryokan has it, "The winds have died, but flowers go on falling; / birds call, but silence penetrates each song." And then there's John Cage's *4'33"*, which consists of four minutes, thirty-three seconds of silence. Cage left Webern in the compositional dust as he pursued the rest to its logical conclusion—just as that wash of white on the

Brooks Range map overwhelms any other cartographic silences that I have experienced. The insistence of that map's silence drew me into the symbolic and vital magnitude of its quiet, in a way that meshed with my personality and history.

Michael Ondaatje writes that "All that I desired was to walk upon such an earth that had no maps." Ah, but by the early 1970s aerial and satellite imagery ensured that there were few, if any, unmapped places on the globe, even if some regions remained inaccessible for political or logistical reasons. Yet other alluring silences still existed, for my early exposure to ecological fieldwork told me that there was a type of blankness, one beyond cartography, which I could explore. I took some joy in understanding the lives of animals and plants, and participating in the process of scientific discovery. There was in me an incipient but growing pleasure in adding the tiniest bits of clarity to our understanding of the natural world, a satisfaction which would lead to obscure scientific papers on additions to local bird faunas, the feeding habits of sparrows, the eggs of pipits, the habitat relations of grassland birds. I could imagine this kind of scientific documentation, but I never hoped to become a cartographer and map unknown geographies, or explore new ways of remapping known ones, for *I did not want the blankness—the silence of the map—to be erased*. Instead, in the face of inevitability, I wanted to preserve cartographic silence. Part of this desire was my fascination with a vanished world, and explorers such as Bob Marshall, who had traveled into unmapped terrain. This nostalgia might partially explain my wilderness misanthropy. Outside, I am happiest when I encounter no one other than my (usually) sole companion. Too many people around me, and I metamorphose into a curmudgeon: for if there are other people, it is less possible to believe, however irrationally, in adventure, and that I am participating in any sort of discovery. Blankness also represents the world of possibilities, in the manner of a highway intersection or trail junction, but with an intensity several orders of magnitude greater—for if even the tiniest portion of the world is unmapped, all paths remain open, all explorations and reinventions possible. Mapping the last of the lost and lonely places would be more than a simple act of filling in a blank space; it would be a potent symbol, an admission that there are personal and collective limits to our options.

Perhaps, too, by 1972 my experiences in the wilderness, which stretched across eight years, had begun to create in me an incipient desire for silence and a world less pummeled by noise than the one in which I normally lived. I was a typical young adult male, longing for loud music and intense physical activity, and not particularly interested in holding still. I liked long days in the mountains — still do, at times — those solid, fifteen or twenty miles of travel, humping a pack over beautifully broken terrain: got to cover ground, walk those blues away. I carried this preference for movement into my thirties, when I worked as a mountaineering instructor for Outward Bound. Late in a course, when my students were on their final expeditions and operating quasi-independently, I might spend the day shadowing a patrol for fifteen miles, set up camp, then go for a four-mile trail run, just to burn off extra energy.

Still, I was not always on the move in the wilderness. Camp was fine, especially when I had burned myself out for the day and was ready to rest. There were times, too, when the world was illumined, and burned with the intensity of its origins. These occasional epiphanies almost always occurred when I stopped to listen, and was quiet. The first came by the shores of Mirror Lake, in Yosemite Valley, when I was thirteen. It was a religious experience that undoubtedly drew me toward the natural world, but although my first few years of wilderness hiking took me into some very beautiful places, I had to wait three years for the second numinous and mystical encounter. I mostly was too preoccupied with movement and adjusting to unfamiliar environments to listen and see well, but when I was almost seventeen I had an intensely spiritual experience near Vogelsang Lake in Yosemite National Park. My friend Dick and I were eight days into a hike that had been more difficult than normal. We'd had three days of continuous rain, and endured a violent, all-night storm at timberline, hunkered down in a leaky tube tent and soaking sleeping bags, as thunder and lightning pounded the alpine cirque where we were camped. Dick was miserably ill and vomited repeatedly during the long and sleepless night, but by the time that we reached Vogelsang Lake the weather had broken, we had dried out, and my friend was well. We stopped early, ate dinner, then climbed to an alpine bench above camp. The bench was bounded by gray granite basins, the evening sky lambent, the ridge blanketed with the yellows, purples, and reds of alpine cinquefoil, lupine, and paintbrush. We were uncharacteristically quiet, two normally chattering teenagers reduced to silence by the solemn beauty of the place. Perhaps we were riding the tail end of endorphin highs, relieved to be out of the rain and healthy, but whatever the cause, we had stumbled into a mystical, multi-dimensional dovetail of sense and emotion. Both Dick and I recognized the experience for what it was, struggled to articulate our feelings, and so lost hold of its essence. Still, we had been there, and *knew*.

Other, similar experiences followed—one on a moonlit autumn evening in my eighteenth year, beneath Rainbow Bridge in southeastern Utah, another when I was twenty-two and descending from a nineteen thousand-foot pass in the Himalayas. We had been through a punishing few days: hauling heavy loads to the pass (two steps forward, rest, two more steps and another rest), then setting up a high camp and climbing a small peak the next day. The altitude had blessed me with nausea and a severe headache, but once we descended from the pass, I felt much better. I let my companions hurry ahead and for awhile I traveled alone through a high, austere glacial valley, a jumble of moraines and ice where no flowers bloomed and no birds sang. The distant peaks of Tramserku and Kang Taiga rose free from a roiling sea of clouds, shining in the last light of day. I was silent and alone and coming into air richer with oxygen, fit and supremely happy, as peaceful and content as I'd ever been, and for an hour or more it was all Theodore Roethke: "I learned not to fear infinity / The far fields, the windy cliffs of forever, / The dying of time in the white light of tomorrow."

By my early twenties I had traveled deep into the Sierra, Utah, and Himalaya, and in these places found some measure of peace and belonging. In doing so I was, in the words of the Quakers, "going into the silence," a silence that I have grown to desire more as I age, and as my youthful predilection for constant movement wanes. I still enjoy the physical exertion that for me is an integral part of being in the wilderness, but now I am drawn, intensely, to the quiet of the natural world, and to "not doing." Instead of making camp at six or seven, as was once my habit, I prefer to stop at four, brew up a cup of tea, lean against my pack, and listen to the world, to the well of silence that bathes each bird song, the trickle of water spilling through a garden of rocks, or most powerfully, the austere and gelid arctic winter, which I first encountered in my twenty-sixth year, deep in the Canadian wilderness:

Thirty below on a windy December night, with the waxing moon high in the sky. I climb out of the spruce, away from Warden's Grove and the Thelon River. Hard snow crunches underfoot, and each inhaled breath is ragged in my nose. Overhead the aurora dances in ribbons of color—purple, yellow, and green curtains streaming through the sky. From the crest of the hill, the Barrens lies clothed in a liquid, silver light—a great, undulating sweep of land locked in the grip of winter. Below, the Thelon gleams gently, its frozen current shining in the brittle night. And everywhere is a silence so deep that it has become palpable; the wind is here, but as a part of the silence that streams out of the desolate land. It is as though I could reach out and hold the silence, cupping it, ever so gently, in my mittened hands. I recall the words of Meister Eckhart, a fourteenth-century German mystic: "There is nothing in creation so like God as stillness." His words hover in the quiet of the expectant night; I huddle in the lee of some stunted trees and drifted snow, desiring warmth yet unwilling to leave the ridge and hear myself move. No matter how many days and nights pass, no matter how many sunrises and sunsets greet me, no matter how many disappointments there are . . . there will always be this view, and a sense of having come to an appointed place, drawn by whatever it is that marks the stillness and the course of my life. I tell myself to hold onto a quiet heart, and the empty land, for they offer the hope of grace at times when grace does not seem possible.

When I become conscious of my shivering, I begin the descent, walking back as quietly as possible, guided by the familiar landmarks and soft lamplight from our cabin—a single beam that rushes out into the night, only to be swallowed by the Barrens, by the empty land that seems to go on forever, until it finally dissolves in the winds of space.

My work as a field biologist, too, has taken me deep into silence, as during one austral spring and summer, when I studied the breeding ecology of the Australian pipit high in the Snowy Mountains. My study site lay in a small alpine basin, less than three miles from the nearest road, and only one mile from a major trail that climbed to the main crest of the range. Hike the trail on a warm summer's day, and you might pass fifty or more people in a few hours, yet I never saw anyone in my trailless basin. There was little reason to go there, unless you were after pipits—no convenient route to the surrounding ridges and peaks, no alpine lakes. I usually worked alone, sometimes for three days, sometimes for ten, while my family lived with my wife's parents, a three-hour drive from my study site. I spent most of my time in an area of less than one square mile, focused on my low-tech study: probing for pipit nests among boulders and tussocks, mapping the birds' territories, weighing and measuring eggs and nestlings, following foraging birds across snowfields and tundra. For day after day I lived quietly and without speech, focused on the lives of the birds and their habitat and repeatedly traveling over the same ground—watching birds for hours in the hopes that an incubating female, or a male with a beak full of food, would lead me to a new nest, while at the same time falling into my mind's ceaseless chatter.

I began fieldwork in October, when my basin was filled with snow and flocks of pipits foraged in the small patches of open ground. As spring turned to summer, the flocks disbanded, pairs formed, and females built their nests. The snows retreated into the lee of cutbanks and ridges, and the tundra moved from brown to green. Wildflowers, mostly a mix of white and yellow, bloomed in the moist meadows, and as the days warmed, great clouds of flies rose into the air—blowflies the size and form of a standard-issue housefly, and large horseflies that Australians paradoxically call "March flies," even though they appear in December. The blowflies did not bite, instead swarming across my exposed hands and into every available crevice of my face—mouth, ears, nose, behind my glasses—seeking whatever it is that blowflies treasure. The March flies, though, were after blood, and as much of it as possible. Quantitative guy that I am, I used calipers to measure the proboscis of several trophy-sized March flies that I killed, and found that their biting parts were a quarter-inch long—sufficiently long to startle me out of an ornithologist's reverie as I focused on tracking a skulking pipit to her nest.

The dedicated attention of the flies, the need to maintain my mental focus in the face of their assaults, and the succession of days without talking—these things also pulled me deep into myself. On those warm and still days when the flies were at their worst and my work forced me to remain still, I felt as though I was collapsing inward and retreating, turtle-like, into a protective shell. After several hours of playing the lead in *Bored of the Flies*, I would become aware of my tightly clenched jaw muscles and rapid, shallow breaths. I carried this tension with me through the long, hot hours, even on those good days when I added two or three new nests to my cache of data. But then would come the glorious evenings, for as soon as the sun sank behind the crest of the Main Range, the flies vanished. Their retreat brought me back to camp, and into stillness. The flocks of little ravens that filled the small valley during the day disappeared, carrying their raucous calls back to their roosts, and the pipits grew quiet—no more arcing, song-filled display flights, no more incessant calls, the insistent *peep peep peep* that filled the soundtrack of my research. I would sit at the edge of the small stream that ran by my tent, pull a chilled ale out of the water, fix a simple meal of "Fantastic Happy Noodles," and climb back out of myself and into the mountains. In the cool and shadowed evening I could tend to the day's last gardens of light, watch as alpenglow embraced the peaks surrounding my basin, and the long eastern slopes fell into night. The dark gathered its presence, the sky a glitter of unfamiliar, southern constellations rising brilliant above the backlit alpine ridges. The little stream gurgled on, a murmur of white noise, but behind the sound was the silence, a silence born out of the days I'd spent alone in my valley. Immersed in the quiet, I could reclaim some measure of peace, and shed my frustrations and tensions—the assault of the flies, my failures as a scientist, the constant mutterings of my mind. For awhile, in the evening and then in the sweetness of night, I could ignore my internal static, focus on the vast, blessedly uncaring world, and feel some measure of wholeness and calm.

What I have discovered in the silence of the natural world, and in the silence promised by wilderness maps, is something akin to the essence of silence that informs most religious traditions, especially those emphasizing mystical experience. Muhammad said that "the first stage of worship is silence," while Martin Buber gives a Hasidic saying as "The altar of earth is the altar of silence." Silence, too, is an essential part of Zen Buddhist practice. The silence of nature—or the nature of silence—also is embraced by what Belden Lane describes as the "Christian exercise of silence in prayer," or the "mystery of silence in the apophatic tradition." Apophatic prayer began in the fourth century as a way of reaching "beyond" (*apo*) every "image" (*phasis*) meant to describe God. Because the divine is ineffable and ultimately incomprehensible, language is inadequate for worship, and prayer must begin with an "embrace of silence." Among the earliest practitioners of apophatic prayer were the Desert Fathers and Mothers, who sought spiritual understanding in the solitude and privations of Wadi El Natrun, a desert region in northern Egypt. In a landscape of renunciation and abandonment, of silence and immense vastness, was the way to God, whose essence lay beyond language. This practice and belief is beautifully described by pseudo-Dionysius the Areopagite (fifth- and sixth-century CE): "the mysteries of God's Word lie simple, absolute and unchangeable in the brilliant darkness of a hidden silence." And, as much as I might try to describe the natural world, both in creative writing and scientific practice, some essential aspect of its existence will always escape me and inhabit "the brilliant darkness of a hidden silence." Beyond the quantitative and qualitative, beyond art and science, lies—what?—the aching beauty of the world's silence, a silence that lives at the center of creation, a silence that nourishes me in a fundamental way. There is truth in the notion that "the things that ignore us save us in the end," and what ignores us more than silence? I've touched the edge of this silence many times—in the desert summer's midday stillness, when the flaring sun forces all life capable of escape into shelter, or in the fierce depth of winter, with fifty degrees of frost settling beneath a crystalline sky. Stand quietly on some frozen lake, with the steep slide of mountains falling into the plane of ice, and the night hard and deep and long. Shiver slightly, as the cold probes your core, then gather your down parka close around you and settle into its thin grace of warmth. Listen to the faint whisper of wind as it drifts downslope, gently stirring the thick stands of spruce and fir, then slips away into the brittle cold. Atheist or true believer, agnostic or acolyte, it is here that you confront a meridian of silence. It is here that you may understand something of the longing of the Desert Fathers, and the great, mysterious blessing of "the things that ignore us."

I believe that we—as a society and as individuals—are too often exiled from silence and bathed in noise, although the notion of what constitutes "noise" is confusing. The common definition of noise as "unwanted sound" illustrates the problem, because one person's music is another person's noise (consider Beethoven and Pearl Jam going mano a mano), while the whine of snowmobile or jet ski may drive Mr. and Mrs. Smith to ecstasy or fury, depending upon their values. Noise also is defined as unmusical, or aperiodic, sound, but this is problematic because the quiet rustle of leaves might qualify as noise, while the piercing, rhythmic pulse of a siren would not. Another definition of noise is simply any loud sound; perhaps this notion is closer to what most people mean by "noise," but certain soft sounds (the scratch of a fork across a dinner plate, the muted hum of traffic pushing through my closed window, as I write) also are noise. Finally, in electronics and engineering, noise refers to "any disturbances which do not represent part of the signal," but again, one person's signal (the roar of engines at a NASCAR race) may be another person's static. The misanthrope in me wants to define noise as "any human-produced, loud sound," but aside from the problem of defining "loudness," which involves subjective intensity, many human sounds are delightful (the sound of a lover's voice in your ear, a baby gurgling in contentment, a choir rising in collective praise), while certain natural sounds (a flock of ten thousand starlings screeching and squawking, or the deafening rasp of cicadas on a thick Kansas night) are irritating beyond belief. And I have gone to sleep on the banks of the Colorado River, contentedly bathed in the roar of a huge rapid, only to awaken eight hours later and find that the water's churn and tumble had been transformed into noise. The problem is that what constitutes "noise" is a matter of quantity and quality, decibels and aesthetics—a situation recognized by R. Murray Schafer's concept of the "soundscape," which is the acoustic equivalent of the human-perceived landscape, and thus a social construct and matter of taste.

Around and around I go, grappling with something that I recognize but cannot quite get hold of. Like Robert Pirsig's notion of "quality" in *Zen and the Art of Motorcycle Maintenance*, noise is an elusive concept—yet even if we have trouble with the definitions, we can recognize quality, and noise, when confronted by them. Well, maybe. Perhaps it would be best to resort to a technical definition of noise as "audible acoustic energy that adversely affects the physiological or psychological well-being of people." Yet there are issues here, too, because something that is psychologically desirable—give me that Hendrix guitar solo—may have negative physical consequences for the listener. One thing is for certain, though. There are thousands of studies documenting the effects of exposure to loud sounds, both periodic and aperiodic, chronic and acute, on the mental and physical well-being of people, many of which are cataloged in Karl Kryter's *The Effects of Noise on Man*. Aside from obvious effects related to hearing impairment, noise—sometimes at levels far below those damaging to hearing—can induce physiological responses indicative of stress, such as elevated blood pressure, pulse rate, blood cortisol and epinephrine levels, and higher rates of cardiac irregularities, as well as difficulty attending to tasks.

Sound pressure levels usually are measured in decibels; on this scale, an increase of ten units means that a sound is ten times more powerful, and sounds twice as loud. The range of human hearing is roughly 0 to 130 decibels, at which point sound sensation is converted to pain. Hearing damage results both from acute exposure to very intense sounds, and chronic, long-term exposure to sound. Many factors contribute to the effects of sound on hearing, including rapidity of onset, length of exposure, frequency and continuity of the sound, and individual differences in sensitivity, but chronic exposure to sounds in excess of 85 decibels, approximately the intensity produced by a steam engine, pose a serious threat to hearing. The Occupational Safety and Health Administration requires that employers have a hearing conservation program if employees are exposed to a time-weighted average of 85 decibels over an eight-hour day, while short-term exposure to sounds in excess of 110 decibels—about the intensity produced by a chain saw—can cause immediate hearing loss. It is ironic that humans living in the Arctic, which in the winter feels like the source of all silence, suffer high levels of hearing loss, in part due to chronic exposure to snowmobile engines. One study indicated that 60 percent of Canadian Inuit suffered significant hearing impairment, and attributed this to early snow machines which produced sounds in excess of 110 decibels at the source.

Another area of concern is the effects on human behavior caused by community noise, a special form of ambient noise that typifies an area. Researchers interested in community noise quantify variables such as L_{dn}, the average day-night sound level, in areas exposed to loud sounds such as those from heavy air and ground traffic. They then calculate descriptively named "annoyance functions" to determine the level of ambient noise that interferes with activities such as speech and sleep. North American and European studies are remarkably consistent, and suggest that L_{dn} levels above about 55 decibels are at least "moderately annoying" to a majority of people. Urban ambient noise levels in cities have risen substantially over time, although the magnitude of this increase is difficult to quantify. One indication, though, might be that the intensity of emergency vehicle sirens rose about 30 decibels in sixty years.

Machines and our cities are getting louder. CD and MP3 players produce sounds with a maximum intensity of 121–139 decibels. Chronic exposure to intense sounds can be harmful to our hearing and general health, and interfere with sleep and conversation. These effects are important, but what concerns me most is not the physical effects of intense sounds, or even their more obvious psychological impacts, but the long-term, psychic effects of constant exposure to sound of all types — even those of relatively low intensity — especially those produced by humans. We are assaulted by sound, immersed in it, plagued by it. Sound intrudes on our lives, with the initial stage of the intrusion known, appropriately, as the "attack phase." As Schafer writes, "Every attack of sound is occasioned by noise, and the more suddenly it appears, the more noise is present." There is the pulse of traffic on the streets outside our home, the hum of refrigerators and whir of laptop fans, the chatter of voices on cell phones, the background music in malls and offices, the constant companionship of MP3 players or iPods, the pounding of "cardio" machines in the gym, the obstinate insistence of television. We adapt to many of these sounds, and the stimulus-filtering systems in our ears and brains essentially render much of the background noise insensible. Yet the sounds — the constant noise — remain with us, and we pay a price for our accommodation. As the title of an article by the American Industrial Hygiene Association has it, we live with "The Inescapable Sound of Noise," and I wonder how, or even if, we can hear ourselves think.

The chronic effect of exposure to even low-level ambient noise may have consequences of which we normally are unaware, or choose to ignore — effects missed by annoyance functions and L_{dn} values. This, partly, is the point of Schafer's "World Soundscape Project," and the wonderfully named "Tranquility Mapping Project," which sounds as though it was undertaken by a cadre of Buddhist geographic information specialists; instead, it is an effort by the Department of Transport and the Council for the Protection of Rural England to map areas away from noise and visual intrusion. My dictionary defines tranquility as the state of being "free from anxiety, tension, or restlessness," and while a Zen monk might be amused by attempts to quantify tranquility, that's what the Tranquility Mapping Project attempted. Tranquility was modeled and mapped using forty-four variables related to noise (from roads, railways, airports), visual intrusions (urban areas, power stations and transmission lines, wind farms, mines, recreational parks, industrial developments), and levels of recreational use. Each five hundred meter by five hundred meter grid of England was given a tranquility score and color-coded—darkest green for locations most likely to induce tranquility and brightest red for those least likely to do so. The resultant map shows tendrils of red snaking out from the major urban centers of England, with the largest hydra centered on London and the deepest green occurring in southwestern Cornwall and the northern border regions. To paraphrase Blake, "And did those maps in modern time / Quantify England's tranquil green." Perhaps any attempt to measure tranquility seems foolish and futile, like trying to quantify beauty or love, but I like the concept and its recognition that tranquility is in short supply in our modern, noisy world.

We are almost never without noise and activity in our multitasking lives, and almost never *with* silence. Such a loss, for even though there are many sounds that soothe us, and the world must have its beautiful voices, my myriad wilderness trips and my work as a field biologist have incubated me in silence and convinced me of its necessity. This chronic exposure to quiet has exerted a cumulative effect on how I view the world, and my attitude toward sound. I have come to love and require a world without noise, even if I cannot or will not live in it always. This quiet world is symbolized by the wilderness maps that have, for so many years, claimed my attention and passion, and drawn me into their intimations of silence. When I was young and lived for a short while in Minnesota, I was not prepared to explore the deeper silences of the map, or of the external and internal worlds. I was unprepared to live comfortably with the type of stillness held by the Brooks Range map that I discovered in 1972, even though I felt its pull so strongly; neither was I willing to encounter the silences of what George Eliot termed "the unmapped country within us." Now, at fifty-seven, I am ready to do so.

Long before I began this book, I lost the details of the map that I had encountered in Mankato. Although I am suspicious of memory, I believed that my recollection of the Brooks Range map was more than myth. Yet to understand the map's claim on my imagination, and its importance to my story, I needed to see and touch it. So, for months I tried to track it down, through "virtual" trips to libraries at Mankato State University, the University of Texas at Austin, the University of California at Berkeley, and the University of Alaska. My search was hampered by a lack of information; I had no specifics, no sheet names or numbers. I wasn't even certain that the map had been published by the Army Map Service; all I distinctly remembered was the Brooks Range, a 1:250,000 scale, and blankness. No map matching my memory was in the current collection at Mankato State. The University of Texas had the index maps to a 1950s-era Army Map Service series, but not the maps themselves. Berkeley was no better, and the University of Alaska a bit more promising, but a continent away.

I was discouraged, but correspondence eventually led me to Cornell University, only a two-hour drive from Brockport. On February 19, 2009, my wife, Melissa, and I walked into the map collection in the Olin Library. Bob Kibee, the map librarian, led us to a gray cabinet, pulled open a tray, and laid several folders before us. I opened one, searched quickly through the maps, and found nothing. But then, in the second folder, I encountered the ghost of my memory, and it was real: Demarcation Point, scale 1:250,000, sheet NR 7, 8–9, Army Map Service Series Q501, edition 1–AMS, hard up against the Yukon Territory in the extreme northeastern corner of Alaska. The map, published in 1951, was based on topographical surveys made between 1906 and 1946, supplemented by "photogrammetric compilation" from 1945. The Demarcation Point quad covered the Romanzof and British Mountains of the Brooks Range, and the arctic coastline in what is now the Arctic National Wildlife Refuge. The United States-Canadian border was a solid north-south vector, with a thick squiggle of contour lines extending roughly three miles to the east, where the contour interval increased suddenly, from two hundred feet to one thousand feet. Vertical angle bench marks (VABMs) traced the border, but ended two miles out, at the limit of detailed survey work. Even with the thousand-foot contour interval, the broad outlines of the country were clear, but the decreased density of contour lines made it appear as though blankness began to claim the map as soon as my eye moved east of the border. And then, as the contours of the Brooks Range fell toward the solid blue triangle of the Beaufort Sea, the mapped world suddenly disappeared. Ridges and slopes ended, and the blue braided channels of the Kongakut, Aichilik, Jago, Okkerokouik, and Okpilak rivers vanished, as if severed by a sharply honed knife. At the coast there was one blue dotted line, tracking the hypothetical course for the Kalokut River toward the mountains. The blankness covered an area of roughly thirty miles by seventy miles and sat directly over the Arctic Coastal Plain. A vast sweep of white dominated the map, but the dashed black lines of the ten thousand-meter Universal Transverse Mercator grid that overlay the silence promised that it eventually would be mapped and brought firmly into our system of knowledge. The area would be known as the calving grounds of the Porcupine caribou herd, and as the repository of the oil that fuels the lustful dreams of British Petroleum, ARCO, Sarah Palin, and George W. Bush. Still, the blankness was compelling and visceral, a vacuum that drew my heart and mind into its depths, a winter of the most brilliant white. The map was an anachronism and I was sunk in nostalgia, but I understood its seductive promise: that I might realize such stillness. For a moment I focused on the emptiness. I held my breath, and in the quiet I prayed that the beautiful silences will remain with us forever, no matter how many maps we create, no matter how much we profess to know.

When I was done with the Demarcation Point map, I carefully placed it in a folder and thanked the librarian. I took my wife's arm and walked back into the rush and noise of life, reassured and, for awhile, quiet.

They Always Knew Their Way

When I was young I worked as a technician on a study of feral burros in what is now Death Valley National Park, near the western edge of the Great Basin. My research took me into the Panamint Mountains, a xeric range of scrub and rock rising eleven thousand feet above the alkali wastelands at Badwater. I spent my days counting burros and tracking them across the canyons that drained the western slopes of the Panamints, trudging over calcined hills and across hardscrabble alluvial fans, wandering through knee-high forests of tough, spiny shrubs with names as harsh as the land itself: thornbush, brittlebush, blackbrush, shadscale, burr-sage. From mid-September through April the days were mostly pleasant and mild, although winter sometimes brought bitter cold and snow to the mountains. But in late spring the desert began to gather its heat, and from May through August torrents of shortwave radiation fell through cloudless skies and rained down upon the parched and empty range. In these, the hardest months, the tourists disappeared and even the ravens sought shade.

In May and June I learned to accept the desert's heat, to welcome it, and to wish for nothing more than enough water to keep me hydrated, plus a little midday shade and a comfortable camp for the night. Disdainful of what the survival manuals said, I forsook sunglasses and sunscreen and took foolish pride in wandering shirtless and hatless across the burning ground for day after day, following the burros into the height of summer. My skin grew dark and leathery, my hair bleached to a light blonde, and the sun baked me dry. I came to believe that I belonged to the desert—but even so, after twelve hours of fieldwork I felt as though I'd shrivel up into desiccated parchment and cartwheel across the desert, blown downslope by the afternoon

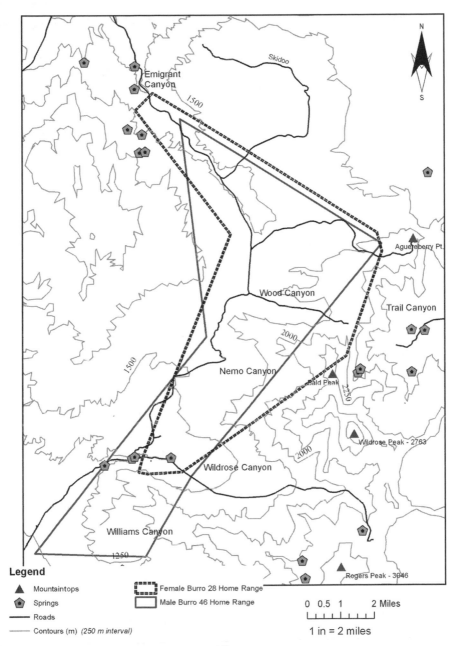

Feral burro home ranges in Death Valley.

winds that swept off the high ridges, five thousand feet or more above my study area.

I needed relief and so, as the apogee of summer approached, I entered into a daily cycle that became a ritual part of my fieldwork. Each morning I would track the burros into the heat-blasted lowlands and each evening I would follow the tidal pull of coolness and retreat to the higher parts of the Panamints. Sometimes I drove up a washed-out road to Piñon Mesa, a lightly forested bench at six thousand feet in Wildrose Canyon; on warmer evenings I sought out the eight-thousand-foot ridge at Mahogany Flat Campground, at the head of the canyon. But on the worst days neither of these places seemed cool enough and I headed for Rogers Peak, another two thousand feet above the campground. A key got me through the locked gate blocking the road to the Park Service repeater on the summit and I wound up the narrow, eroded track to the ridge running south toward Telescope Peak, the highest point in the range.

An hour of driving from Wildrose brought me to a solitary camp high above the lowlands, where mountain bluebirds nested, and brilliant orange paintbrush and delicate, sky-blue flax grew among the limber pine and sagebrush. After downing a quart of water I would cook dinner, write up my field notes, and emerge from the mental refuge where I had sheltered from the onslaught of heat and glaring sun. Then, as evening slipped over the land and a cool breeze rippled through the quickened air, I would watch midday's bleached colors regain their radiance. As the day rebounded into clarity, I relaxed and reacquainted myself with the dimensions of the Great Basin. To the west, Wildrose Canyon fell away, dropping through sparse forests of piñon pine into soft brown arroyos and shrubby flats. Down lower the burning playas and drowsy, heat-soaked scrublands of Panamint Valley sank into velvet softness. Beyond the lowlands were the back-lit Argus, Coso, Inyo and White Mountains, foreshortened in the slanting light and merging into a single, laminated range of rock and shadow. And on the horizon, sixty miles away, was the snow-capped crest of the High Sierra, with its faraway mountain meadows and cracked granite cirques. East, beyond Death Valley, were the Funeral Mountains, Grapevine Mountains, Black Mountains, and Amargosa Range, rolling into the vast basin and range country of Nevada, parallel sets of fractured, fault-block ridges stacked against one another, rising out of deep and hazy valleys.

On Rogers Peak I told myself a story about the Great Basin, all two hundred thousand square miles of it, all six hundred of its mountain ranges and intervening basins. It was a story of endless views and fractals of space and light and heat, of vast geometries of shadscale and blackbrush, a story born from days spent baking in the Panamint's valleys and then rising into evening's coolness, and of other views from other years: of cold scrub basins dusted with snow on a moonlit March night, or the long reach of the White Pine Range marking the boundary of an expansive desert plain, washed with an ephemeral grace of green on a June day. It was a story, too, of the burros that I tracked through the Panamints, as they moved with the demands of the desert and the insistence of their flesh. I saw them through the brittle days of January and February, when Orion hung high above the stark and arid ridges, followed them through the brief burst of spring and into summer's furnace. High on Rogers Peak, as I listened to the soft susurrus of the deep night country and felt the solace of cool winds drifting through the mountains, I could understand the orientation of my days. From the crest of the Panamints, I mapped the boundaries of my world, imagined tracing the paths of the burros through those desiccated mountains, deeper and deeper into that endless, empty realm of basin and range.

I came to the burro study in June 1975, three years after abandoning Mankato for the West. I worked for awhile as a gas station attendant in Portland, Oregon, spent another summer doing ornithological research in Arizona, then headed off to the Himalayas. In January 1974 I enrolled at Southern Oregon State College in Ashland, where I spent one-and-one half years completing a B.S. in biology, before beginning what I thought of as my first real job. My main responsibility as a technician with the Cooperative National Park Resources Studies Unit at the University of Nevada, Las Vegas, was to conduct fieldwork on a Death Valley burro population considered by the U.S. National Park Service to "exceed the environmental capability to sustain feral populations without significant, possibly irreparable damage." The burros were at home and happy in the Panamint and Cottonwood Mountains, on the western side of the monument; biologists had counted almost thirteen hundred during an April 1975 helicopter survey of areas above three thousand feet, and their population in Death Valley probably was as high as anywhere in the United States. Officials were concerned that the animals' presence was both an ecological disaster and a violation of Park Service management objectives, which included "restor[ing] conditions conducive to the perpetuation of natural resources as they functioned before disruption by technological man or competition from nonnative plants or animals."

And nonnative they were. *Equus asinus*, the African wild ass, donkey, or burro, is native to northern Africa and southwestern Asia, where wild populations once ranged from Morocco to Somalia, and Mesopotamia to Oman. However, wild ass populations have been decimated by hunting, habitat destruction, war, disease transmission from livestock, and interbreeding with domestic donkeys, and only a few hundred remain in scattered populations in the southern Sudan, Ethiopia, and Somalia, hanging on in one of the more desolate and strife-ridden parts of the world. Now, most wild populations are descendants of individuals that escaped from domestication or were released when they were no longer useful. Beginning in the 1870s, burros were used as "beasts of burden" in mining operations in the Panamint Mountains, and some must have escaped from captivity along the way. Later, when mining declined and the automobile claimed the transportation niche previously filled by burros, horses, and mules, others were released to fend for themselves. Mules, burdened by the inconvenience of sterility, would have died out quickly, while feral horses would have thrived only in areas with relatively high precipitation, good water, and more food. But when old Shorty, that crusty, farting, bushy-bearded prospector, went bust or succumbed to the seductive convenience of a Model T, he faced an option: give faithful Brighty a bullet to the brain, or a slap on the rear and commit him or her to the desert. The latter choice, being cheaper by a bullet and seemingly more humane, must have sent many animals into an environment that felt like home, and where they thrived. Although feral burros once ranged from Mexico north to Idaho and east to Texas, the core of their range was in the arid and semiarid Southwest, including Death Valley. By 1938 an estimated fifteen hundred burros roamed the monument, mostly in the Amargosa Range to the east and the

Panamint and Cottonwood Mountains to the west, where they caused substantial range damage, particularly near permanent water sources. The Park Service began shooting burros in 1939, and by 1953, when control efforts were abandoned, 3,578 burros had been "removed," eliminating them from the Amargosa Range and halving the monument's population. However, burros are very good at getting by in arid places where most hoofed mammals would perish, and by the early 1970s their populations had returned to pre-control levels, although they remained absent from the east side of the monument.

Most biologists and resource managers were convinced that burros damaged desert habitat, and native plants and animals. One frequently quoted 1958 review paper characterized burros as "wasteful foragers, frequently pulling up entire plants by the roots, eating only one or two mouthfuls, and dropping the remains to the ground." Of particular concern was how burros were suspected to interact with declining native desert bighorn sheep, either through competition for food or by preventing sheep from accessing water: "The bighorn is shy, flighty, nervous, and intolerant. It is inclined to vacate a competitive situation. Burro concentrations around water holes are avoided by the bighorn. Rather than tolerate such conditions, the bighorn frequently will move to another area." The options were obvious, as described in sensational language vaguely reminiscent of 1950s-era hyperbole about the Red Menace: "Either eliminate the burro from actual or potential bighorn ranges or else write the desert bighorn off as another lost American game animal." The same paper also reported, incorrectly, that "there seems to be a tendency to breed every year, even if range conditions are poor, a situation that discourages breeding by other ungulates."

While management agencies saw feral burros as an equine equivalent to Attila the Hun, there were almost no detailed studies available, either on their basic behavior and ecology, or their impact on native flora and fauna. This dearth of scientific information spawned numerous research projects in locations including Bandelier National Monument, New Mexico; the Grand Canyon; along the lower Colorado River in Arizona and California; and Death Valley. By 1975, results of these studies were beginning to appear, occasionally in peer-reviewed papers, but mostly in the "gray" literature—unpublished government and university reports. The general consensus was that, although feral burros might not be one of the Four Equids of the Apocalypse, and some of what passed for information on the subject was actually misinformation, they were a serious threat to the ecological integrity of public lands in the Southwest.

The Park Service wanted the burros removed from Death Valley in the most efficient way possible (shooting would do the job), but some in the general public saw them very differently: "From time beyond memory, the humble, gentle burro has been man's uncomplaining servant and playmate of his children. There is a legend that because he carried Mary to Bethlehem and Jesus along the desert trails of Palestine he was given the mark of the Cross—which you can see along his back and shoulders." Burros not only bore a religious connotation; along with wild horses, they were potent symbols of the mythic West, a status enshrined in the Wild Free-roaming Horses and Burros Act of 1971: "Congress finds and declares that wild free-roaming horses and burros are living symbols of the historic and pioneer spirit of the West; that they contribute to the diversity of forms within the Nation and enrich the lives of the American people; and that these horses and burros are fast disappearing from the American scene." Although the act applied only to lands administered by the Bureau of Land Management and Forest Service, its implications for Death Valley and other Park Service units were clear: feral burros and horses were not only animals requiring management, they also were icons of a powerful myth, the Old West. And so it was difficult for the Park Service to go toe to toe with a symbol beloved by a small but vocal public constituency, which beheld in the burro some compelling combination of cultural imagery and cuteness.

The management situation, circa 1975, also had been confused by conclusions from a PhD project on burro behavior conducted by Patricia Moehlman in the Panamint Mountains between 1971 and 1973. In both her dissertation and a 1972 article in *National Geographic*, Moehlman argued against any major effects of burros on Death Valley's habitat: "At this stage of my research, I see no ecological basis for the elimination of Death Valley's burros. Contrary to widely held belief [i.e., the Park Service's] the burros I observed did not strip the land, foul water holes, or endanger other animals." Moehlman ended her article with an emotional plea for the burros' preservation: "I recall the sights and sounds I remember best of Death Valley: the humor and furry charm of the long-eared foals, the fierceness and bluff of the adult males, the gentle, no-nonsense attitude of the proud jennies. How much longer, I wonder, will Death Valley's burros enjoy their free-ranging state? How long will others be able to see them as I have? For many years, I hope." I can only imagine the apoplectic shock this article must have generated at the monument's Furnace Creek headquarters—a biologist supported by the Park Service via research permits, accommodations, and other logistical considerations arguing strongly against the agency's position, and in a very public manner. "Et tu, Brute?"

Because Moehlman's work focused mostly on behavior, a study dealing with burro ecology was begun in 1974, under auspices of the Cooperative National Park Resources Studies Unit at the University of Nevada, Las Vegas, which is how I became involved. Among our research objectives was a clearer understanding of movement patterns in the Panamint Mountains—where did the burros go, and when? This was best accomplished by tracking marked animals, and to mark them we first had to capture them. For this we used a trap at Wildrose Spring, in the southern part of the study area, which had been constructed to capture burros for adoption, as part of the program to reduce their numbers. The trap consisted of a corral surrounding a watering trough, with a one-way, spring-loaded gate. Thirsty burros could push open the gate and enter the corral, but their lack of advanced problem-solving skills and opposable thumbs meant that they could not escape once they had entered the trap.

Free-ranging adult burros were less than enthusiastic about being handled and so we anesthetized them with a dose of M99 (etorphine hydrochloride), administered with a dart fired from a tranquilizer gun. The darts had a vicious barbed point, and I'd wince when one slammed into a burro's hindquarters with a loud "whack!" The unfortunate animal would startle and prance around the corral; a few minutes later it would begin staggering, much like the drunken college students who now reel past our house on Saturday nights. Tranquilized burros stumbled around the corral for ten minutes or more, banging into the fence and lurching sideways, before collapsing. Once a burro was unconscious, we blindfolded it to protect its eyes from the sun, and hobbled it to protect us from its hooves. We then measured and weighed it; noted tooth wear and eruption, sex and coloration;

searched for ectoparasites; collected blood, and attached an identification device. All burros received a numbered, yellow plastic ear tag; five adults also were given radio telemetry collars. Because the plastic ear tags were impossible to read from a distance, the last twenty-three animals that we captured were outfitted with collars constructed from four-inch-wide nylon strapping, with heavy, color-coded vinyl cloth sewn to the outside—yellow for males, yellow and red for females—and large, numbered metal plates riveted to the side. Once we had finished "processing" a tranquilized burro, we administered a dose of M50–50 (diprenorphine), the antidote to M99. While the tranquilizer took up to twenty minutes to work, the antidote acted very quickly, and within a minute the woozy burro was back on its feet. We then waited ten minutes to insure that the animal had recovered its equilibrium, before opening the corral gate and sending the newly accessorized animal back into the Panamints.

Feral burros are tough, and they—especially males—were hard on the marking devices. They often broke the plastic ear tags, and even though the radio transmitters had a battery life of eighteen to twenty-four months, and were encased in a thick coating of urethane, those on males functioned only for short periods, probably until a kick to the chest destroyed the device. Collars fared better, although males, through kicking and biting, eventually destroyed many of the numbered plates. In contrast, two of three transmitters on females lasted for at least a year, and they were gentler on the numbered collars as well. In spite of the difficulties of keeping numbered animals numbered, I usually could identify burros by some combination of ear tag, radio transmitter, collar, coat color, and markings. The collars were particularly useful because I could tell from a mile or more away if a burro was marked, and then approach closely enough to identify it with a spotting scope or binoculars.

Because the main part of Wildrose Canyon extends from an elevation of around four thousand feet to six thousand feet, conditions were milder there than in Death Valley proper, although they still were hot and dry. Temperatures could reach 105°F, and virtually no rain fell between May and late September. But even by the Panamint's extreme standards, 1975 was dry, with only 3.5 inches of precipitation falling in Wildrose Canyon during the year, about half the annual average. As light tumbled from the cloudless sky, moisture retreated from the broad, treeless basin to the east of Wildrose Spring, which headed in the steep slopes leading toward the crest of the range. Spring's sparse green carpet of annuals, which graced favored sites where moisture might collect, quickly faded into a lifeless brown shadow on the desert pavement. Perennial grasses and wildflowers, many of which blossomed in April and May, slid into senescence, and shrubs lost their leaves and flowers.

I drove the roads of my study area throughout those months of drought, getting to know the animals and their country: counting burros, stopping to look for marked individuals, sweeping my receiver's antenna across the landscape, listening for the blip of a transmitter signal rising out of the vastness. The route to the Panamints took me north from Las Vegas in my puke-green government service Dodge Powerwagon, with enough food and equipment for five days of fieldwork. I'd hurtle past the Nevada Nuclear Test Site and the ramshackle combination bar/gas-station/brothel at Lathrop Wells, slide west on Nevada 58 at the small town of Beatty, cross Daylight Pass and then Death Valley before reaching the mountains. At the north end of the study area I'd snake south through Emigrant Canyon to higher ground before crossing the broad expanse of Harrisburg Flats on the paved road leading to Wildrose. I'd bounce up dirt roads to Skidoo and Augerberry Point, grind along washed-out tracks to Piñon Mesa and Tuber Canyon in compound low, always on the lookout for marked animals, counting herds and recording their composition, elevational distribution, and distance from water, learning the names of the plants, noting the quality of vegetation. As I tracked the burros across the Panamints, through the dog days of July and August, my idioms were heat and dust and light, the numbers and locations of marked animals, Latin binomials (*Equus asinus, Lycium andersonii, Coleogyne ramosissima*), data. And in this process of naming and numbering, watching and following, the burros' home ranges became my home range, too.

Although I drove more than fifty miles of roads during each count, I spent most of my time in Emigrant and Wildrose Canyons, where there was permanent water and most of the animals summered. Males were often solitary, while females usually were alone with their foals or in the company of one or two other females. Regardless of sex, the summer home ranges of marked animals were almost always smaller than during the fall and winter, when the weather was cooler and wetter. This behavior was governed by the animals' need for water. Although adult burros can survive for a day or more without drinking, even when air temperatures are above 100°F, the Wildrose animals hung close to water, within two miles of the spring. The restricted movement pattern was particularly true for females nursing foals less than three months old. While foals could meet their need for fluids simply by nursing, lactating females generally watered two or three times per day.

Unless they were travelling toward water, the burros were mostly quiet. They fed slowly, moved deliberately, and rested, especially during the hottest part of the day. Number 31, a grayish-white female with a radio transmitter, birthed in May, and she and her foal mostly stayed within a mile of Wildrose Spring. Adult females 36 and 28, neither of whom foaled in 1975, remained together near the spring, where they often drank in the evening. Like the females, the males generally stayed close to water. Male 14 occupied a small territory immediately to the south of the spring, where he defended any sexually receptive (estrous) female who wandered through the area, while males 29 and 46 ranged across Wildrose Canyon, either alone or in the company of several other males. When the burros weren't resting or watering, they fed on whatever they could find in that heat-ravaged landscape. Unlike ruminants, with their four-chambered stomachs and recycled cud, burros and other equids have a high rate of what nutritional ecologists term "gut passage." They move food through their system quickly, getting what nourishment they can, emphasizing quantity rather than quality, teenaged boys of the ungulate world. For a demonstration of these strategies, compare a pile of horse dung, with its half-digested bits of stems and leaves, to the smooth, consistent texture of a standard-issue cow pie. Not a bad approach for a large plant-eater in the desert, where primary productivity and the growing season are limited by aridity. And so the burros got by on withered wildflowers and scraggly shrubs, some of which were little more than a collection of twigs and spines, as suggested by their common or scientific names: *Tetradymia spinescens, Grayia spinosa*, Anderson thornbush. Moehlman had even seen Wildrose animals feeding on cottontop cactus, which is defended by clusters of thick spines, and I'd heard of burros in low-elevation areas, when pressed for food, stripping the bark from ocotillo, a tough Mojave plant with a rosette of thorny-stemmed, woody "canes." Imagine finding sustenance in a one-by-two studded with nails, and you will understand what it must be like to eat ocotillo.

On hot summer days there was an aura of patient determination about the burros, a sense of resignation and lethargy in the face of the heat and aridity. One thing, though, pulled the males out of steadiness and into agitated aggregations—the presence of an estrous female. Although burros in our population foaled every month of the year, the peak occurred between May and July, and because gestation time in burros is roughly 365 days, many of the Wildrose females, both with and without foals, entered heat in early summer. When a receptive female was present, the general atmosphere among the burros was one of unquiet, the antithesis of their ordinary summer behavior: an entropic mosh pit, animals braying and jostling with one another, kicking and biting, always on the move. The rule of thumb for male burros was "whither the female goes, so go I." Gaggles of males pestered estrous females like flocks of demented geese—haggling with each other and obsessively approaching the object of their affection, who more often than not wanted only to be left alone, and so showed her displeasure by flattening her ears, lowering her head, and kicking with one leg at any harassing male's chest. Foals, out of some equine form of jealousy, would place themselves between their mother and any amorous male, shoving against the intruder or kicking at him. Although there was a dominance hierarchy among the males, they fought frequently. Males pushed and shoved each other, grunted, bit, and kicked in a constant turmoil of aggressive lust. Subordinate males tested their superiors, dominant males mounted subordinates, subordinates attempted to sneak copulations while the dominant male was otherwise occupied. The males were amazingly persistent with their squabbles; even when one landed a solid, both-hooves kick in the chest of an antagonist, the recipient might react only by moving off a few feet before again attempting to mount the female. And in any large aggregations, there always seemed to be a "last guy," some small, poor bastard with one ear torn half away and a mass of scars across his chest. Skittish and prone to flinching, he hung about at the fringe of the herd, retreating in the face of every attack, never able to reach the female of his temporary, hormone-driven desire, like the kid in high school everyone picked on, and who never got the girl of his dreams, or any girl.

In the early afternoon of an August day I spot a herd of burros on an alluvial fan across the valley. I park my truck, set up my spotting scope, and count eight burros, including three adults with numbered collars. Heat waves rise from the rocky, barren ground; through the lens the burros and the creosote bushes shimmer, a mirage suspended above the terrain. The herd is near the lower edge of the population's summer range and I need to know which individuals are out there, but I can't read the numbers on the collars. The burros are too far away, the metal plates are in bad shape, and heat waves distort the image. Although the temperature is about one hundred degrees and it looks like I'll have to walk over a mile before I can identify the burros, I resign myself to the hike and set off into the heat.

At first I move quickly, holding my binoculars at arm's length and weaving among the scattered shrubs. I don't worry about rattlesnakes; the surface temperature must be at least one hundred and thirty degrees and the snakes won't emerge from their dens until evening. After twenty minutes I'm close enough to read what's left of the numbers; I stop to scan the herd and copy my observations into a notebook. I am reluctant to begin trudging back to the truck, and so I watch the burros for an hour. A few are feeding, but most stand quietly, looking vaguely depressed, patient heads bent slightly toward the ground and eyes closed against the sun's assault. Gradually it dawns on me that, like the burros, I have been out in the sun all day, and that it is HOT. My feet feel like baked potatoes in a $425\,°F$ oven. Sweat collects in the shaded corners of my eyes, but otherwise my skin is completely dry, any sensible moisture having been sucked away by the unrelenting sun. I squint toward the truck, into the waves of hazy heat, my eyes narrow slits: the mile back seems like four and I wish that I was there, now. I begin walking. My pace is much slower than on the way out, as if I'm sinking into torpor and soon will be absorbed by the searing landscape.

The cobbled ground is hard beneath my boots, the air thick with dried heat and the viscid smell of creosote. I feel each breath of air as it moves into my lungs, dehydrating me from the inside out. I wander through fields of stone, follow vague trails into narrow washes, lose my route amidst a tumble of boulders. There is no sound except my own breathing and the crunch of pebbles underfoot. The smaller animals are in hiding; no sparrows call, no insects rasp. Out in the valley I am alone with the burros, like me silent and too large to escape from the sun.

The heat is bad, but it's the light that affects me the most. I feel it burning into my brain, forcing its way deep into my chest and abdomen. I wish for the shirt and hat that I left in the truck—or better yet, the gentle shade of a cottonwood, a trickle of water from a small spring. But there is no cooling refuge and I am impaled by the desert's onslaught. The land is nothing except light and heat and broken rock and the pulse of blood in my skull. I stop and shut my eyes and try to imagine a cooler, more welcoming world, but there is only the naked soil, the ineluctable, blinding avalanche of photons. Cottonwoods, willows, running water: all are lies. Life itself seems tenuous. How do I survive? How do the burros endure, and move through this unforgiving world? As Octavio Paz writes:

> Close your eyes and hear the song of light
> Noon takes shelter in your inner ear.
> Close your eyes and open them:
> There is nobody not even yourself.
> Whatever is not stone is light.

My mouth feels like I've been chewing on polyester batting for the last hour. I stop walking, unscrew the top of my water bottle, take a long drink. The water is warm and tastes of plastic. It does little to refresh me, other than banishing my immediate thirst. I know the relentless vector: liquid flowing into my intestines and then into my blood, before being sucked, almost immediately, from the pores of my skin. The day reminds me of one from earlier in the summer, when I stopped at the Park Service compound at Furnace Creek to gas up my truck. It had been hot in the Panamints, but the heat was of a different magnitude down below. The handle of the gas nozzle was too hot to touch without wrapping a bandana around my hand, the melting asphalt soft and ugly beneath my boots. When I stepped out of the truck I shuddered under the impact of the sun's violence, giddy and vulnerable, and a glance at a nearby thermometer told me why: 123°F in the shade. It's not so bad now, but the sensations are similar, and as I stand in the desert's furnace I wonder about value—in my research, in this particular piece of real estate. Surely there is a better place to be.

I trudge on. The truck seems no closer. A peculiar sensation creeps into my consciousness, a detachment between my mind and body, as though I am an impassive observer watching some automaton plod toward an unknown destination. Perhaps dehydration and a slight rise in my body temperature are having a hallucinatory effect, but the heat begins to lose its oppressiveness. Maybe it's just the overwhelming power of the sun, but I touch the edge of a wonderful lightness of being, as if uncoupling my mental and physical processes has freed me from some restrictive weight. I feel cleansed. The sweat vanishes from my skin without a trace, the boundary between my breath and the surrounding air disappears. Parched and weary, as I approach the truck, I touch the essence of the desert—this scorched and bitter place, this land of thorn scrub, burnt sleep, and the raven's guttural croak, where light and heat tumble from the sky and shear off the gesso ground. In summer it is a place where, if they can, the larger creatures seek shade and rest; the smaller ones emerge only at night, crawling and skittering from their refuges into a cooler, more humid and welcoming world. I have lain on my sleeping pad in places such as this as they cooled into darkness, watching as legions of scorpions scuttled past me, weaving among the withered plants and shattered rocks, stingers arched above pale abdomens. And yet, in spite of the inhospitable essence of Death Valley on a summer's day, I feel oddly at home here, wandering through these wasted mountains—much like the burros, I think.

In the desert, the imperative is water. A mammal's need for it is governed by an adaptive strategy for regulating its body temperature and the interaction between many environmental factors, including solar and thermal radiation regimes, and wind. Take humans. We are what physiological ecologists call "regulators," and must maintain our body temperature and water concentration in our tissues within a narrow range. We are intolerant of both dehydration and hyperthermia—an inconvenient situation in the heat, because evaporation of the desert's most precious resource, water, keeps us cool. In contrast, feral burros, like their wild progenitors, African wild asses, are "tolerators." Creatures of arid lands, they are admirably suited to life in the heat, capable of withstanding a water loss corresponding to 30 percent of their body weight, while appearing mostly unaffected by losses of 12 to 15 percent of body weight, much like the camel. In contrast a 4 percent loss in humans causes "functional derangement," while a 10 percent loss results in severe mental and physical impairment, with death following at about 18 percent loss. Burros also have an astounding capacity to rehydrate quickly; one 320-pound animal drank 28.5 quarts of water in less than five minutes, equivalent to a 150-pound person consuming about 13.5 quarts of water at once. Try drinking a quart of water without stopping, even if you are racked by thirst, and so consider these numbers. Unlike humans, burros also can eat while dehydrated. In humans a 4 percent water loss renders the mouth dry, and an 8 percent loss completely inhibits salivary gland function. Burros, though, will continue to eat low-quality forage like straw even when dehydrated, although they will reduce their food intake when their water loss reaches 15 percent of their body weight. Finally, burros, unlike humans, can tolerate "pronounced heterothermy"—daily body temperature fluctuations that average about 3.5°F in arid environments, although the range of summer body temperatures for five free-ranging burros in the Mojave Desert spanned an impressive 11.9°F.

Perhaps this cavalcade of numbers is alienating, and doesn't adequately illustrate the different physiological responses of humans and burros to heat and dehydration. So imagine yourself as a test subject on a mildly hot, cloudless summer day in the Panamint Mountains, with shade temperatures of 100°F. At dawn you strip off your clothes and walk naked into the desert. Your feet are tender, so you're allowed shoes, but that's it—no hat, shirt, or pants. Leave that canteen behind, because you won't be drinking any water. As the lovely morning light laves the scrub-covered valley and the land rises into heat, hike two miles out from the spring. It's not too bad at first, of course. The air carries a hint of coolness, the light has not yet gone nuclear, your body retains most of its water. To conserve bodily fluids and energy, you are allowed to stay still, if you can, at least until the mental impairment and restlessness caused by dehydration set in; perhaps you then will begin to wander aimlessly. You're permitted to seek refuge from the sun, although in this barren valley there is no shadowed cave, no verdant copse of cottonwoods, their sheltering canopy a gentle, comforting rustle in the hot air. So, huddle beneath the scraggly, virtually leafless branches of a creosote bush (carefully avoiding those cactus spines and sharp rocks) and pass the time of day. Listen as the last, desultory song of a black-throated sparrow dies away into the thermal silence. Remain still. Focus on survival.

Although the air is so dry that your water loss is mostly insensible, you understand the imperative of concentration gradients, how water is being sucked from the pores of your skin and into the air's great arid void. When your water loss is only 2 percent of your weight, your body temperature begins to rise. Remember that inactive humans on a hot desert day may require two gallons of water to replace their body fluids, and that lethal body temperature is around 107°F. By the time that your water loss has reached 4 percent of body weight, you are apathetic, sleepy, impatient. You imagine relief, endless glasses of water, fantasize about snow, the sweet caress of an air-conditioned breeze on your skin. You curl into yourself, as a way to pass the creep of time. Soon your water loss has reached 8 percent of your body weight. Your tongue feels swollen and sticky, and speech is almost impossible—although who would you talk to, out in that empty, hardscrabble, heat-scourged valley? Notice that you've stopped urinating; your kidneys have shut down in a desperate effort to conserve water and maintain blood volume. Notice, too, that your pulse is up about forty beats per minute over its normal resting rate. Your hypothalamus, at the base of the forebrain, has noted an alarming increase in your body temperature, which is now about 102°F, and is attempting to compensate by instructing the heart to pump more blood from your core to the skin. But there is a fundamental problem here, because most of your water loss has come from your plasma, unlike in camels and burros, which can maintain blood volume under short-term, severe dehydration. Thus your blood is thicker and much less efficient at transferring heat to your skin, where it can be off-loaded via sweat—a process which is failing, too, as you become progressively more dehydrated.

You know where this experiment is going, of course. You have no water, it is damned hot, and you are trapped in a positive feedback loop: as you lose water, your body temperature rises, and as your body temperature increases, the only way to cool is to evaporate more water, which causes your plasma volume to drop, which causes. . . . Eventually, when your body runs out of the water necessary for evaporative cooling, its temperature will rise explosively and death will follow. But perhaps there is a humane researcher supervising your experiment, unlike in the early, unregulated days of environmental physiology, when nonhuman test subjects were pushed well beyond their physiological tolerances and fried or frozen to death, and too many scientists accumulated too much karmic debt. So the trial is terminated when your water loss is only 10 percent of your body weight, and recovery is possible. The problem is, it's only mid-afternoon. You can't wait until dark—you've lost too much water already—and you will have to walk the two miles back to water in the full sun, even though the temperature is well over 100°F and at 10 percent weight loss, "man is physically and mentally unable to take care of himself." You have the will to live, but it's impossible to cover a distance that normally would take less than an hour, when your body has shut down and is plunging toward death. As much as you desire that spring, that life-giving trickle of water, as much as you long for family and friends, you cannot force your body to overcome its water deficit, and hyperthermia. You rise and stumble toward salvation, but you are cooked, both figuratively and literally.

In early September of 1975, the Panamints hovered on the edge of autumn. Evenings slid more quickly into relief than during August, and mornings climbed more slowly toward the searing, midday heat. At dawn, when I rose from my sleeping bag on Piñon Mesa and looked out over Wildrose Canyon, a slight fragrance hung in the cool air, a mix of moisture and sage and pine. I would brew my tea and watch the lovely colors of morning, a soft, rich palette of gold and brown and grayish green, lilac and rose, spread across the valley. The Panamints had lost their summer's edge, but the land was still sere. No rain had fallen on Wildrose Canyon since April and down lower, near the spring, the vegetation was desiccated. The poor quality of the forage wasn't due only to the heat and lack of moisture. The burros, tied to water, had remained near the springs in Wildrose Canyon, and hammered the plants. The herbaceous annuals and perennials preferred by the burros were mostly gone; the few surviving individuals of Indian rice grass, desert speargrass, and desert mallow were little more than nubs, while many shrubs had a well-rounded, manicured look, as though attended to by a legion of hyper-efficient Japanese gardeners. Although scattered individuals of favored browse species, such as

Shockley goldenhead, burr-sage, and indigo bush, hung on near Wild-rose Spring, most survivors had been trimmed back to near ground level and consisted of a few sad, leafless branches. Only species dis-dained by the burros—Mormon tea and Cooper goldenbush—were robust. The situation was different, though, farther from Wildrose Spring, in areas such as Wood and Nemo Canyons, and inside a small exclosure about two miles east of Wildrose Spring, which pre-vented burro access. There, the shrubs were more vigorous, the pe-rennial grasses and wildflowers, although brown, more abundant and healthy.

The burros, hobbled during the summer by their need for water, were shaping Wildrose plant communities, preferentially remov-ing desired species, sculpting surviving shrubs, compacting the soil, and carving dense networks of trails into slopes and benches near the spring. Their actions also impacted small mammals, contrary to the implications of Moehlman's dissertation. She had tallied burrows, presumably occupied by small mammals, along transects at increasing distance from Wildrose Spring, and found no effect, which she took as evidence that feral burros were not affecting small mammal pop-ulations. However, my data from two live-trapping grids, one near Wildrose Spring, the other at a similar elevation in a burro-free part of Death Valley, showed that almost three times as many small mam-mals, mostly long-tailed pocket mice and canyon deer mice, resided in the burro-free area. I knew of similar effects at two study sites in the Grand Canyon on opposite sides of the Colorado River, one with burros and one without. There, biologists found higher rodent species diversity, and almost four times the density, at the site without bur-ros. These effects were due to an inverse trickle-down principle, à la Ronald Reagan, as it influenced the "economy of nature." In both the Grand Canyon and Death Valley, there were healthier plant commu-nities in burro-free locations, with more plant species, robust shrubs, and well-developed understories of sub-shrubs, perennials, and an-nuals. Preferred foods, such as globe mallow, plantain, and perennial grasses, were rare or absent at sites where burros were abundant. The burros ate the plants that, directly or indirectly, supported the small mammals, and the small mammals, mostly nocturnal species that few people see, suffered in turn.

And so data describing the effects of burros on vegetation and small mammals, when combined with the mission of the National Park Service and goals set out in the 1963 "Leopold Report," which proposed maintaining parks in the condition they would have been in at the time of European discovery of North America, supported removing burros from Death Valley. As much as I had come to admire burros—for their physical and behavioral adaptations to the desert's harsh environment; their tenacity; their ability to eat plants that I could hardly touch, without getting stabbed by a thorn or spine; their patient stillness in the furnace of summer; the manner in which they moved across the land; their ridiculous brays and chaotic mating antics; and the sheer otherness of their lives—I believed that they did not belong in Death Valley. Although equids evolved in the New World and immigrated to the Old World some three million to two-and-one-half million years ago, native species had been absent from the region for at least thirteen thousand years, since the great megafaunal extinctions of the late Pleistocene. The lineage that included burros had evolved only after equids had colonized the Old World, and so I saw feral burros as being of the desert, but not of the Panamints.

There were those, like Moehlman, who argued that feral burros should remain in Death Valley and the Grand Canyon. Some, such as Paul Martin, a paleoecologist at the University of Arizona, have advocated for a "Pleistocene rewilding," the reintroduction of descendants of Pleistocene megafauna or their close ecological equivalents, including modern horses and burros. Proponents of rewilding see it as a way to fill niches vacated during the extinctions following the last major glaciation, when perhaps forty large mammal genera, including mammoths, camels, giant ground sloths, short-faced bears, and saber-toothed cats, padded and lumbered into the dustbin of evolutionary history. In 1979 Martin chartered a helicopter and paid a short visit to the same Grand Canyon location where plant and small mammal communities had been compared in sites with and without burros. On the basis of his cursory inspection, he concluded that burro impacts were not "alarming or intolerable," even though data from the eleven-month study demonstrated substantial damage. I had visited the same locations in 1975, and in my field notebook described "much evidence of severe overgrazing, with very few annuals or small perennials present, and most large shrubs showing signs of heavy browsing in 209 Mile Canyon [the side of the river with burros]." Perhaps our different impressions were another case of "same planet, different worlds," in which contrasting conclusions were driven more by preconceptions than by reality—but the data on burro impacts were out there, in a peer-reviewed paper, and its conclusions have been supported by numerous other studies in the region. I wonder if Martin's belief that feral horses and burros in the Southwest were "returning to their phylogenetic homeland," and his refusal to "stand back passively in the face of efforts to throttle back reintroduced equids," influenced what he saw along the Colorado River, among the mesquite and creosote bushes. Sometimes we ignore what we do not care to see. It is easy enough to do.

Other burro advocates included supporters of the Wild Free-Ranging Horse and Burro Act, with its allusions to the mythic nature of the American West. The passion of their advocacy is captured by the present-day Wild Mustang Coalition's website, with its wallpaper featuring an American flag, bald eagle, and Statue of Liberty, and description of lives "transformed by their [burros'] magical presence and the passionate devotion that these special beings have inspired." Others wanted the burros protected because they were one of the few highly visible mammals in a landscape that to the casual observer appears almost devoid of living things other than small, scraggly shrubs. In the mid-1970s, a drive through the Panamints from Emigrant Canyon to Wildrose Canyon usually yielded a herd or two of burros, some of whom approached cars and pleaded for handouts from the tourists. Among the most effective beggars were jennies with their young foals, undeniably cute and effective poster animals for feral burro preservation.

Ultimately, I felt that advocates for allowing feral burros to roam desert ecosystems of the Southwest were wrong. Proponents of "rewilding" were wrong because southwestern ecosystems had changed over the last thirteen thousand years, and were no longer the functional equivalents of what they had been in the Pleistocene. Those who argued that the burros did not damage desert environments were ignoring data from studies in Death Valley, the Grand Canyon, and elsewhere. Those who saw them only as a loveable attraction or symbol of pioneer spirit did not understand the ways in which burros altered ecosystems. They either could not see, or did not care to see. Feral burros may not have been harbingers of ecological disaster, as they sometimes were portrayed, but they affected the habitat, in places severely. Perhaps it was easy to love the burro, just as it was easy to love the wild mustang; it was more difficult to feel affinity for the mice that scuttled and hopped silently through the darkness, their lives lost to us, or for the spindly shrubs and ephemeral wildflowers that bloomed quickly and withered into sleep. As the ecologist Paul Shepard wrote about feral horses:

> The destructive aspect of the horse is a subdued theme in the modern world. When the U.S. government decided to reduce the number of feral horses on public lands by killing them, a great outcry arose for their protection that resulted in relocation plans that had only limited success. The inability of the defenders of those horses to feel as deeply for the larger community of life, which the horse destroys, demonstrated the depth of its power... as well as the difficulty of weighing that abstract "community" against the most vivid of all animal figures.

By August 1975 some parts of Wildrose Canyon looked like an abandoned parking lot, with scattered, scraggly shrubs poking out from holes in the neglected pavement. Little remained for the burros to eat and in early September, as the weather turned milder and the burros were unshackled from their need to water daily, they began to move. Female 31 traveled north with her foal. By September 12 they were near the old mill in Emigrant Canyon, about ten miles north of Wildrose Spring, where there was permanent water, but where fewer burros lived during the summer. Other adult females, including 28 and 36, who would remain together until the following spring, moved into the broad expanses of Nemo and Wood Canyons, and Harrisburg Flats, as did males 14, 39, and 46. The burros probably wandered because, across much of the northern part of the Panamints, the vegetation was in better shape than near Wildrose Spring. In many places annuals carpeted the ground, although most were shriveled ghosts and of little nutritive value. More important, shrubs comprising the majority of the burros' diet did not have the domed, symmetrical shape characteristic of those near Wildrose Spring, and held forage of higher nutritive value.

In late September heavy but localized rains fell in parts of the Panamints. Wildrose Canyon remained dry, but Emigrant Canyon and higher areas north of Wildrose received good — by Death Valley standards — soakings. Within two weeks a wash of green had spread across the alluvial fans and flats. Thornbush, goldenhead, burr-sage, and brittlebush were flush with succulent leaves and shoots, and small, lush pockets of annuals sprouted amongst the cobbles. By mid-October the young leaves and shoots of the three main browse species in Emigrant Canyon had an average protein content of 13 percent, and a moisture content of 66 percent, while major browse species in Wildrose Canyon averaged 6 percent protein and 25 percent moisture. Female 31 and her foal moved farther north down Emigrant Canyon to an elevation of three thousand feet, where rains had prodded the vegetation into renewed growth, and where they would remain through the winter.

As fall moved into winter, and winter into early spring, Wildrose burros spread into parts of the Panamints where they were rarely or never seen during the late spring and summer. Wood and Nemo Canyons, and Harrisburg Flats, continued to hold animals, and in late November large numbers of burros, including eight marked animals, moved to near the vanished mining camp of Skidoo. The area is almost six thousand feet high, and night-time temperatures often fell to well-below freezing, but there was plenty of fresh growth on south-facing slopes, which was where I found the burros. These places were about four miles from the nearest water, but with cooler weather and lush vegetation, the burros could afford to roam. Several marked animals moved further north than 31 and her foal, working their way down Emigrant Canyon and west onto the alluvial fans west of Towne Pass. Although the straight-line distance from Wildrose to their "furthest out" was only ten miles, their movements indicated that they had traveled more than thirty miles from where they were marked. Other burros descended into the broad sweep of Panamint Valley, directly west of the mountains. But by late March, burros began returning to Emigrant Canyon, Wildrose Canyon, or Tuber Canyon, two miles south of Wildrose Spring, where there also was permanent water. In April females 28 and 36 went their separate ways, with 28 moving to Emigrant Canyon and 36 returning to Wildrose. By mid-April, when female 31 and her foal — now almost one year old — appeared in Wildrose Canyon, the vegetation, stimulated by sporadic rain and snow, had revived.

Most marked burros remained near Wildrose Spring during the summer of 1976, their movements again restricted by their need to water daily, even as the plants sank into senescence. Female 31 foaled again, and her yearling was on its own. In June female 36 was found dead near the spring, having died while foaling. Males 14 and 46 also spent another summer in the Wildrose Canyon area. The summer of 1976 looked like a repeat of 1975 and so I expected the burros to again move out of Wildrose once the weather cooled, but most did not. Instead, unusually heavy rains fell in Wildrose Canyon in late August and September, reviving the dormant vegetation, unlike during the previous year. Most marked animals, including female 31, remained in Wildrose Canyon, or left briefly before returning in early October.

The lives of the Panamint burros were tidal, an irregular ebb-and-flow governed by food and water. They showed a strong fidelity to small, dry season ranges near permanent springs, where seasonal drought and the concentrated animals reduced the quality and quantity of forage, but once the weather cooled, diminished physiological stress freed the burros to wander farther afield, seeking areas where food was more abundant and nutritious. The burros were flexible, their movements unpredictable in time and space. A roiling cluster of dark cumulonimbus clouds building over the mountains, a sweet gray curtain drawn down upon some dusty, scrub-covered flat or boulder-strewn arroyo: there would be rain, and the plants would grab enough of it to rise from their sleep. Less burdened by heat, the burros would move with the promise of moisture and a flush of succulent new leaves, a covenant of green climbing out of drought-ridden grays and browns.

I watched burros spill out of Wildrose Canyon, traverse Harrisburg Flats, wander into Emigrant Canyon and then over Towne Pass. They descended into Panamint Valley or climbed onto the broad ridges along the crest of the mountains. Some disappeared for months on end, roaming into parts of the Panamints where I could not follow, only to reappear six months later. A few marked animals vanished, tracking their inclinations into some waterless oblivion, or traveling until they found other burros elsewhere in the Panamints, or in playas and mountains to the west. But most burros knew enough to find their way home, and I wondered about what potent combination of sense and memory drew them across the broken ground. It was 1976 and I was almost twenty years shy of acquiring the appropriate technical language, but what I was considering was spatial orientation and the cognitive maps of animals.

Most neurobiologists believe that, in mammals, the seat of spatial orientation and memory is located in the hippocampus, although a few dissent from the majority view. The hippocampus is a mass of neurons at the base of the forebrain; in humans it is shaped vaguely like a seahorse—hence the name, which is derived from the Greek *hippos* for horse and *kampos* for sea monster. The mammalian hippocampus is larger in species and sexes that range over larger areas, and must deal with more complex spatial tasks such as navigation and retrieving stored food. One study illustrating this effect involves the meadow vole and closely related pine vole, small rodents with different mating systems and ranging habits. Meadow voles are polygynous, and during the breeding season males cover four to five times as much space as do females, in their restless search for multiple partners. In contrast, the monogamous pine vole lacks seasonal, sex-related differences in home-range size, as males have no need to wander. Laboratory studies also demonstrate that males of polygynous vole species perform better in mazes than do females, while males of monogamous species do not. Differences in ranging behavior and spatial abilities are mirrored by differences in hippocampal volumes, which during the breeding season are larger only in males of the polygynous meadow vole. Lest we consider the relationship between hippocampal volume and spatial experience an attribute of non-human mammals only, the volumes of the hippocampal region thought to store spatial information are larger in London taxi drivers than in other London drivers.

If there is some dissension in the neurobiological ranks about the role of the hippocampus in storing and processing spatial information, there is even more debate about cognitive maps in nonhuman animals—what they are, and even if they exist. One definition of a cognitive map is "a powerful memory of landmarks which allows novel short-cutting to occur"; a second, less restrictive definition involves "any representation of space held by an animal." The argument is conducted in technical journals that I do not read regularly, using language that I can only partly grasp, but my sense is that animals as diverse as honeybees, pigeons, rats, and monkeys do possess cognitive maps; if not involving "novel short-cutting," at least of the "spatial representation" variety. This belief comes partly from my imperfect understanding of the technical literature, but more importantly, from my fieldwork on burros in Death Valley, Harris's sparrows in the Canadian Arctic, and Australian pipits in the Snowy Mountains. I have marked burros, sparrows, and pipits, lived with them for months on end, and witnessed how they move through their worlds. In doing so, I have become convinced that these animals carry some sophisticated representation of space in their brains. They must have their "hippocampal topographical maps," as different, complex, and ultimately incomprehensible as they might be to humans—maps which keep their lives centered on the bits of space that they occupy. For a Harris's sparrow, there must be a map that helps a returning, migrant male recognize the particular copse of stunted trees and shrubs where he bred the year before—a tiny patch of dwarf birch and black spruce, set back a quarter mile from the Thelon River and lost in the expanse of the Barren Grounds, some sixteen hundred miles from where he wintered. For a female Australian pipit, there must be a map that allows her to quickly locate her nest, hidden beneath a fifteen-inch-tall shrub in the midst of a fifty-yard by one-hundred-yard patch of shrubby *Grevillea*—all of the plants of a similar height, the patch lost in a mosaic of tundra vegetation cradled in a high alpine basin, the basin held deep within the Snowy Mountains. For a feral burro in Death Valley, there must be a map that leads it back to Wildrose Canyon, across thirty miles or more of dry arroyos, scrub-covered flats, and desert ridges, past springs where it will drink but not reside, alongside burros with which it travels for awhile but then abandons.

Although I know that the burros were good at navigating through the Panamints, I do not know how they did so, and here the technical literature is not very helpful, as little is known about spatial memory in equids. Horses can navigate mazes well, and recall solutions to spatial problems weeks or months after learning how to solve them. Humans have millennia of experience with domestic horses and their use of space. Some of us have herded them and ridden them; more of us have heard anecdotes about Old Joe and how he carried a comatose cowboy (perhaps festooned with arrows) back to the ranch, and safety. Legions of field biologists have followed zebras, wild horses, and wild burros across the veldt, or through the thorn scrub and high desert, documenting their migrations, home ranges, and territories. We know that livestock recall good grazing sites and repeatedly seek them out. We have watched and measured and ridden, but we still do not understand much about "the ability of horses [and other equids] to remember relative spatial information, develop spatial maps of familiar areas, and navigate over long distances." We assume, but evidently do not know for certain, that the hippocampus is the repository for spatial information in equids, as it most likely is for other mammals. The requisite studies have not been done; not only are horses large and expensive to maintain, they have a very passionate constituency. It would be difficult to conduct the kinds of neurological studies that have been done on voles. No one's going to run a horse through a series of mazes, and then kill it and thin section its brain; neither would it be easy to track down an MRI machine of the sort used with the London taxi drivers, large enough and available for a study of horse hippocampi.

Still, I wonder about the burros: how did their brains respond to the topography of the Panamints? How did they build their maps? How did they *know*? Foals might follow their mothers for a year, and so become accustomed to their space, but then, how did their mothers know where to go? There must have been more than some sort of tautological progression in which one burro follows another, which follows another, and so on. There must have been some powerful mix of sensory stimuli and memory that drew them into Wildrose Canyon in the spring, and led them out of it in the autumn: a cascade of events in which the world, with its myriad stimuli, was rendered first as flashes of action potentials along neurons and fluxes of neurotransmitters between axons and dendrites, before target cells translated the language of DNA into the language of proteins. Out of this alchemy, a burro would understand where to go and would know some place as home. What complex nexus of memory (where I was, before) and sight (there—that ragged ridge, breaking against the horizon just so) and scent (there—the faintest odor of water drifting downwind, miles from that tiny trickle of a spring) and sound (there—the song of a Bullock's oriole given out on a bright May morning, from that verdant cluster of cottonwoods) told them where they were and where they needed to go?

No matter; it was enough to understand that the burros knew their way. I envied the patient and steady manner with which they moved through their desert world. They seemed certain of their maps in a way that I was not, for when I worked in Death Valley, and despite my desire for the desert, and the joys and satisfactions of my work, I felt unsure of my path and place. The Panamints, for all their arid beauty, were never quite enough. From Rogers Peak I could survey the length and breadth of my study area, the canyons and salt pans, arroyos and mountains where I spent so many of my days, and which I had come to love. Yet I often looked farther afield and yearned for other geographies. Back in Las Vegas I poured over maps, and sought out the lands of my imagination. In my abundant free time I ranged far and wide into the Sierra, the slickrock country of Utah, the Grand Canyon. Partly my restlessness was a product of my distaste for Las Vegas, the physical and psychological expressions of its ethos. I knew, too, that my temporary position with the Park Service would end in 1977. I toyed with the idea of graduate school, went so far as contacting potential faculty advisors and applying to several programs. I did so because I couldn't conceive of any attractive alternatives, but my hesitant intentions did not resonate well. Despite my love of fieldwork and the world of the intellect, and what I saw as the inevitability of an academic path, I could not imagine returning to tests and an avalanche of technical journal articles. I was quietly agitated; I desired an anchor, but nothing of much certainty waited beyond the end of my Park Service contract. Perhaps this restlessness led me, in late 1976, into a fascination with the Canadian Arctic. During the days I worked on the final report on my Death Valley research, but in the evenings I read Vilhjalmur Stefansson on the High Arctic, R. M. Patterson on the Nahanni River, Sir John Franklin on the Barren Lands—acts foreshadowing a year-long journey that I would begin only seven months later, one that would take me just about as far away from the desert as I could get, deep into the wilderness of the Northwest Territories.

Had anyone at the time asked me if I was happy, I would have replied, honestly, that I was. I embraced my work and where it took me. I had a steady girlfriend and some very close friends. In my abundant free time I ranged far and wide into the wilderness—climbing, rowing rivers, and backpacking, finding solace and excitement in the lost lands. The debris of my childhood was still there, but I sought as much distance from the past as I could muster, and for the most part I held that my flight was successful. But I was at times anxious, aware of a subtle dissatisfaction that could blossom into full-blown angst without apparent reason—unless my stepfather made one of his miserable cameo appearances as a refugee fleeing bill collectors, perceived persecutors, and his demons. I met him once at a motel in Las Vegas, when he and his fourth wife, Helen, were on their way to California. They struggled to maintain a jovial façade, but the tension between them was as thick as the fog of cigarette smoke and alcohol fumes that choked the room. For a few hours I inhabited a world of false levity and awkward, halting conversation, wanting nothing more than to make my escape, yet bound by some painful sense of duty and embarrassment to remain, tethered by my subconscious mantra: "Do not disturb." Stay calm and quiet, maintain your defenses: all of it will pass and nobody will get hurt. Soon you will walk out of the room, into the bright light of a Las Vegas afternoon, and the visit will be behind you. You will look northwest, toward the Spring Mountains, rising ten thousand feet above the city and half-hidden by a haze of smog, and you will be cleansed, and free. I would carry this desire for freedom from my stepfather, and the effects of his behavior, far beyond his lonely death in a Fort Wayne, Indiana, apartment in 1988. Even now there are moments when his ghost is with me, and I must struggle with an inchoate manifestation of what Faulkner once wrote: "The past isn't dead. It isn't even past." But this story is tied to another set of maps, I suppose, and not for the telling, here. Instead, let the focus be on the deserts, the mountains, and the high, wind-scoured plains of this world. Let those places, and their maps, carry me forward. . . .

In the final pages of our report, "Ecological Studies of Feral Burros in Death Valley," the leading scientist on the project and I argued that feral burros did not belong in Death Valley National Monument and wrote that "direct reduction by shooting appears to be the least expensive, most effective and humane method available." I believe, strongly, that we were correct about removing feral burros from Death Valley, but I am not so confident about the shooting. Perhaps capture, adoption, and transport to places far from the desert was the better option, despite its expense and inefficiency. I really don't know

what the best answer was, or even if one existed. Remove the burros, either by shooting or trapping, and others might migrate in from
populations outside the park. Let the burro populations build once
again, then use helicopters costing $1,000 per hour to round up some
of the burros, while knowing that the Park Service doesn't have the
money to spend on a project that won't work in the long run. Rifles,
on the other hand, cost much less and would reduce burro populations to a level at which their environmental impact is limited. Regularly scheduled rounds of herd reduction by shooting would most
likely be a more efficient and cost-effective option, but I am much
less certain about life than I was in 1977, and far more aware of death
and suffering. The world is too burdened by these things, both among
humans and nonhuman animals, and one of our roles should be to
reduce the net amount of pain on this planet. I know that I chose, and
will always choose, the long-tailed pocket mouse and desert mallow
over the burro, and that burros should be kept out of Death Valley. I
also know that shooting would be the easiest way to accomplish this
objective, but I do not know if lethal means are ethically preferable.

Besides, for awhile I lived with the burros. Although I had my refuges, I felt the same heat and light; walked among the same tough
and thorny shrubs; responded in some similar but inchoate way to
the ineluctable pull toward water and the grace of rain; slept beneath
the same winter sky, that ocean of gelid stars; felt the land exhale as it
turned from winter toward spring, and the delightful manner in which
summer slowly folded into autumn, when the rabbit-brush bloomed.
My job required that I watch and measure, and travel with the burros through their annual cycle. After each day of fieldwork I sought
out a camp, where I sat cross-legged on the ground and cooked a
simple meal. I was almost always alone and still; and as the desert
fell into twilight and I fell into the quiet, I would write up my notes,
and consider what I had seen, and what I did not understand. I carried these thoughts with me, out of Death Valley to a desk at the university, where I summarized my data, ran statistical tests, read scientific reports, and searched for patterns in the lives of the burros. The
template of my days, a mix of fieldwork and analysis, physical activity and contemplation, was one of the chief pleasures of my work. It
was wonderful to inhabit the world of direct experience, and wonderful to understand something of the patterns sequestered within

the tables, graphs, and technical papers. The burros moved through the Panamints, along interwoven paths of sight and sound and scent and touch, through a land of light and desert scrub, and I followed. I moved with the data, as well as with the animals and plants, and I was blessed by them all: a cartography of the aesthetic and analytical, a way of mapping the sensual and sensuous world. Together, the burros and I made our maps of the Panamints. We traced the paths of the seasons, were drawn into that harsh and lovely land by the pull of body and mind, the insistence of heat and history. We adapted as best we could, and in the simple act of perseverance there was some grace, a sweetness that bound us to the world.

The Truth Shall Be Revealed

t is raining, much as it has been for the last five days. It is late June in 1982, and I am standing next to my Outward Bound patrol, watching as they work out just where we are on the west side of the Oregon Cascades, and where it is that we need to go. Rain plummets from a leaden sky, leaks through the thick canopy of mountain hemlocks and onto the hood of my rain jacket. I stand with my legs splayed, hitch my pack higher on my back and tighten the gut strap, trying to find a more comfortable stance. I catch my coinstructor's eye, throw a look of resignation her way: this is the students' problem, not ours. Not yet. In our current roles in the experiential education game, we shall remain detached bystanders and wait for the students to make their decision. The patrol's two "navigators for the day" hunker over their topographic map, which is protected by a plastic pouch, and try to divine our location. They rotate the map, working to get the orientation right, then fiddle with their compasses, which hang like plastic pendants around their necks. In the rain and thick trees, and at the end of a tough day, none of this is easy: to know your place and your way when you are new to the task. A few of the more impatient students cluster round the navigators, gesticulating, trying to help. Other members of the patrol stand hunched beneath their packs, in various postures of impatience or forbearance—silent and slightly miserable, contemplating the rain, waiting.

Waiting: I am tired, but the students look exhausted. It has been a long day. It is early evening and we have been walking since eight in the morning, climbing through thick forests and across an occasional meadow, hauling our fifty- to seventy-pound packs over trailless ground and late-lying snow. We are headed toward the lower slopes of the South Sister, which we hope to climb the day after tomorrow, if the weather clears. If it ever clears. For five days we have seen nothing but gray skies, except for the occasional "sucker hole"—those ephemeral patches of blue that breed tiny flashes of hope, only to vanish in the roiling swirl of clouds, their disappearance first generating disappointment, then resignation. We should know better: the rains will remain, like the unwelcome guest who comes for dinner but stays for a week.

The ground is either saturated or snow-covered. The thick coniferous foliage drips constantly, even when the rains cease for an hour or two. Even the relatively sheltered bark of the trees is wet, in places squishy to the touch of my wrinkled fingertips. We are sandwiched between the fog that rises from the lowland valleys and the swirl of thick gray clouds above, tiny figures lost in a sixteenth-century Chinese landscape painting: a craggy, cloud-sheathed world rendered in black, white, and gray, forests and mountain hillsides wreathed in thick, ragged tendrils of mist. We have good equipment, but it seems like everything we are wearing is soaked. Our leather boots are sodden, wool socks wet, long underwear and wool outer layers damp. Cold feet and hands warm only at night, in our synthetic sleeping bags. In camp, rain splatters against our tarps, a constant dirge, and we sleep in a world without stars. We look west, down valley, cast furtive glances at the clouds, hoping for hints of a clearing, but find nothing in the sky on which to hang our hopes.

The rain continues. I shift the weight of my pack again, contemplate the dankness that envelopes us and permeates our soggy world. Fool that I am, I am seduced by thoughts of a soft, warm bed and a hot shower, or better yet, the desert in spring—but I'd settle for shedding this damned pack, a sheltering tarp, and steaming cup of tea. The patrol is restless; the students look disconsolate, one or two might be on the verge of incipient hypothermia. We must move, find a good camp spot, and seek refuge from the rain. Our navigators need to determine where the patrol is, and quickly—if not, we'll have to intervene. It's not the right moment for a mutiny, the instructors strung up by a climbing rope from the nearest yardarm (though a handy fir would do just as well). But finally the navigators quit muddling with the map and announce that they know (well, maybe) where we are, that it's only about a quarter mile to our goal for the day. We plod over to them and discuss the map's orientation, contours, and landmarks,

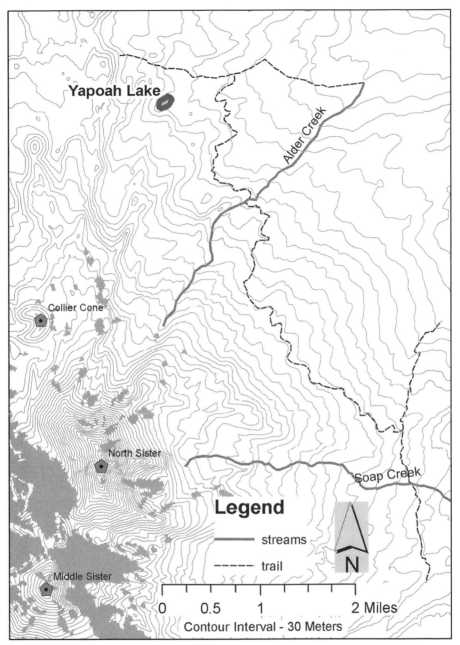

Three Sisters area in the Oregon Cascades.

the route ahead. The navigators *do* know where we are: I congratulate them, and tell them that it's time to move and get to camp.

Fifteen minutes later, the patrol finds a nice patch of level, well-drained, snow-free ground. The students know the drill, and four tarps go up quickly, taut and nicely strung. We scavenge enough dry tinder and kindling to start a smoky, tentative fire, then slowly nurse it into a crackling bonfire. The rains cease, at least for a few hours, and we dry our clothes and gear by the blaze. We fire up the stoves and fill our bellies with a slurry of hot cocoa, noodles, cheese and tuna, and tell war stories about the day's hike. Before going to bed we pull out the maps and discuss the day's route, note our camp spot, and plot tomorrow's probable path. Everyone is happy to be warm and dry and full of food, and we crawl into our sleeping bags, content. The conversations continue, quieter now: words whispered, sporadic drops of rain spattering against our shelters, the hushed forest slipping into silence, the fire dying into darkness. Talk grows desultory and the patrol settles into stillness, anchored to the world by coordinates of latitude and longitude, experience and desire. The map may not be "the territory," but it feels very good to know how we are and where we are: comfortable and supremely tired, in this particular spot of snow and fir and hemlock, rain and cloud, Douglas squirrel and mountain chickadee. The map tells me that we are camped at 6,300 feet in the upper Hinton Creek drainage, directly below and west of the South Sister: *This place. Here.*

I began teaching for Northwest Outward Bound in June of 1979, less than a year after finishing a fifteen-month canoe expedition across the Northwest Territories of Canada. My life was an ecotone of circumstance, a transition from rootless wanderer to husband and graduate student. In August I would marry my fiancée, Melissa, and in September begin a master's program in zoology at Washington State University. I had laid aside concerns about commitment—both to graduate school and marriage—and soon would settle into a life focused on academics, research, and domesticity. Still, over the next four years I found enough free time to work as a mountaineering instructor on a number of Outward Bound courses, most of them in the Oregon Cascades or North Cascades of Washington. The work was demanding, satisfying, and almost always enjoyable, at times even more so than field research. What could be better than getting paid to be in the wilderness, and teaching about what I loved?

The Outward Bound students whom I taught were a disparate lot, but most were novices with little outdoor experience. I told them that my main goal, other than getting everyone through the course in one piece, was to help them learn how to travel safely on nontechnical routes in any mountain wilderness in the lower forty-eight states. And so, on the twenty-four-day courses that I liked best, the first nine days were dedicated to physical conditioning and teaching the basic skills necessary to live well, as a small community, in the wilderness: packing and carrying a heavy load, first aid, setting up a taut tarp and keeping dry, cooking over a small camp stove, elementary climbing techniques, map-and-compass, group dynamics and communication. The patrol, which usually consisted of ten students and two instructors, would move deep into the mountains, first on trails and then cross-country, the students struggling under heavy packs, working through sore muscles and blisters, and seeking the best ways of adapting to an unfamiliar and at times intimidating physical and social environment. My assistant and I taught as we traveled: knots after dinner, a first-aid scenario during an afternoon halt, a two-hour lesson on ice axe use before lunch, route-finding questions while munching on raisins and peanuts during a morning break.

We devoted a lot of time to map-and-compass training because knowing where we are is perhaps the most fundamental aspect of our relationship to the enviroment, and the most essential wilderness skill of all. We began with the basics: what the symbols on our 1:62,500 scale topographic maps meant; how to interpret contour lines (valleys and ridges, the steepness and shape of terrain features); the nomenclature of a compass, and how to use one to orient a map, identify landmarks, and determine cardinal directions and one's location. We gave the students route-finding problems, first on trails and then on progressively more challenging cross-country routes, and gradually weaned them from depending on our knowledge and advice. We also tried to get the students to cultivate a sense of direction and dead-reckoning skills, without referring to a map: north, south, east and west, approximately this many miles traveled in three hours. Each day we appointed two students to act as navigators; they carried the maps and held primary responsibility for making route-finding decisions.

And sometimes we followed the patrol into confusion, let them get lost (but not too lost), and then work out where they were and how to get back on route.

There was a logical progression to teaching map-and-compass skills, which I recognized. Yet I never thought much about how students might learn about maps and why some students had more trouble than others. I'd picked up the skills on my own, in California's Coast Range and High Sierra, through trial and error and modeling those who knew more than I. For whatever reasons, the learning had come easily—perhaps because at an early age, along Saratoga Creek, I had ranged far and wide, and grown comfortable navigating by instinct through a world of orchards and oaks. My fascination with road maps and long-distance driving also had cultivated an instinctual sense of map orientation, and how maps depicted direction and distance. For many of my students, though, their map was an arcane object, their compass an alchemist's tool. They mostly were novices, both in the wilderness and with the topographic maps they carried. They were embarked upon what was, for many, one of the great adventures of their life, abandoning roads and traveling through exotic terrain, moving deep into an unknown and spectacular geography. One of the imperatives of their journey was to know where they were and where they were going, and few had much understanding of how to do so.

The basic problem with map use is to link the world of direct experience (in the middle ground, that sinuous river valley; beyond, a serrated ridge rising toward a conical peak) to the representation of the same world that we hold in our hands. If the map is accurate, then the problem for the map reader is to understand the "relational correspondence" between the world and the map, as arbitrated by our knowledge, senses, and desire. To use a map well one must know how to transition between the map and the real-world objects it represents, which requires mastering three types of relational correspondence: representational, configurational, and directional. Representational correspondence involves matching map symbols with objects in the external world—understanding that the map's narrowing, concentric circles of contour lines depict that conical peak on the horizon. Configurational correspondence requires visualizing spatial relationships among a constellation of features displayed on a map, and their corresponding features in the external world: on the map, the narrowing band of concentric rings lies just to the right (or better yet, east) of the sharp "v" of contour lines pointing downslope, toward a meandering blue line, just as that conical peak rises to the right of a jagged ridge-line, which knifes into the river valley below. The competent map user also must position the map so that it is aligned with the world it represents. Bearings on the map must match those in space: if I turn the map just so, the concentric rings and thin "v" of contour lines are oriented in the same manner as the conical peak, serrated ridge, and river valley. Another important aspect of spatial ability and map use is that of perspective: being able to envision views from different positions. Imagine that you are standing at this point and looking off to your right; what would those squiggles and circles of contour lines look like, in the world of rock and snow? To fail at any of these tasks will make it difficult for the map user to locate himself in space, or find her way from A to B—and so wander lost through an uncertain and threatening world.

Maps, for all their utility, have difficulty depicting a large and complex world in a small, planar image. These limitations have to do with symbolization, scale, and projection. Issues of scale and projection were not important for my students and the map-use tasks they faced. Our USGS topographic maps were either 1:62,500 or 1:24,000 scale, which showed plenty of detail for accurate navigation. Likewise, distortions due to map projection, or displaying the spherical representation of the earth on a flat surface, become important only when dealing with extremely small-scale maps, such as those of the world. Instead, my students had to contend mostly with the curse of the third dimension: translating a limited, two-dimensional image into a three-dimensional view. My job, then, was one of helping students understand the nature of our topographical maps' symbols, and how to position these symbols relative to the lay of the land—in other words, teaching them how to "see through the map to the world behind it."

I began by laying out a topographic map and discussing what each symbol meant, and how much useful information was contained on a map: dashed black lines for trails, solid blue lines and polygons for water, irregular white polygons dissected by blue lines for glaciers, brown lines for elevation contours, dotted red squares for the surveyed sections of township and range, mottled brown-and-white patches for lava, green overlay for forest cover. This much was easy; it was more difficult to envision what the contour lines represented: how the thickening squiggle of closely-spaced contours meant a steepening slope, a "v" of lines pointing uphill depicted a valley, or a series of irregular, narrowing polygons indicated a peak. Once we'd covered the basics of map symbols, I'd ask the students to draw their own contour maps, based on a verbal description: "Give me a basin opening to the west, broadly curved at the bottom, narrowing and steeper toward the crest of a pyramidal peak, with a sharp ridge trending to the east."

Once my students were proficient at visualizing how contour lines worked, I would take them to a vantage point and demonstrate how to orient the map, so that its symbols were aligned properly, relative to the view. This was challenging, for it required understanding the correspondence between the host of symbols before them, and the external world that spread outward from their perch. At first I had them work by sight alone; correctly orienting a map without a compass meant that they understood the relationship between map representations and the terrain. Finally, I'd introduce the compass, beginning with its nomenclature (housing, needle, dial, orienting arrow, base plate, direction of travel arrow), then demonstrate how to determine magnetic north and geographic north—another important skill, because it provided another way of orienting the map with the terrain. This was a pesky task though, because it meant dealing with the issue of declination, or the angle between true north and magnetic north. Maps are aligned relative to true north (the geographic north pole), while the north end of a compass needle points toward the magnetic north pole, which currently lies near Ellesmere Island in the Canadian Arctic. Thus, in most places in the world, the angle between the observer, true north, and magnetic north is not zero—unless one is positioned along what's known as the agonic line, which in the continental United States runs between Lake Superior and the Florida panhandle. East of the agonic line, the north end of the compass needle points west of true north, while west of this line the needle points east of true north. So an Outward Bound student in the Oregon Cascades, where the declination was roughly 20° east, needed to add 20° to her magnetic bearing to obtain a true bearing—which she could do by simply rotating the compass housing. Another way of describing this relationship is to say that the orientation of a topographic map aligned with magnetic north would be about 20° off. To complicate matters, the magnetic north pole wanders; what had been a 20° declination in 1959, when our maps were produced, by 1982 had become an 18° declination. To explain all of this in two dimensions was difficult, so I would take a pencil and my climbing helmet, inscribe it with lines of latitude and longitude, add a north pole and magnetic pole, and get students to visualize the relationship between their position and the North Pole, and hopefully understand how their compasses needed to be adjusted in order to orient the map correctly.

Orientation, declination, compass nomenclature, map symbols, relational correspondence and perspective, and cardinal directions made for a confusing conceptual stew. Some students were adept at applying what we taught them, while others were less successful. A few had been exposed to map-and-compass work before their course; they tended to master the skills quickly, although experience wasn't always a good predictor of how someone would do with route-finding and other map tasks — a situation implied by some research on learning and recalling map information. Other research, more directly focused on the spatial skills necessary to use maps well, suggests that gender has some effect on spatial ability, with males often, but not always, scoring higher on tests evaluating mental rotation and related tasks. However, there usually is a large overlap between distributions of male and female scores on tests of spatial ability. In other words, the variability *within* groups is larger than the difference *between* groups, so that gender has little or no predictive power relative to individual performance. Statistical issues also make navigating through the technical literature on gender differences difficult. In some studies examining gender differences in map-use skills or wayfinding ability, the analyses, while statistically significant, explain such a small proportion of the difference among individuals that gender again has little predictive power. Interestingly, most experimental tests of map-using skills seem to involve road maps, world maps, or other maps displaying only two dimensions of the earth's surface, rather than contour maps.

As I plow through the technical literature on spatial ability and consider my experiences teaching map-and-compass skills, my sense is that individual differences in understanding and using maps cannot be explained entirely by experience or gender, given the equalizer of proper instruction. Some of my female students may have been at a disadvantage at the start of a course because they'd had less exposure to maps, and ranged less widely, than their male compatriots. Yet many soon became adept at using maps. Conversely, some males never quite mastered the skills necessary to become good navigators. There were strong individual differences in navigational and map-use skills, though, which sometimes persisted in the face of intense instruction and repeated practice. It was a bit of a mystery: why were some students more adept at finding their way through the world than others? Success at map use and navigational tasks seemed to depend upon problem-solving and spatial visualization skills, but facility with these tasks resisted easy categorizations like male-female or experienced-inexperienced. Some students appeared to possess an innate sense of where they were, and it was difficult to identify the source of this facility.

It is day sixteen of another Outward Bound course. The students have been through a lot: they've climbed three peaks, two of them technical and exposed enough to require ropes; thrashed through thick forests and across a storm-wracked pass; survived a seventeen-hour "death march"; spent three days alone on "solo," with only a sleeping bag, a bit of plastic for shelter, and a few handfuls of nuts and raisins for food; and dealt with the emotional fallout from a student who was terrified of heights, terribly slow and weak, and a bit of a walking cartoon. Hell, *I've* been through a lot, too. I worked the first nine days of the course alone, and I'd had no opportunity to relax and step back from my role. I was on for twenty-four hours per day: teaching, alert, watching. Fortunately another instructor, Sue, joined me after the first resupply and since then the work's been easier. Yesterday the patrol covered nine miles in about twelve hours — not much distance, but all of it cross-country, with forty-seven hundred feet of elevation gain, three miles of roped glacier travel, and a technical peak climb. In the late afternoon we swung around the north side of the North Sister, traveling across trailless, broken volcanic terrain, through fog and a light, driving rain pushed out of the west by gusty winds. The country was an eerie kaleidoscope of umber rock and stark white snowbanks rising out of swirling fog — cinders and pumice, barren valleys almost devoid of life, a study in white and brown and gray.

Patches of alpine whitlow grass—a tiny, mound-shaped mustard with small yellow flowers—dotted the volcanic soil, tiny flashes of color blinking in the mist. We were headed east, into the headwaters of Alder Creek, and the students were responsible for route-finding. They were navigating mostly by compass, as there were few visible landmarks to guide them through the shrouded world. The two navigators were exhausted and their work was slow and halting, but they successfully led us through that confusing and alien territory. It was difficult, though, for Sue and me to remain silent and let the students work through their uncertainty. We, too, were tired and yearned to move quickly into a refuge from the rain where we could throw down our packs and STOP. It would have been easy—and wrong—to lead them across the pass, and to camp; instead, we allowed their decisions to become ours. Eventually, they worked through the problem and crossed to the leeward side of the divide, and a more benign world. The clouds dissipated. To the east were the lowlands of eastern Oregon, warm and brilliant in the evening light. Alder Creek was close at hand, flowing out of the volcanic wastes, through scattered krummholz and the small, sheltered valley where we claimed our rest.

Today's hike will take the patrol to a trailhead resupply and the start of "finals," when the different patrols will be mixed together in groups of four or five students, then travel independently from the instructors. Sue and I want to give them a final route-finding problem, one that demonstrates their competence with off-trail navigation. We tell them that they need to walk from the headwaters of Alder Creek to Yapoah Lake, which lies about twenty degrees east of true north and sixteen hundred feet below our camp, in thick coniferous forest. From there it's only one-quarter mile north to a trail, which we can follow east to a trailhead and the resupply point. Two younger women, Mary and Charlene, are the patrol's navigators for the day. They're competent enough, but quiet; they will lead the way, with the rest of the students helping out if need be. Sue and I will remain quiet and go where we are led. It's the students' game.

From camp the students descend Alder Creek for a mile before heading cross-country toward Yapoah Lake, about two miles north of the creek. I ask how long it will take the patrol to reach the lake. The navigators estimate about two hours once they leave Alder Creek—the students are fit, but when traveling off trail the patrol never moves at much more than one mile per hour. Mary and Charlene lead the patrol down valley, then head north, aiming along a compass bearing of 340°, having correctly adjusted for the declination. It's ten A.M., so we should eat lunch at Yapoah Lake, if it's not some fetid, mosquito-plagued swamp. The country is typical eastside terrain — reddish-brown volcanic soil and open lodgepole pine forest with little understory and only moderate relief. At first there are several distant landmarks by which to orient, enough to locate ourselves on the 15-minute map. All is well and the patrol makes good time. Mary and Charlene take us across an open plain; we descend slightly into a broad, U-shaped valley, then cross a gentle, northeast-trending ridge. Sue and I notice that the group is wandering to the northeast, perhaps pulled downhill by gravity's seduction, but we say nothing and let them drift. There is little conversation about the route; Mary and Charlene are not consulting their map and compass frequently enough, and it's as if the patrol's collective psyche has determined their course. Sue and I hang back and let them go where they will, as we don't want our body language or discussions to influence the students. One of the males, Will, gradually works his way to the front of the patrol, where he prefers to be. Apparently, he believes that he knows the correct route. Quietly but insistently, he leads the patrol further into confusion, continuing northeast into deeper forest. Mary and Charlene cast furtive glances at one another; they understand that their role is being usurped, but they say nothing, and gradually melt back into the group.

Sue and I know that the patrol is misled, and that the rightful navigators have stopped doing their job. We let them walk for another twenty minutes, then suggest a break; it's hot, and folks are thirsty and tired. We've been walking for the better part of two hours, yet Yapoah Lake is nowhere in sight. The patrol halts in a relatively open area, where there are a few, limited views of high country to the north and west. From here it should be possible to estimate our bearing relative to an identifiable landmark, and get some sense of our location. Sue asks the students how they're doing, and where they are. The patrol clusters around Mary and Charlene, passes the map back and forth, and discusses the situation. Will and a few others think that we're still on the correct course, Mary and Charlene are less certain. The conversation gathers momentum and the patrol assembles itself into a familiar arrangement, almost as if the students are molecules passively responding to forces of charge, mass, and shape: males (particularly the larger ones) cluster toward the middle, women move to the outside. Mary and Charlene, by virtue of their appointed roles, must remain near the center of the circle, but around them it's pure X and Y chromosomes. What's operating is the principle of "Biggest, Loudest, and Deepest," or BLD. In a situation demanding a decision, the largest individuals, with the loudest and most authoritative voices, are most likely to take charge. BLD has been operative from the first day of the course, when we gave our patrol a series of initiative tests as a way to introduce the students to one another. Will and several other large males were ready to make decisions, solve problems, and direct everyone, while the women and a few of the less-confident males hung back, quiet and passive. They'd seen this dynamic before and knew their expected roles. Yet the ideas of the followers generally were at least as good as, and sometimes better than, those of their more assertive compatriots. Given this dynamic, Sue and I would push the quiet, less-confident students, such as Mary and Charlene, into leadership positions, even if they were reluctant to do so—hence our "navigator for the day" scenario.

The gender dynamics of my Outward Bound patrol, as they related to route-finding and map work, mirrored research results that would be published almost twenty years later. In one study, which took place in Boston, college students rated themselves as having a good, neutral, or poor sense of direction. Equal numbers of males and females who described themselves as having good or poor senses of direction were then driven to a distant park, along a route with no familiar cues. To track their position, participants could use only geocentric dead reckoning—an internal map—to stay on course. Once at the park, subjects were asked to point south, and then to a set of invisible landmarks with which they were familiar. They then were shown the correct direction to the landmarks and to south, before being led along a winding path to a second location, where they again were asked to point south, to the same set of landmarks, and to the start of the path. Women subjects in the study tended to rate themselves more negatively in terms of their directional sense than did men and, in most comparisons within the self-described sense-of-direction groups, women were less confident of their directional choices than were

men. Another interesting result was that there were few sex-based differences, within the sense-of-direction groups, in errors made when
pointing for target landmarks, although men tended to outperform
woman when identifying south.

The BLD dynamic continues, with Will arguing stridently for his
map interpretation, while Mary and Charlene appear intimidated. I
suggest that they shoot a bearing on the North Sister, the obvious
peak to the southwest, partly visible through the trees. They take a
magnetic bearing, determine the bearing relative to true north, and
then pencil it in on the map. Other students repeat the process and
agree with the navigators' results — and sure enough, we're east of
where we should be, although exactly where isn't clear. We could be
any number of places along the line running northeast from the
North Sister, but there's no other recognizable feature visible, and so
triangulation isn't possible. Instead, the students will have to read
the topographic map carefully. They do not want to compound their
route-finding error and divine their location with a guess — or in the
wonderfully opaque academic language of one scholarly paper, an
"insufficiently constrained solution path." So Mary and Charlene use
their compasses to orient the map, then try to work out the message
of the contour lines. It's difficult, though, because the terrain shows
relatively little relief and the 1:62,500 scale doesn't clearly depict the
subtle play of gentle valleys and ridges in the area.

Here again there is disagreement. Mary and Charlene are the pessi-
mists; their reading of the map places the patrol further along the bearing from the North Sister, and thus east and downhill from Yapoah
Lake. According to them, it will take an uphill slog through loose soil
to reach our destination. Will, although chastened by his earlier error,
holds out for an optimistic interpretation, which situates the patrol
more to the south of, and a bit closer to, Yapoah Lake, and at about
the same elevation. The student factions glance at Sue and me, in a
silent appeal for support, but we remain sphinx-like. As much as we
want lunch, they need to decide. It's an interesting problem from both
an applied standpoint ("Just where is that damned lake?") and a more
theoretical perspective ("What is the best general approach to solving
this riddle, and other similar ones?"). In thinking about these issues,
and even larger ones, such as how we might make good choices in

our lives, I am drawn to the research of H. L. Pick and his coworkers. Pick *et al.* recruited twenty-nine experienced map readers for their
project, which reads like an academic riff on a classic fraternity hazing
prank. Each participant was blindfolded and driven separately to a location in gently rolling terrain, about thirty miles from the University
of Minnesota, where they were led to a point on a hill. The blindfold
was removed and each subject given a segment of a U.S. Geological
Survey map from which all nontopographic information had been removed. There were no roads, no vegetation symbols—only confusing squiggles of contour lines, a few elevations, a scale, and a diagram
showing the direction to true and magnetic north. They then were
asked to work out their location on the map while thinking out loud
about the process. Most map readers employed two types of information while attempting to identify their position: the relative size,
shape, slope and elevation of features (large vs. small, narrow vs. wide,
and so on); and the relational configuration among features (in front
of, behind, next to, etc.). Almost none of the participants used units
of distance or degrees of slope in their analyses—even though I immediately imagined doing so when I first read the paper. In the end,
only seven of the twenty-nine subjects correctly identified their position. Those who did so employed a number of strategies, the most
crucial being the evaluation of multiple hypotheses about the viewpoint: attempting to disprove, rather than confirm, hypotheses about
a viewpoint, and then changing their viewpoint by moving around in
the field. In other words: consider multiple explanations, be skepti-
cal, and evaluate the problem from different perspectives. One wonders how different history might have been if Bush the Younger had
adopted a similar strategy before invading Iraq in 2003.

The students are having none of this. Instead, each group is advo-
cating its own solution and trying to disprove their adversary's position, rather than showing skepticism about their own. Will and his
small cadre of supporters see only what they want to see in the relationship between the terrain and map features; Mary and Charlene,
and their supporters, are convinced of something different. What's
partly at play here is pride—each group wants to be right—but
there's also the issue of desire. Will's cohort *wants* to be closer to their
goal than they may actually be, and so interprets the map in a way that

provides the answer they seek. I've seen this behavior before—and, I'll sheepishly admit, occasionally in myself. Given the right circumstances, we can become mental alchemists, and through sheer force of will attempt to transform the particular, sinuous weave of contour lines, and dip and sway of the land, enough so that they fit our template of desire. Those "insufficiently constrained solution paths" seductively beckon, urging us to create our own pseudoreality, even if the land and the map will have none of it. Given sufficient hunger, tiredness, or arrogance, it's hard to be a dispassionate, analytical observer, even though an incorrect answer will only lead one farther into the Big Muddy.

It wasn't that our students lacked sufficient information; everything they needed was there before them, and they possessed the requisite skills and equipment. Instead, some of them were behaving like perfect postmodernists, trying to fashion their own, preferred stories from the map, or rather, text. To quote Sarah Bednarz *et al.* from a 2006 paper, "In the context of maps and map learning, it is important that students and teachers understand that maps are social constructions; just as texts are written by individuals with different points of view, and can be read and interpreted in different ways and for different purposes, maps, too, are not objective representations of reality but social productions that can be subject to critical analysis." Well, there is some truth to this statement. Maps are not completely "objective representations of reality," because they must offer a selective, incomplete view of the world. A second and more potentially sinister reason why maps are sometimes less than objective is that, as Mark Monmonier argues in *How to Lie with Maps*, they may be used as propaganda, and to lie. For example, the Nazis used maps to distort the proportional representation of Germans in other European countries and to curry anti-British sentiment in the United States, while the Transverse Mercator projection, which increases the apparent size of high-latitude land masses, was used to emphasize the threat posed by Eastern Bloc nations during the Cold War.

The postmodernist wave that swept through academia during the last three decades of the twentieth century exerted its effect on geography, as well as English, departments. Monmonier's *How to Lie with Maps* was heavily influenced by this perspective, as was Denis Wood's *The Power of Maps*. But perhaps the most influential proponent of postmodernist cartography was Brian Harley, an expatriate British academic who settled at the University of Wisconsin–Milwaukee. Titles from a 2001 posthumous collection of Harley's essays, *The New Nature of Maps*, illustrate Harley's general attitude: "Texts and Contexts in the Interpretation of Early Maps," "Maps, Knowledge, and Power," and "Deconstructing the Map." Harley invoked the names of postmodern theorists like Foucault, Derrida, and Panofsky in his passionate attacks on what he described as cartographic "positivism," or the view that cartography is objective, detached, accurate and exact, and progresses toward greater accuracy. Like any good postmodernist he surrounded terms like "truth," "fact," and "reality" with quotation marks meant to "break the assumed link between reality and representation." Sarah Bednarz and her coauthors were channeling Harley's ghost when they insisted that maps "are not objective representations of reality but social productions."

To my untrained and admittedly prejudiced scientific ear, the language of Harley and Bednarz sounds suspiciously like that of "science studies," whose postmodern practitioners view science in much the same way as Harley did cartography. One prominent advocate of this position is Sandra Harding, who depicts modern science as the "ethnoscience of the West," one culturally constructed discourse among many possible "borderland epistemologies." As we slog deeper into the tangled thicket of science studies we encounter the same language as in any deconstructionist/postmodern work: "text," "hermeneutics," "transgressing," "interrogate," "semiotic," "hegemonic," "discursive," "discourse," etc. A classic work of science studies is *Laboratory Life: The Social Construction of Scientific Facts* by Bruno Latour and Steve Woolgar, who describe activities of scientists investigating the structure of a hormone called thyrotropin releasing factor (TRF or TRH), which is produced by the hypothalamus. According to Latour and Woolgar, TRF is socially constructed: "The artificial reality, which participants describe in terms of an objective entity, has in fact been constructed by the use of inscription devices [instrumentation]." Latour and Woolgar "do not conceive of scientists . . . as pulling back the curtain on pregiven, but hitherto concealed, truths. Rather, objects (in this case substances) are constituted through the artful creativity of scientists." Thus TRH(F) "exists as a 'newly discovered substance' within the confines of networks of endocrinologists. . . . Outside of these networks TRH simply does not exist." Never mind the effects of the molecule TRH — or whatever name we attach to it — on the pituitary gland, which in turn produces a thyroid-stimulating hormone, which causes the thyroid to produce hormones necessary for proper growth, development, and metabolism. To use a term by Edward Slingerland, Latour and Woolgar's worldview creates a curious situation in which a substance such as TRF is dangerously "disembodied." For the disembodied practitioner of science studies, human cognition is disconnected from the body and its sensory-motor systems — and in a larger context, from nature itself. Thus the possibility of both extreme relativism, in which one view of the natural world is as valid as any other (HIV causes AIDS, HIV does not cause AIDS), and a curious anthropocentrism, in which natural objects and processes exist only through the grace of the human mind. How else to interpret the statement, "Outside of these networks TRH simply does not exist"? In an identical manner, the disembodied practitioner of what I'll call "cartographic studies" sees the map as disconnected from the reality of the terrain, if such a thing can even be said to exist. "We begin to learn that cartographic facts are only facts within a specific cultural perspective," writes Harley. Never mind the particular tumble of the meltwater stream spilling from the Collier Glacier, the sharp, dark-hued east arête of the North Sister, or the specific set of Cartesian coordinates that position a body at one, and only one, position in space.

Yes, there are limits to our understanding. Yes, science and cartography are not always, or even usually, entirely dispassionate and objective endeavors. Facts as we know them are not immutable; hypotheses once proven are disproven, theories once accepted are discarded. Knowledge evolves. Modern physics, with its reference to quantum mechanics and Heisenberg's Uncertainty Principle, asserts that there is a fundamental unpredictability to the world and what we may know about its structure and function. And yet Newtonian laws work extremely well in predicting how a billiard ball reacts to a cue ball, or how a climber's body, when separated from a rope and arcing through space, will respond to the tumbled talus two thousand feet below. There is an objective reality out there, even if it is difficult or impossible to fully apprehend. Although we only can achieve successive approximations of the truth, some views of the physical world are more accurate and useful than others. Progress is possible in both science and cartography, and we can know the world in better and more complete ways. To put it plainly, throw a rock at a strident practitioner of science studies; if she ducks, she's a liar. Or blindfold a postmodernist cartographer and set him down in the Three Sisters wilderness—a place he has never been. Remove the blindfold and ask him to find his way home. Do so when there's a storm coming up, hard off the Pacific Ocean, and hold off on the food—hunger can be a great motivator with humans, as it is with pigeons and monkeys in Skinner boxes. But be nice; place a 15-minute USGS quad in his hand, and a compass around his neck. If he hasn't spent too much time in the academy, perusing back issues of *Social Text*, knows how to use a map and compass, and is able to work out his position and where he should go to reach a road—well, he's a liar, too.

According to Harley, "Maps are never value-free images; except in the narrowest Euclidian sense they are not in themselves either true or false." *Except in the narrowest Euclidian sense.* In other words, if maps are true only in the most fundamental, important, and powerful way. Our misplaced postmodern cartographer has two options: either ignore what Harley describes as "an intricate, controlled fiction," and wander lost and starving through the thick wilderness woods; or abandon ideology and use the map to find his way to a trailhead, food, and shelter. If our postmodernist geographer is interested in survival he will have to admit that the 15-minute USGS Three Sisters, Oregon quadrangle, 1959 edition, 1:62,500 scale, represents more than a "specific cultural perspective," just as the science-studies ideologue must acknowledge the velocity and vector of the rock that's speeding toward her head, or someone with a metabolic disorder just might want to accept the reality of TRF. Call the Three Sisters quad an "an intricate, controlled fiction" or "lie," if you like, but you still must use it to find out where you are and where you will go.

The debate between Will, and Mary and Charlene is winding down. They've stopped glancing at Sue and me; folks are nodding, and everyone is getting ready to hike. Sue and I hoist our packs, wander over to the patrol, and ask what they've decided. Mary and Charlene have held their ground—or rather, their understanding of the ground. They have convinced the patrol that we are due east of Yapoah Lake, and that if we walk on a magnetic bearing of 250° for about twenty minutes we should locate the lake. The patrol has foolishly embraced the assumption that there is a link between "representation and reality," and compared their different interpretations of the compass bearings and map contours to the terrain around them. In reaching their decision, the crucial steps were to transcend expectations about where they were, desire about where they would like to be, and the ego, which insisted that their answer was the best one. Will, Mary, and Charlene abandoned any inarticulate tendencies they might have had to interpret the map as a postmodern "text," open to several equally valid interpretations. Instead, they were in and on the land fully, and used their map skills to work out their location. "Insufficiently constrained solution paths" vanished, and the truth, in all of its limited but comforting presence, was revealed.

Mary and Charlene lead the way, and just about twenty minutes later the patrol runs headlong into Yapoah Lake. Upon their first view of the lake, as seen through a filter of trees, the students whoop, Mary and Charlene grin, and Will good-naturedly admits that he was wrong. Although Yapoah Lake is not as aesthetically pleasing as some of the lakes we've seen—too hemmed in by trees for my tastes—the water looks fine and the mosquitoes are mostly absent. It's a grand place for lunch, and so the patrol settles down for cheese, pilot biscuits, peanut butter, sardines, and lemonade. They are happy to be here, and Sue and I are pleased that they've worked through the problem. Most of them, we think, will do well in their finals groups, when they'll travel through the Three Sisters wilderness on their own. Alone, I'll track some of the finals patrols south as everyone heads toward the course end at Frissell Crossing. Ready to be done with the Oregon Cascades for awhile, after two courses and forty-six days in the mountains, I'll cover twenty-five miles on the last day of hiking, racing through low-lying meadows and across dry ridges thick with lodgepole pine, dust squirting from beneath my boots, chugging though pockets of whining mosquitoes, the mid-August air hotter and more humid than usual, chanting, softly and to myself, the names of the places that I was passing for the last time that summer: Platt Lake, Lookout Lake, Cabin Meadows, Beaver Marsh, Junction Lake, Rock Lake. On and on, recalling a line from Han-shan: "Body asking shadow, how do you keep up?" Across the gentle country south of the Three Sisters, finishing the final ten miles in less than three hours, the balls of my feet tender from too much pounding, hurtling southwest and dropping over the edge of the plateau west of Corral Flat and switchbacking down to the South Fork of the McKenzie River, through bay laurel, madrone, and manzanita, pockets of Douglas fir here and there, the air thick with the sweet, viscid scent of buckbrush, the checkerboard desolation of clear-cuts marching up the western approaches. Road's end: finals groups dissolve and patrols reassemble; everyone runs thirteen miles on trails and dirt roads, then finishes the course with a feast of fresh food and a closing ceremony that lasts late into the night. Among the students, there's a melancholy mix of nostalgia and excitement, the intensity and comradeship of their adventures already verging on history, the pleasures of memory leavened by the anticipation of clean sheets and showers, reunions with family and friends: *Look what I did, and who I have become.*

The chartered bus arrives early the next morning, while the Mc-Kenzie Valley is still sunk in shadow. We say our goodbyes before the students and staff scatter, and follow their personal maps into future lives, new directions, and old habits. Melissa and I head north, work September courses in the Washington Cascades, then drive east to Connecticut before embarking on a five-month bicycling and hiking trip in New Zealand and Australia. For us there would be a new set of maps: road maps of the South Island, New South Wales, and Victoria, topographic maps of the Snowy Mountains and the Southern Alps. At thirty-one I still felt young and insouciant, fit and happy after a summer in the mountains. I had finished my master's program at Washington State and was ready for adventures of my own. My knees were not yet creaky, my lower back years away from rebellion, my sun-bleached beard still free of gray.

I had no clear idea about where we would live and work once we were done with Outward Bound and our overseas travels, but still the world felt predictable and secure, my location in it as certain as it had been five weeks earlier, when my first patrol of the summer was bivouacked on the alpine col between the North Sister and Middle Sister, on a brilliantly clear, windless evening. I sat off from the group, enjoying the post-dinner quiet, a map spread upon my lap, contemplating the country. To the east, glaciers plunged into a chaotic tumble of brown and red volcanic debris, moraines trailed from the flanks of the mountains, tongues of trees rose from the thick forest to greet the rock and ice. And as the sun slid toward the horizon there came a moment when its last light poured through the pass and the surrounding shadows of the North Sister and Middle Sister pushed far out into the darkening lowlands of eastern Oregon, and so formed a huge "V" perhaps one hundred miles long, stretching all the way to the horizon, with its base at my perch. It seemed, then, that the world quivered with meaning and that all of its tumblers had clicked suddenly into place, for that immense and magnificent "V" was pointing directly at the pass where I sat. It illumined my location with a wonderful, portentous precision, which was enhanced by a small but pleasing coincidence — that at the time I just happened to be reading Thomas Pynchon's novel, *V.* Those vectors of sunlight and shadow marked a particular point on the map, and its degrees of latitude and longitude anchored me to this life: 44°06'12"N, 121°49'09"W. For a short while, in the dying light of that luminous mountain day, as the crystalline cold crept over the land and the long blue shadows of night claimed the basin below, I believed that I could see the world with clarity, and knew everything that I needed to know about where I was, who I was, and what I would become.

Late Maps

Fathering the Map

e moved to Lawrence, Kansas, in August of 1988, riding a rental truck west from the solid, maple-covered hills of Connecticut to the eastern edge of the Great Plains — from a suburban, slightly claustrophobic New England village to a cosmopolitan university town enveloped by an aching sweep of field and sky. The horizons opened up, as did the summer heat, and in that drive we transitioned not only from New England to the Midwest, but also from a secure world to a much less certain one. We moved so that I could begin a PhD program at the University of Kansas, and in doing so, Melissa and I abandoned good jobs at Westover School, a private girl's secondary school where we had worked since 1983. Melissa was dean of students, while I taught science and ran the school's outdoor program, and although there sometimes was too much of it, the work was good. We had a cadre of wonderful friends, and a comfortable colonial house on the village green, across the street from the school. Our daughter, Liza, had been born on Groundhog Day in 1987, near the end of a reproductive pulse by other young Westover faculty. There were lots of small children for Liza to grow up with, an unlimited supply of eager baby-sitters among the Westover girls, and convenient day care on campus. We could have been settled, as many of our Westover friends seemed to be, but I was restless in my job and where we lived. I'd had trouble deciding on a career path, and my uncertainty had made it difficult to remain in Connecticut.

It was a time of stress. The loss of income, separation from good friends, and an unfamiliar environment contributed to a sense of impermanence and vulnerability. It is rarely easy to migrate. I felt guilty for having dragged my family out of a comfortable New England life and into an uncertain world, and this uncomfortable sense of accountability was the fourth passenger in the cab of our truck as we swung south around Kansas City and across the Missouri line: just what state had I brought us into? We followed Kansas State Highway 10 across the caprock hills, through scattered pockets of oak and hickory, and miles of pasture and agricultural fields sweltering in the August sun. In the distance was Lawrence, an island rising from the rolling plains. Ahead lay the suburbs and sprawl spreading eastward along 29th Street, the low crest of Mount Oread capped by a ragged crown of university buildings: our home, or at least where we would live for the foreseeable future. We found our apartment, then worked late into the night unloading the rental truck in the thick heat, a chorus of cicadas rasping in the viscid air.

We were not soothed by where we lived during that first year in Lawrence — in a triplex among other rental units and private homes dating to the late 1960s or early 1970s. The apartment was clean and spacious enough, and the roaches under reasonable control, but the ambience of our suburban space firmly resisted the concept of "neighborhood." There were no spacious porches on any of the single-story houses, no sidewalks, few large trees, and a slightly shabby, depressing uniformity to the ranch-style architecture. The subdivision's design had been influenced by economy and the internal combustion engine, and its aesthetic had more in common with the strip malls and fast-food restaurants lining 29th Street than with the older, tree-shaded neighborhoods surrounding the university. It was the sort of place where cars, trucks, and RVs seemed to be an integral part of the architecture, fulfilling decorative as well as structural roles. The lack of sidewalks made it difficult to walk anywhere, but there weren't many places to walk *to*. There were no local services — no nearby stores or restaurants or library — and no destinations other than the park a few blocks from our apartment. After work and on the weekends, Melissa and I would wheel Liza to the park in her stroller. In the playground, we would help her climb to the top of a rusting metal rocket, perhaps fifteen feet high, and look out over our domain: in the foreground, oaks and withered grass; to the west and north, the subdivisions; to the south, open country, where the farms began.

Perhaps it was our busyness, or our status as renters and recent academic immigrants, but we made few friends that first year in Law-

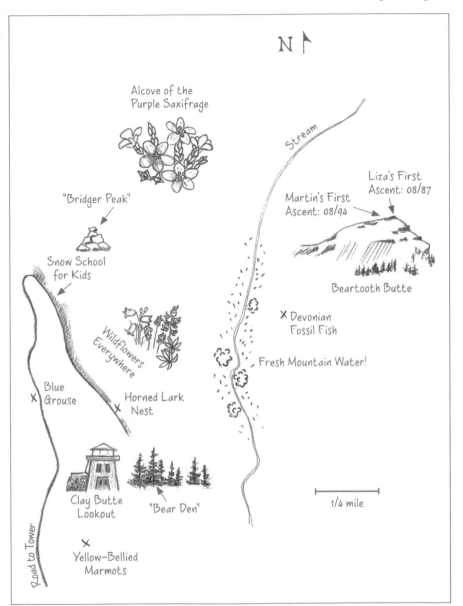

Clay Butte area in the Beartooth Mountains in Wyoming.

rence. Those few with whom we did find some common ground were connected to our work—either with the university or the Lawrence School District, where Melissa found a temporary job in a classroom for children with behavioral disorders. We knew few people in our neighborhood, other than the Iranian family who lived next door to us, refugees from Khomeini and the Islamic revolution. Even the family renting the ground floor unit of the triplex remained little more than an abstraction formed by the muffled arguments and odor of cigarette smoke that crept into our downstairs study through the heating vents. Most of our neighbors were wraiths, going about their insular lives as we went about ours. Nobody walked much of anywhere, except to and from their vehicles, and there was little to draw anyone outside. Our "lawn" was a landlord-cultivated plot of crabgrass and bare dirt, and while some neighborhood yards were well-kept, no one ever seemed to be out in them. During the work week, I would strap Liza into the child seat on my bicycle and pedal off to the university, through a featureless suburban world that in memory has faded to the color of sun-bleached grass. There was little to recommend our apartment, other than its location on the outskirts of town, for on long runs I could slip quickly out of the suburbs and onto the back roads south of Lawrence. There, among fields of corn and hedgerows of Osage orange and oak, and in the heartbeats and rhythm of my work, I found some connection to the place in which I lived.

When our lease was up we decided not to renew it; instead, we house-sat for my major professor during the fall while he was away on a sabbatical, and looked to buy a place of our own. Melissa and I had few financial resources—my first year of graduate school, childcare costs, and Melissa's own graduate work had seen to that—but Melissa found a permanent position as an itinerant teacher of visually impaired students in northeastern Kansas, my graduate position brought with it both a fellowship and a teaching assistantship, and her parents fronted us the money for a down payment. These assets allowed us to qualify for a modest loan, and so we went house hunting. We knew what we did not want, which was a home in the quasi-modern suburban uniformity south or west of downtown Lawrence, and what we hoped for—a place within walking distance of the university, in the older part of Lawrence. We could not afford one of those beautifully restored Victorian homes that graced the historic district, and there wasn't much on the market that suited the combined imperatives of our budget and taste. But after much looking we found a run-down, two-story Victorian, circa 1870, on Louisiana Street, just north of West Sixth Street. It was a classic "needs work/fixer-upper/starter/sweat-equity" house, in desperate need of the thirty-something energy (if not carpentry skills) that Melissa and I had, and it was rumored (incorrectly, as it turned out) to have been the childhood home of Langston Hughes.

We closed on the house in the fall of 1989. The first weekend that the place was ours, we put crowbars and sledgehammers in the hands of our friends and gave them leave to play demolition derby. By the end of the day most of the interior walls were stripped down to studs, we were knee-deep in lath and rotten plaster, and we looked and coughed like coal miners after a twelve-hour shift in the pits. What followed, with the help of contractors and Melissa's father, was a six-week dash to render the interior space livable: new sheetrock in many rooms, a new heating and cooling system, new electrical and plumbing, refinished floors, and innumerable coats of paint, applied late at night, after long days at the university or on the roads of northeastern Kansas. We moved into our new home in early December, impelled by the early return of my professor from his sabbatical and the desire to be settled in our own place. In the next several years, as finances, time, and the availability of Melissa's dad allowed, we replaced the roof and front porch, and added an upstairs bathroom, backyard fence, raised flower beds, and swing set for Liza. We coaxed the neglected lawn back into life, painted the exterior sage green with dark green trim, threw in a splash of bright color with a refurbished, brick-red front door. And just about one year after we moved into our home, our son, Martin, was born.

We lived on Louisiana Street for three-and-one-half years, while I completed my PhD program, spent a postdoctoral year scurrying between part-time positions at the University of Kansas and the University of Missouri–Kansas City, and searched for a permanent academic job. In that time we came to understand something about the meaning of the word "neighborhood," and the pleasure of living in a place built in a manner that catered more to human needs than did the subdivision where we had first lived in Lawrence. We were drawn into this understanding by the work that we devoted to our home; by Martin and Liza, and the scale and needs of their lives; by the design of our home, and our neighbors' homes; and by the landscape of our neighborhood—its structure and location in the context of Lawrence. In spite of my innate difficulty with settling, like some sort of larval invertebrate adrift on oceanic currents, our Louisiana Street neighborhood was, in the most positive sense of the word, "a place." And in this place was Lucy Lippard's "lure of the local," a landscape conducive to connection, intimacy, and cultivating personal history. Along the maple-lined streets and sidewalks of our world, it was possible to find, and make, our maps.

Our Lawrence home was situated in a place with many of the positive attributes described in *Great Neighborhoods: How to Bring Them Home*, a handbook published by a Madison advocacy group, 1000 Friends of Wisconsin. Most important, the scale of our neighborhood, and its design and location, favored walking, which increased contact with our neighbors and the physical environment. There were sidewalks down both sides of every street; the blocks were short, which offered a variety of walking routes; and many amenities, such as the library, park, and community pool, were within a quarter-mile of our home. Just beyond this quarter-mile radius were the downtown shops and restaurants of Massachusetts Street, and our pediatrician's office, where we always seemed to be taking Martin and Liza, who were plagued by earaches. The only major impediment to walking was West Sixth Street, a major traffic artery linking downtown Lawrence and the western parts of the city, although we could safely cross it at traffic lights to the east, or via an underground passageway to the west, of our home.

A quarter-mile radius represents the distance that most people are willing to walk on a regular basis, although they can be induced to walk a bit farther by "magnet" destinations. A circle inscribed by a quarter-mile radius encompasses 160 acres, which planners term a "pedestrian shed," and the scale of our neighborhood reduced our reliance on the automobile. We needed to drive several miles to a grocery store and pharmacy, and busyness and tiredness sometimes pushed us into our van when we should have walked, but we were oriented toward transportation that put us on our feet, rather than our butts. And when I did ride somewhere, it was often on my bicycle. It was only one-and-one-half miles to the Museum of Natural History on the KU campus, where I had my office, and Liza's day care was across the street, so I could strap her into the child seat and be at work in ten minutes. We would negotiate the vehicular hazards of Sixth Street, ride up Louisiana for a block, turn west to Indiana, and then climb the steep northern "face" of Mount Oread—Liza sometimes urging me to "Ride faster, Daddy!" when I could maintain my forward momentum only by shifting into first gear and standing on the pedals.

We walked a lot, and in the walking it was possible for Melissa and me to decompress a bit, and for Martin and Liza to burn off some childhood energy and explore their world. We walked to swimming lessons at the community pool; to the doctor's office; to check out books at the library; to the playground at Pinckney School, where in the limestone gravel there were fossil crinoids to be found; to what Liza named the "lonely train park," where there was an old steam locomotive that children could clamber around on. We could walk to Liberty Hall, where there were great independent films, to the Freestate Brewery, with its wonderful beer, or to the Paradise Café, where there were hearty breakfasts. In Martin's first months, we placed him in a chest carrier during our walks, although he demanded to sit in a forward-facing position, to better see the world. Then came the baby backpack, which he rarely tolerated. Instead, he pulled himself upright and used my hair for handholds to mantle up and over my head. Once Martin went vertical we abandoned the backpack and let him move under his own power. As his language came on, and no matter the time of day or weather, he would clamor for "ouside" [outside], and "walk, walk!" Most of our expeditions never went much of anywhere—just into the backyard or around the block, stopping to sit on a favorite rock or try out an interesting-looking tricycle at a neighbor's house. There were cats, dogs, squirrels, and sticks to attract his attention, or the work of collecting old nails that generated spontaneously in the alley behind our house. In the spring, summer, and fall, preparations for "ouside" were minimal, but in cold weather I sometimes felt as though I was readying Martin for an attempt on Mount Everest: overalls and then overpants, turtleneck and thick fleece jacket, windbreaker, scarf, wool hat, and mittens. The mittens and hat generally came off two or three times before we made it out the door, but eventually we would be off, with Martin decked out in a blue balaclava and turquoise windbreaker that fell to his knees, trundling down Louisiana Street and passionately interested in everything.

The walking brought us to parks, the library, cafés, and the pool, but also to our neighbors, a process enhanced by the design of homes and arrangement of building lots in older Lawrence. The most important feature of most neighborhood homes, but one not mentioned in *Great Neighborhoods*, was the presence of ample, glorious porches. In the days before air conditioning, a porch would have been a necessity—a place to escape the sweltering heat that settles over Lawrence in July and August. I imagine porches as places where people gathered and sat and talked late into the evening, amidst a cacophony of cicadas, as they waited for their houses to cool. Because people collected on porches and did not have air conditioning, television, and other electronic devices with social R-values equivalent to the thickest insulation, they would have spent more time visiting. Porches must have been social focal points, a function enhanced by the size of the building lots and where houses were situated. In all but the wealthiest sections of old Lawrence, lots were small and houses sat near to the sidewalks. We got to know our neighbors because in the evenings we sat outside, and they sat outside, and we were not separated from one another by too much space. I was able to overcome my intrinsic shyness and talk casually of the weather, and work, and children, of those things that form the fabric of our lives. On many evenings Melissa, Liza, Martin, and I would walk our block and adjacent blocks and talk with friends, or people who would become friends. Sometimes it took us an hour or two to navigate our route, for we would stop to visit with Tom and Virginia, or Stephano and Susan, or Madeline, or Eric and Debbie, or our babysitter's family, and everyone's children and pets. There might be lemonade for the kids, and exotic toys for them to play with, and cold beer for the adults, and stories for everyone. For me this visiting was easy and relaxed because I never had to knock, never had to ask—because if folks were on their porches, it felt like a tacit acknowledgment that they were available, and open to conversation. And if on some evenings they did not want company, they could retreat, like we sometimes did, to their backyards, which were mostly fenced and private. In all of this, it is significant that the people in our neighborhood whom we never got to know were those who lived in houses set farther back from the sidewalk, or which lacked front porches. Our orbits rarely overlapped, and so we did not interact.

The winnowing effects of time and memory are such that I am wary of recalling our Lawrence neighborhood through a nostalgic haze. (Cue up the soft, old-time fiddle music, open an album full of sepia-toned photographs, narrate the reminiscence with a Ken Burns documentary voice-over.) It wasn't perfection. Having homes built close together meant that we could not avoid the unpleasant family that, for awhile, lived next door in a Smurf-blue house. Their late-night arguments and parties; intransigence about our shared driveway, which they blocked with a derelict car; and defensiveness whenever we tried to talk about the noise or car, made them difficult neighbors. And there was a tendency for folks to want to know everyone else's business. During our initial renovations, one neighbor reported us to the building inspector for using an unlicensed plumbing and electrical contractor—admittedly our mistake, although we were unaware of the situation when we contracted with him. And two years later, another neighbor complained to the city about a housing-ordinance violation we did not commit, without first talking to us. (It may be a spurious correlation, but he was one of the few people on the block who lived in a porchless house, and with whom we'd had little contact.) These incidents gave us an uncomfortable sense that we were under constant surveillance, and that informants were everywhere. But some of the same people who became over-involved in their neighbors' lives also cooked meals for Madeline, when her husband was stricken with brain cancer. And once, when Martin was just a few months old and colicky, and had been screaming for hours, the wife of the neighbor who complained about the unlicensed plumber gently asked Melissa if she could hold Martin for an hour, just to give her a break. Such small acts of quiet generosity are one of the best things about living in a good neighborhood.

Melissa and I walked because we had chosen (and could afford) to live in a safe neighborhood that encouraged walking, because we did not own a television, because our children wanted to see the world, and because we owned only one car and were sometimes forced into foot travel. We walked because the good citizens of Lawrence had worked to save the downtown, banished the big box stores and strip malls to the periphery of the city, and put money into their parks. We walked beneath the brutal noon sun and deep maple-shade of summer, and through the drifting, silent snows of winter. We walked among the snowdrops that colonized March gardens, past the rockered front porches of our neighbors. And as we walked, our children walked with us. We would hold their hands, or let them run ahead when it was safe to do so, and walk to the places where the streets and parks and shops and neighbors pulled us together. As we walked, Liza and Martin created their childhood cartographies, of "ouside" and "lonely train parks," of fossil crinoids scattered amongst playground swing sets, and of the pool where they learned to swim and played late into the softening summer evenings, after the numbing midday heat.

For all of us, Lawrence was full of good maps, and a wonderful place to live, but it was difficult to stay there after I finished my PhD in 1992. I was not qualified for any academic jobs in the area, and so in July of 1993 we moved east so that I could take a tenure-track position at the State University of New York campus in Brockport. It was a wrenching change, for we loved our house, our neighborhood, and Lawrence. Liza was most affected. She had grown up in Lawrence, and spent five years at the Hilltop Child Development Center at the university, where she was very close to a group of four girls. On our last morning in Lawrence, as we drove out of town, she turned to Melissa, and with tearful fury shouted, "I *never* want to do this again!" In Brockport it took the better part of three years for her to recover her joy; it was not until fourth grade, when she found a best friend, and had a teacher whom she loved, that she again seemed truly and consistently happy.

We drove east to Brockport through a heartland flooded by a summer of extraordinary rains, threw all of our belongings into storage, and searched for a place to buy. In October we closed on a 1930s-era, Cape-style house across the street from the campus, with an expansive backyard that backed up on the Erie Canal. Our house has its attractions and we have made it our own, but in living there we have never felt as though we were part of a neighborhood, in the manner of Lawrence. Although there are the requisite sidewalks, our Brockport house lacks a front porch, as do many in the village. We front a busy street, and as the college gobbles up nearby private homes and converts them into parking lots, we have become increasingly encroached upon and isolated by the automobile. During the 1990s the best playgrounds were beyond convenient walking distance, so there was no nearby version of the "lonely train park" where Liza and Martin could play. As our children grew and our lives were increasingly taken up with their activities, we got out of the habit of walking, and began driving everywhere. We sunk time into everything but walking and visiting—house renovations, jobs, school activities and lessons. The winters in western New York are longer and harder than in Lawrence, which drives everyone indoors and further away from one another. And we bought a television.

For awhile though, our family did have its neighborhood — only it lay two thousand miles west of Brockport, in the Beartooth Mountains of northwestern Wyoming. There, at almost ten thousand feet, the four of us lived for parts of three summers in the Clay Butte lookout tower, most recently when Liza was nine and Martin was five. Melissa and I also had served there for four summers during the 1980s, two of those before we had children, and two with Liza, and so we knew the area well. Our temporary home was perched on the edge of a three-thousand-foot precipice, at the uppermost limit of trees, where the land tipped away into the valley of the Clarks Fork of the Yellowstone River. Surrounding the tower was a vast, unbroken panorama of mountains: to the south and west, Windy Mountain, the dramatic pyramid of Pilot Peak, and the dark-brown volcanic rock of the Absaroka Mountains; to the north and east, the main crest of the Beartooths, a long, massive crest of cirques, glaciers, ridges, and towers that included the highest point in Montana, Granite Peak. Immediately to the north of the lookout was a broad alpine ridge that ran for three miles through gardens of purple lupine and larkspur, creamy yellow locoweed, white bistort. The sunsets were stunning, the crashing thunderstorms that built out of the west were spectacular and sometimes intimidating, the rainbows that followed the rains, brilliant.

At Clay Butte, our neighborhood was both huge and intimate, built on a scale that ranged from thousands of square miles (the 360° circle of mountains and river valleys that extended west to Yellowstone, north into Montana, and southeast almost to Cody) to less than one square foot (the horned lark's nest at our feet, or the white blossom of a marsh marigold in the soggy ground below a melting snowbank). And we had two magnificent porches — the large deck in front of our living quarters, immediately below the glassed-in observation cab where we spent our duty hours, and also the catwalk surrounding the cab. Although our lookout was miles from the nearest habitation, we had our neighbors, too — the white-crowned sparrows that sung from the small clumps of krummholz, the elk herds that wandered across the alpine meadow behind the lookout, the yellow-bellied marmots that sunned on the rocks below the tower, the U.S. Forest Service personnel at the Crandall Ranger Station about twenty miles down valley. We also had many visitors, because a dirt road leading from U.S. 212 to the tower drew lots of traffic during the height of summer. But in the evenings and early mornings, and when the road was blocked by late-lying snow, the neighborhood was quiet, and ours.

Unless we needed to buy groceries, do laundry, or take showers, we mostly left our car alone and remained at Clay Butte. Because we had left behind our jobs, the reams of chores that come with home ownership, and the kids' lessons, teams, and schools, there was time to walk and watch. When we were not on lookout duty Melissa and I would take Liza and Martin and explore the valley immediately below the tower, where they played in the small stream that wound through meadows and patches of scrubby willow; or we would hike farther east toward Beartooth Butte, and prospect for Devonian-aged fish fossils. Most often, though, we walked about one-half mile north to a high point where the main crest of the Beartooths rose before us and we could look down upon the lonely tower, perched on its soft, meadow-green rib. Sometimes Liza would bring along her sketchbook and draw wildflowers. If there was running water along our route, Martin would stop—constantly—to fill and refill his waterbottle, take a small drink, and exclaim, "Ah, fresh mountain water!" Or I'd tie the kids into a climbing rope, give them ice axes, and ascend a gentle snowslope, and we'd imagine being high on some Himalayan peak. And there always were questions: Is that tiny rivulet of snowmelt good for floating grass blades over mini-waterfalls? What animal deposited that pile of sawdust-colored droppings? Why are there clumps of ladybugs clustered among those boulders? What does a jumping spider feel like when it's scuttling across your palm? Where does a white-crowned sparrow build its nest?

What I recall most strongly about our lookout home were the mountains beyond mountains, the huge and endless sweep of rock and sky radiating out into that magnificent space and distance. But twelve years later, when I asked Liza about her memories of the landscape around the tower, she recalled the following: "The valley with a stream; heavy rocks, with iron in them; hiking out along the ridge, to the point overlooking the tower; burnt snags; how the trees released clouds of pollen; dried cow patties in the meadows; scaring up a blue grouse; finding pieces of coral fossils in the limestone; the grove of fir by the lookout tower, where we played." Martin's memories of the place he had last seen when he was five were more local than his older sister's: "Green; lots of snow; flowers; wind; the 'bear den' of trees near the tower, where we played; the stream where we played; fish fossils." Neither Liza nor Martin mentioned the world that spiraled out from our perch, the spectacular spread of mountains beneath an endless sky of light and cloud. As it had been with my sister and me in that Saratoga orchard some thirty-five years before, there was in our children that same focus on the immediate landscape, the view at their feet rather than toward the far horizon.

More often than seemed reasonable, a visitor might ask, "Do you have a television?" And when we explained that no, we did not and could not and would not have one, they then wondered, "Don't you ever get bored?" And truthfully—I'll speak for Melissa and the kids, too—no, we never were at a loss for things to do, although Liza did at times pine for her friends. We had endless iterations of sky and mountain, a substantial library, daily maintenance activities and look-out duties, and the most wonderful of backyards to explore. Instead of being held captive by lookout-tower ennui, my innate tendencies and academic-year inertia sometimes leaked into my life, and I was much too driven to accomplish "things." One summer I came to Clay Butte with the following list of projects: locate and monitor white-crowned sparrow nests, count breeding birds at Beartooth Pass, work on a survey of Clay Butte plants, write a short article for a journal, revise syllabi for my classes, continue research on monument plant ecology, work on a series of poems on the elements, and exercise regularly, with the goal of running over Beartooth Pass. This was silly. I could never accomplish half of these goals, and obsessing over them made it difficult to relax with my family or jettison the stress that accumulated during the academic year. The self-imposed pressure sometimes left me anxious and incapable of letting Martin and Liza establish the agenda for a day, or even an afternoon. Too often I lived with my obsessions, within a cycle of inarticulate frustration and tension that waxed and waned at unpredictable intervals. Ah, but when I could shed my fixation with goals, then it was possible to enjoy our neighborhood, and let the children, and myself, just *be*. . . .

It is afternoon; Liza is reading, while Melissa has pulled lookout duty. Martin is full of his five-year-old boyish energy, and I suggest a walk. We pack snacks, water, and raingear. I extract a promise from Martin to not "cry, whine, or plead," slather him with sunscreen, and off we go. Martin wears a baseball cap, his trademark turquoise windbreaker, shorts, and carries a small hiking stick. At first he moves quickly across the tundra, but his energies soon flag and he wants to stop for a rest. I give him a goal—the small summit up the abandoned jeep trail that runs along the ridge behind the tower. To take his mind off the ascent, I ask him about his latest obsession, Jim Bridger. He lapses into "Bridgerese," and his best western drawl: "Pardon me, ma'am. Know where a feller might rustle up some grub? Been on the trail, and got myself a mighty big hunger. Seen any Injuns 'round these here parts?" The improvisational skill of Martin's Jim Bridger riffs rival those of a Jerry Garcia guitar solo. They drive his sister absolutely wild, but Melissa and I think they're pretty funny, and encourage them whenever Liza's sibling rage isn't too explosive. We reach the top of the hill, which we christen "Bridger Peak," and I suggest that Jim and I take a break by the cairn, maybe sit our horses for awhile and chew on some pemmican and bison hide, search out what lies down the Oregon Trail. Martin plops down, high-grades our trail mix for M&M's, and drinks some water. He transforms his walking stick into a musket, then picks through the rocks between his legs, and driven by an innate imperative common to all little boys, begins throwing them at nothing in particular—and given the target, his aim is spectacular.

After a few minutes of rock-tossing Martin is ready to go again, and we wander off in search of a spot where there's a delightful, luxurious carpet of tiny alpine willows. It lies sheltered against a block of beige limestone, in a hollow where snow accumulates during the winter and provides enough meltwater to keep the willows happy. Martin and I lie on the firm mat, in the warm and welcoming sun, protected from the wind, and I search for the three dwarf species that grow here: *Salix reticulata, S. rotundifolia,* and *S. arctica.* The Latin is, well, Greek to Martin, and so I give each species a common name, such as arctic willow and round-leaved willow, so that we can talk about them. I show him the imbricated pattern of veins on the leaves of *S. reticulata,* and a tiny flower cluster from *S. rotundifolia,* no more than one-half-inch long. I tell him how these tiny plants are related to the weeping willow that grows in our Brockport backyard, which is seventy feet tall and over thirty feet in circumference at its base. I don't want to play the role of professor with my son, but I am excited by the close relationship between the minuscule, cold-hammered willows that cover our resting spot, and the messy, massive tree that I spend days cleaning up after each autumn. I try to tell Martin how this makes me feel, and for a moment he's vaguely interested. Then he's up and wandering around, searching among the rocks for the yellow-bellied marmot that, a few minutes ago, announced our approach to the alpine willow garden with a shrill whistle. I lie in the lee of the limestone, enjoying the deliciously warm sun, relaxed but every few seconds glancing around to make certain that Mr. Bridger's explorations aren't going to land him in a heap of trouble. I call Martin back to where I lie, and after a little more trail mix we move on, along the ridge leading north, which narrows beyond the willow patch.

We descend to a small pass, then climb to a pinnacle of eroded rock, where there's another plant I want to see. Over the seven summers that I've spent at Clay Butte, I've explored every nook and cranny along the three-mile ridge leading north from the tower, and this is one of my favorite spots: a shallow, north-facing alcove eroded out of a limestone pinnacle, with a cooler microclimate than on most of Clay Butte. And there, on a small shelf of decaying rock, I find what I'm after: purple saxifrage, *Saxifraga oppositifolia*, a small, densely-matted cushion plant with brilliant blossoms. What moves me most about this plant is the fact that it has a circumpolar distribution, with populations that extend to $83°N$. This tiny plant is a vehicle that transports me to Greenland and Ellesmere Island, to the furthest limit of plant distribution and my imagined Arctic, to a world that I may never see, but which is suddenly before me. It's hard to communicate what I'm feeling to the five-year-old boy beside me, but I point out the purple blossoms, mention bumble bee pollinators and Ellesmere Island, and hope that some small bit of the wonder will stick with him, be nurtured, and eventually develop into his own joy.

I am in my element and would love to continue down the ridge, but Jim's getting tired and there are thunderheads building to the west. It's been a great walk, and I do not want to ruin the experience by pushing him. I've learned that much over the years of parenting small kids. Martin tends to be more persnickety than his sister—when he was a toddler, his favorite words were "No!" and "Mine!"—but he also has a wonderful sense of humor. When he's amused by something, as he has been much of this afternoon, his face crinkles up and his brown eyes disappear behind a mask of laugh lines. I do not want him to lose this mood and crash, and so I ask if he's ready to head back to camp and see if the women folk have rustled us up some grub. Martin looks south toward the lookout, hooks his thumbs over the pockets of his shorts, then spits on the ground. In his very best Jim Bridger voice, he simply says, "Yup," and so we turn toward home.

When we lived in Lawrence, Liza and Martin wandered through our neighborhood, but always with Melissa and me. In Brockport, our family wandered much less. We never let our children explore on their own, even when they were ten or twelve. Such behavior was dangerous—there was a busy street in front of our house, the constant passage of strangers bound for the college, the threat of injury or abduction: the fodder of newspaper and television news, stimuli for our darkest parental angst. We knew, or thought that we knew, that only children with negligent or missing parents wandered. We would see them downtown or outside a rundown rental property, feral kids running in packs, practicing for the trouble they'd have in school and eventually with the police. And so Liza and Martin never had the chance to run free, as Melissa and I did when we were growing up in rural Connecticut and suburban California. By the time that Liza was ten and Martin was six, they had traveled halfway around the world, to Australia and the South Pacific. Yet their independent Brockport home ranges were small, and grew little until they reached adolescence. They had few chances to explore what Michael Chabon calls the "wilderness of childhood," to be adventurers in their own right and own neighborhood, free of adult supervision. "Childhood," Chabon writes, "is a branch of cartography," and although we helped them explore the world, and took them many places, in Brockport they had little freedom to draw their own maps. For Martin and Liza, there were no adult-free analogs to the plum orchard or Saratoga Creek, no irrigation ditches to wade in, or bicycle expeditions to the village square. Their lives were constrained, with little independent movement, and too often confined to—as Chabon observes—a system of "reservations," such as the Discovery Zone, to which I would add school, Scouts, dance studios, and fields where they played team sports. Our kids, like our friends' children, had more than enough to do, but they almost always were doing these things with adults watching over them, or in the confines of their homes or backyards. They had few opportunities to explore the dangerous world. We could teach Liza and Martin to ride their bicycles, but once they'd learned, where could they ride to, on their own? Where were the alleyways, woods, and creek bottoms where they could run, walk, cycle, crawl, skin their knees, get dirty and maybe scared? There were books, of course—a world that Liza, in particular, embraced—and the electronic Sirens that later would seduce Martin, but there was no glorious, independent *out there*.

The effect of our culture's persistent theme of childhood endangerment, and adult-imposed boundaries on childhood adventure, risk-taking, and imagination were made clear to us in 1996, during our last summer at Clay Butte. It was early July, and the road to the tower was blocked by snow. Because there were no potential abductors about, and it was a beautifully clear afternoon, our parental fears were calmed and we suggested that Liza, who was nine, take her five-year-old brother and climb the small hill north of the tower. The small summit was in plain view and about three-quarters of a mile away, along a gentle ridge. This was familiar ground—they'd probably walked there with us a dozen times or more. We helped them pack small daypacks, then waved them off on their adventure. They walked about fifty yards, stopped, and gazed back at the tower, where Melissa and I were standing on the catwalk. They looked anxious, and wanted our approval. "Go ahead," we said, urging them on with a wave of the hand. "Go!" They walked another fifty yards, then again halted and glanced back at us. They repeated this process several more times, until they finally advanced, timidly but on their own, to their destination. We had trained them well. Liza and Martin were uncomfortable with their tiny taste of freedom. They repeatedly sought our endorsement as they walked away from the tower, even though they knew the ground well and we watched them the entire time. Given the same opportunity, a nine-year-old Chris or Melissa, circa 1961, would have been gone, and not once looked back at their parents, except perhaps to wonder at how far they had run and how much farther they could roam.

Now, though, I'd like to think that our family walks, the time we spent at Clay Butte, and all the hiking, camping, and international travel, compensated for how we monitored and constrained our children's wanderings. Time spent outside must count for something, even if it was mostly with adults; for Martin and Liza there still was the unpredictable wild, the world of sparrows and mountain meadows and thunderstorms, trails tracking unexplored landscapes and wandering far from Chabon's "reservations" and the insidious permutations of electronic media. Their childhood experiences flowed outward from Lawrence and Brockport, into the Beartooth Mountains of Wyoming and the North Cascades of Washington, to Australia, New Zealand, and the South Pacific islands, to the Grand Canyon and Adirondacks. I hope that our family's explorations taught them enough about the color and spirit of good terrain, gave them their own cartographies, allowed them sufficient access to the great and uncertain world, and so nurtured their desire for the wild. I hope that the maps Melissa and I gave them are like "moonlight seething on the sea," or the luminous spread of the Southern Cross. Now in their early adulthood, both of our children have found passion in the outdoors and in travel. They are drawing their own maps of Tasmanian and Grand Canyon trails, and the churning rivers of the Adirondacks, Chile, and Mexico. It's a good feeling, to see them out there. But as most any parent can tell you, there is a cost to having independent and adventurous children. For if they learn to be cartographers in their own right, they will rarely look back at their parents, who are left behind, watching. Sometimes this is a painful thing—to know that your kids do not need much reassurance, or to glance back at you very often. And so it seems that the only solace for your children's independence is to wave them on their way and hold them in your prayers. Then it's best to unfold your own maps, survey the terrain, and begin walking—out along that alpine ridge that stretches north, through beautiful wildflower meadows, past sheltered willow gardens and north-facing alcoves, toward the far, far hills.

In the Fullness of Time

In the Fullness of Time

Above all else, there is the full-throated, bass roar of the rapids. We are immersed in sound. It permeates the Grand Canyon's air, washes us in the reflected violence of water pounding against rock, against other molecules of water. We will be lulled to sleep by liquid pulses of white noise, wake to their insistent thrum. Taken for twenty-four hours or so, the noise is oddly soothing, but if there were nothing but the sound of rapids for day after day—well, it would begin to wear. But there will be no sensory overload for Liza and me. Tonight my daughter and I are camped beside Boucher Rapids, but in the morning we will hike away from the Colorado River, toward the South Rim. Ten minutes or so of walking, a few turns and twists up the narrow slot of Boucher Creek, and the river's brawl will fade into the silence that claims the Canyon on most days, in most places.

It is a late afternoon in mid-March, on the third day of our hike. To get here, we descended the Hermit Trail for eight miles, swung west along the Tonto Trail for another five miles, and tracked Boucher Creek for a mile or so to the south bank of the Colorado. We have moved at a leisurely pace, partly out of a desire to relax, partly out of a necessity enforced by Liza's blistered feet, which resemble three-dimensional replicas of Craters of the Moon National Monument. Now, at five o'clock, Liza has assumed her customary position for this time of the day—reading in the tent—while I have assumed mine, propped against my pack, waiting for water to boil on our tiny camp stove. I brew my afternoon cup of tea, extinguish the stove's thin roar, and take all of this in: brushstrokes of dried grass sweeping across the sand, the rich riparian smell drifting up from the water's edge, the expansive, aching view. From where I sit I can see the North Rim and Point Sublime, fifty-three hundred feet and six miles north of Boucher Rapids. Between Point Sublime and the Colorado River is the broken pyramid of Mencius Temple, which guards the west side of Crystal Creek. Upriver, below Pima Point, are the golden-beige walls of Coconino Sandstone and blood-red cliffs of the Supai Formation, brilliant in the afternoon light. Beyond Pima Point, a few shreds of rain hang from a drift of broken cumulus clouds, suspended above the Canyon. And then there is the Colorado, which is the color of thin chocolate milk. It gathers in a quiet pool just to the east of camp, hesitates and eddies in a swirl of confused currents, then tumbles into the maelstrom of Boucher Rapids: noise, an explosive froth of water, and more noise.

Across the river, after a fall and winter of unusually heavy rains, the brittlebush are blooming, flashing electric yellow against the black, fluted walls and gullies of Vishnu Schist, metamorphic rocks from the deep vault of time, 1.7 billion years old. There is time—seconds, minutes, hours, days, weeks, even a lifetime—and then, as in the Canyon, there is TIME. From rim to river, from the 270-million-year-old Kaibab Limestone to the basement rocks that surround us, I can track roughly one-third of the earth's history. Down here, amidst the rock and seep willow, time is more than physics or psychology; it is something palpable and elemental, a motion and a presence. We walk in it, sleep in it, breathe it. Sometimes, I even think that I can taste it. I sip my tea, close my eyes, and imagine slipping below the surface of time, as if sliding into a deep desert pool, the cool grace of water on my skin. The noise of the river and the scent of seep willow fade away, and I am washed by seconds, hours, days, years, decades, centuries, eons. There is this moment. There is my life and the life of my daughter, the lives of trilobites and nautiloids, the cycles of folding and faulting, deposition and erosion. For a few seconds I brush the edge of time's essence, and then this sense is gone, like the waters which drift past our camp, headed toward the Gulf of Mexico, or more likely, a golf course in Las Vegas, a subdivision in Phoenix, or a lettuce field in the Imperial Valley.

The roar of Boucher Rapids: the present floods back in. I glance at my watch and realize that it is time for dinner. I rise and call out to Liza, who reads on.

In the morning we start toward the rim. We plan to hike a ways up Boucher Creek, ditch our packs at its junction with Topaz Canyon,

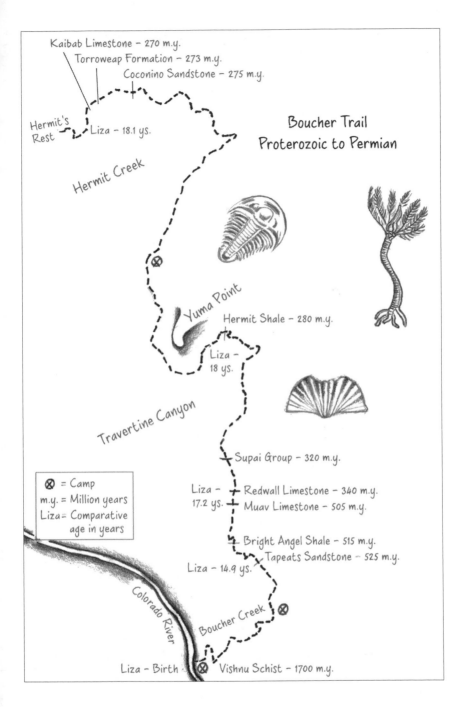

Kaibab Limestone – 270 m.y.

Torroweap Formation – 273 m.y.

Coconino Sandstone – 275 m.y.

Hermit's Rest

Liza – 18.1 ys.

Hermit Creek

Boucher Trail
Proterozoic to Permian

Yuma Point

Hermit Shale – 280 m.y.

Liza – 18 ys.

Travertine Canyon

⊗ = Camp
m.y. = Million years
Liza = Comparative
        age in years

Supai Group – 320 m.y.

Liza – 17.2 ys.

Redwall Limestone – 340 m.y.

Muav Limestone – 505 m.y.

Bright Angel Shale – 515 m.y.

Tapeats Sandstone – 525 m.y.

Liza – 14.9 ys.

Colorado River

Boucher Creek

Liza – Birth

Vishnu Schist – 1700 m.y.

Boucher Trail in the Grand Canyon.

then head west on the Tonto Trail for the day. Tomorrow, we will begin the steep climb through the last of the Precambrian schists, followed by the Tapeats Sandstone, Bright Angel Shale, Muav and Redwall Limestone, Supai Group, Hermit Shale, Coconino Sandstone, Toroweap Formation, and Kaibab Limestone. We plan to spend another night camped near the top of the Supai and finish up early the next day. Liza needs to get back to Westover School, where she's in her senior year of high school, and I have classes to teach. We have our imperatives.

We track Boucher Creek south as it meanders through some narrows, and the river's roar quickly recedes into stillness. A rock wren sings, then another: "*keree-keree-keree, chair, chair, deedle, deedle, deedle, tur, tur, tur.*" The creek is little more than a slip of water a few inches deep and several feet wide, a gentle murmur across small cobbles. I stoop and pick up a small stone from beneath its surface — a thin, oblong piece of Vishnu Schist, a shimmer of grayish silver with minute black dots, maybe three inches long and two inches wide. There's no particular reason why I seize on this particular rock, and there is nothing special about my prize — no spectacular colors or smooth, water-washed symmetry. Except, of course, that it is 1.7 billion years old. I decide that it will be my talisman for the remainder of the trip, my date with time. In clear violation of the Federal Antiquities Act, I place the stone in my pocket, where every now and then I rub my thumb and fingers across its slightly roughened surface, trace its irregular edge. For something that only weighs a few ounces, I think it has remarkable heft.

Liza walks ahead, head slightly bent, quiet in herself. She is wearing tan shorts and a blue T-shirt, has her light-brown hair pulled back into a ponytail. Her mangled feet are better after a day of rest, but her tentative gait suggests that they are still tender. One of Liza's traits is a refusal to complain. She is a mere slip of a young woman, no more than 5'2" tall and 105 pounds, but she is tough. Not rugby-playing, drill sergeant tough, but silent-and-determined tough. As a cross-country runner in high school, she trained and competed with stress fractures and chronic arch ailments that sometimes reduced her to quiet tears of pain and frustration by the end of a run. I don't know that such silent suffering is always a good thing, but it's how Liza is, and so every so often I'll ask her how she's doing, and if she needs to rest or treat her blisters. I know that, once asked, she'll tell me if things get bad enough.

Liza has been, for most of her life, relatively quiet — at least around her parents. Melissa and I are certain, though, that there is another side of her demeanor, one that she keeps mostly secret from us, but sometimes reveals to her friends. Our sense has developed, in part, from an appreciation of her insouciant humor, which is illustrated by a recent photographic portrait. Liza stands in the desert, with a cross section of watermelon held in front of her face, a fetching frown etched in the red fruit. Whenever she is amused by something, which is often, she flashes a small smile and a characteristic set of subdued chuckles, as when she scratched an abbreviated form of the following math proof in the sand during a lunch break:

$$\text{Study} = \text{Not Fail}$$
$$\text{Not Study} = \text{Fail}$$
$$\text{Study} + \text{Not Study} = \text{Fail} + \text{Not Fail}$$
$$\text{Study} \; \cancel{(1 + \text{Not})} = \text{Fail} \; \cancel{(1 + \text{Not})}$$
$$\text{Study} = \text{Fail}$$

Liza's humor showed itself early on, although she figured out the form of jokes before she understood their dependence on ironic tension. Witness an exchange that Melissa recorded when Liza was three-and-one-half:

Liza: "Knock! Knock!"
Melissa: "Who's there?"
Liza: "Wall."
Melissa: "Wall who?"
Liza: "Wall, ceiling. Isn't that funny?" (This followed by delighted laughter.)

Before long, though, Liza understood how jokes operated, and she soon besieged us with legions of knock-knock jokes and amusing stories. She was voluble and demonstrative around us with her humor, and with her anger. When she was two-and-one-half, and upset with one of our decisions, she would stand with her tiny fists clenched, look up at us with a pout and declare, very loudly and directly, "I don't like that!" And when she was just four, she sent a tennis ball whizzing past my ear when she felt that I was paying too much attention to her six-week-old brother; I turned around to see a small girl with a look of absolute fury upon her face. Now, though, she has a mostly quiet presence that meshes well with her love of tight places. She's always been comfortable in small, dark spaces; when she was young and upset, we would sometimes find her curled up beneath her bed, in the corner against the wall. Now she enjoys caving, which seems to me an acquired taste, much like eating marinated fish offal. She is relaxed in spots that I must force myself to enter, like one sixty-foot-long slot not much wider than my body, so tight at one end that I had to remove my helmet to worm my way through. Liza dove right into the entrance, while I knelt there, eyes closed, gathering my breath, determined to follow her into the close and claustrophobic darkness.

It's easy to talk to Liza about her passions, like books, music, politics, or the outdoors, but with rare exceptions it's impossible to carry on a conversation about her emotional, interior life, not that I'm exactly the Dr. Phil of personal explication. If Melissa or I ask her, "Liza, how are you feeling about X?" her invariable response is, "I don't like questions like that." On this trip, I've tried to have several "meaningful" father-daughter talks about her impending graduation from high school and transition to college, or the vagaries of her friendships. However, my efforts always end in what I call a "knee conversation": I ask the personal question, Liza reacts by staring at her legs, and says nothing. So I've let go of my efforts to delve into her interior life, because it is enough — more than enough — to be together and happy in this place. Even if she is quiet about the big issues, she is smiling and relaxed, at least when her feet aren't throbbing, and her voice has this soft lilt to it, a note of pleasure and satisfaction. Still, I worry that she is too much like me, that some combination of genes and environment has rendered her too independent and afraid of showing emotion, reluctant to ever confront someone directly, either in anger or in love, and ask for what she wants and needs. I often see myself as the Neville Chamberlain of interpersonal politics, always willing to compromise and avoid conflict at all costs, to settle for "peace in our time," and I don't want this for Liza. For the lack of immediate conflict doesn't equate with peace, and there is no easy end run around the tectonic forces of our emotions and relationships. You may take your trip to Munich, but eventually there will be a Dunkirk, and the Blitz.

Boucher Creek begins to widen. The Vishnu Schist that bounds the creek is still steep, but its walls have lain back enough so that a determined hiker could find places to scramble up to the base of the cliffy Tapeats Sandstone, some four hundred feet above us. The schist here is mostly black and dark gray, and marbled with white and pink intrusions of younger, granitic rock. The dark rock and steep, confined walls render canyons such as this one brutal and oppressively claustrophobic on a 110°F July day. Now, though, the walking is easy. There is the warm and gentle sun, the soothing flow of Boucher Creek, and a flush of wildflowers on the canyon slopes, crowned by the vibrant yellow of brittlebush. I stop to take a photograph, then pull out the 15-minute Bright Angel quad. It's a standard USGS topographical map, but it reveals much more than contours and elevations, and the route of the Boucher Trail, for it also marks our route through time. At the moment we're sunk deeply in Precambrian rock; in making our way from Boucher Rapids to the Tapeats, the lowest Cambrian rocks, we will gain only eight hundred feet of elevation and cover just 15 percent of the 10.5 miles that the trail takes to climb from river to rim. Yet in that one-and-one-half miles we will traverse something on the order of 1.2 billion years, which is about 82 percent of the temporal distance between the Vishnu Schist and the 270-million-year-old Kaibab Limestone that caps the sequence of Grand Canyon rocks. That's a long way to travel in such a short distance; in Liza time, it is equivalent to moving through almost fifteen of her eighteen years.

The lower reaches of Boucher Creek make for a good meditative environment, and as we walk I contemplate the rocks, and my daughter's life. The schists that we are traveling through were most likely deposited as submarine sediments, then deformed by thrusting and folding; the great pressure and heat—roughly 1000°F—would have destroyed any fossils present. Too bad, for the middle Precambrian was a time of great evolutionary innovation. Although evidence of the first primitive, prokaryotic cells—those without a nucleus and membrane-bound organelles—appears in the fossil record about 3.4 billion years ago, the first eukaryotic cells—those possessing a nucleus and organelles—did not arrive on the scene for another 1.8 billion years or so, around the time that the original rocks comprising the Vishnu Schist were formed. The Vishnu Schist is part of the Granite Gorge Metamorphic Suite, which sounds like a composition for strings and horns by Ferde Grofé, rather than a complex stew of Proterozoic metamorphic and igneous rocks. Intense heat, folding and faulting, and pressure: it must have been a tremendous burst of geologic activity, and we are walking through evidence of that turmoil—vertical deformations, sheer bands, tortuous foldings. Imagine a crumpled piece of thick paper, and you have some idea of the rock's fabric. So much tectonic noise, a history of violence, now enveloped by such quiet. . . .

In the evening we camp at the junction of Boucher Creek and Topaz Canyon, after a ramble west into the Slate Creek drainage. We've had bouts of wind and rain these last few days, but tonight it is perfectly still and clear, and so we dispense with the tent and sleep beneath the stars. After a dinner of Jaipur vegetables and rice we lie in our sleeping bags, the cold and infinite sprawl of heaven above us, talking quietly of novels, music, and constellations. I am relaxed, and Liza seems much the same. Today she mentioned that she was "glad she came along," which is about as much as she will ever say about her internal state, and it is good enough for me.

Liza and her brother grew up spending time outside, and in spite of her balky feet she carries herself as if she is entirely comfortable out here. Melissa and I took Liza camping in the Mojave Desert only six weeks after she was born, an act meant to demonstrate that having a child was not going to change *our* lifestyle. (Fools!) Between the ages of six months and nine years, Liza spent parts of five summers living in a fire lookout tower in the Beartooth Mountains of Wyoming. Her playground was a copse of subalpine fir, which she called the "bear den," and the alpine flower garden that ran north from the tower. She "climbed" her first peak when she was just six months old, and I have a picture of her on the summit, sitting in her baby backpack, looking small and vulnerable amidst the sweep of the Beartooths, yet smiling from beneath her red sunbonnet. Her first overnight backpacking trip came when she was seven, when the family wandered three miles up the West Fork of Rock Creek in Montana on an easy trail through lodgepole pine and spruce. She carried her own small pack and did well, her only vice being a strong predilection to forage for strawberries, raspberries, and even tiny whortleberries. But she could walk quickly and never complained, and most likely could have covered six or eight miles, if her three-year-old brother had not slowed the pace considerably. It was Martin's first overnight hike, too, and he needed constant reinforcement with M&M's and games to coax him to the first decent camp spot.

And so, from an early age, Liza was incubated in mountains and deserts. She spent many nights on the ground, went on countless day hikes, ate innumerable meals cooked on a camp stove, and carried packs across Adirondack portages. She had to make do with her parents, brother, and books as companions for weeks at a time, and amuse herself without the pervasive electronica that now clutters most kids' lives. I like to think that her immersion in the natural world nurtured her in some fundamental way. Along with what I take to be an inclination similar to mine, her early exposure to the natural world granted her an outdoor ease, a fundamental sense of contentedness and ability to transcend blisters, bugs, and hard work. Sometimes it's difficult to know what's going on inside her, but she seems at home amongst the rocks and desert scrub, beneath the stars.

We say our good-nights, switch on our headlamps and read for awhile, then drift off to sleep. Nearby, tiny Boucher Creek gurgles on, cutting slowly through the canyon's cobbles, slicing its way ever so patiently through the deepest layers of time.

Liza and I break camp by nine, walk a short distance up Boucher Creek, then begin climbing toward the rim. Shortly after leaving the water and cottonwoods behind, we reach the Tapeats Sandstone, and here, in a few short steps, we leap across almost 1.2 billion years, from the Vishnu Schist into Cambrian rocks about 525 million years old. We have crossed what John Wesley Powell termed the Great Unconformity, which was created by the erosion of perhaps six miles of rock. Our hike out of the Canyon will take us across many unconformities, or breaks in the geological record, but this is the Mother of All Unconformities. The Boucher Trail climbs into the Tapeats through erosional debris, which obscures the contact between the strata, but in many places along Boucher Creek the transition between the Vishnu Schist and younger rocks is visually dramatic: fine-grained, black metamorphic rock, riddled with a complex latticework of white and pink igneous intrusions — wonderfully termed "dike swarms" — running hard into dark brown, horizontal sandstone bands, and simply vanishing. A few feet of steep trail not only carries us from a geology of metamorphic and igneous rocks to one of sedimentary deposits, but also from a world of microscopic, prokaryotic organisms to one of large, complex creatures. We have moved, quite suddenly, into the Cambrian explosion, which began some 542–543 million years ago, a burst of evolutionary innovation that led to the appearance of essentially all major, extant body types. Over some twenty million years, and following by about 300 million years an explosion of photosynthetic activity and rise in global oxygen, life embarked upon a period of accelerated and unprecedented innovation, and general increase in body size and complexity. Prior to the Cambrian explosion, most animals were small and weakly skeletonized. Fossilized remains of these early life forms are generally rare, and so our knowledge of Precambrian life is sketchy. But very quickly after the Cambrian transition came highly skeletonized forms: mollusks, echinoderms, arthropods, and the first vertebrates. Animals invaded the substrate, tracked the ocean floor, swam through the seas and, by 450 million years ago, were up to one million times as big as they had been in the late Precambrian. Unfortunately, the metamorphic forces that created the Precambrian rocks destroyed any fossils once present in their parent material; along with the accompanying Great Unconformity, this means that there is no evidence along Boucher Creek with which we can track Precambrian life. So we must look elsewhere for evidence of life's early development, such as in the Grand Canyon Supergroup, a series of strata in the eastern part of the Canyon that span a portion of the Great Unconformity, from 1.2 billion to 740 million years ago.

Even without the fossils, all of this is stunning. As we climb through the Tapeats, my pace slows, I finger my piece of Vishnu Schist, and consider the history of life and human lives, their transitions. In Liza equivalents, the time gap we have crossed has taken us from her first days of life into ninth grade. It's as if she instantaneously leapt from nursing, the tiniest diapers, unfocused vision and naked helplessness, to the *Lord of the Rings* trilogy, high school, and her first Grand Canyon backpacking trip, which she took with her friend Kathy and Melissa—a three-day hike down the South Kaibab Trail to Phantom Ranch, and then up the Bright Angel Trail. For me, it's as if I have jumped from infancy to being the father of two small children and beginning, far too late in life, a career in academia. Memory and personal history, human development, the Cambrian explosion and Great Unconformity; I've stepped into a vortex of time, which races by, slows to a crawl, spirals back on itself, convulses. Actually, it's not time that does this, but my perception of time, which is alternately *adagio* and *allegro*, linear and circular, while the physics of time remains inexorable and constant. While "the second" is a human construct, our technical definition is based on the invariant oscillations of the cesium atom. And so the atomic clock at the National Institute of Standards and Technology lab in Boulder, Colorado, which uses the resonance frequency of the cesium atom as its timekeeper, ticks on, accurate to one second across twenty million years. Or take the radioactive decay of the isotope potassium-40, in which an electron is captured by a proton in the nucleus, resulting in the formation of a neutron and a new element, argon-40. The constant exponential decay function of potassium-40 has a half-life of 1.248 billion years; cook or squeeze an atom, subject it to the heat and pressure that the Vishnu Schist must have seen, and the rate of electron decay stays the same.

Time flows on, dismissive of human categories — of seconds, minutes, weeks, months, decades, centuries, millennia, eons. Relativity and what's called "time dilation" might have some effect on time's velocity, but only at speeds approaching that of light. Here on earth, even at orbital velocities, its current is a constant oscillation of cesium atoms, an invariant flux of isotopes: and potassium-40 shall beget argon-40, and rubidium-87 shall beget strontium-87 . . . But as we experience this relentless, elemental cascade — whether in the present, past, or future — we cross unconformities, encounter strata which vary in their thickness and rate of deposition. The summers of my youth lasted forever. During those hot and languid days in the Santa Clara Valley, I knew something of boredom, when time turned as torpid as an August afternoon in the deep sycamore shade along Saratoga Creek. But years later, after Liza and Martin were born, our diminutive time machines catapulted Melissa and me across the years, through a haze of diapers and sleepless nights, dance classes and baseball games, full-time jobs and overtime parenthood. One moment, it's a gray and bitter winter day in Connecticut, and Liza is just home from the hospital, weighing all of five pounds. She's buried deep within layers of blankets, a fortress against the cold. Who knows what she was thinking about, but it must have involved some primal, inchoate vision of mammal milk, snuggly warmth, and a clean bottom. Look again, and she is climbing through sandstone on a bright and warm March morning. Now her thoughts turn to calculus, a class that she loves passionately, and to the novels of Tolstoy and Michael Chabon. She's suddenly eighteen and ready for college; I'm suddenly fifty-four and almost ready for Social Security. In 1969, I wanted to ratchet up life's speed. I wanted legal beer, voting privileges, independence. Now I'd like the pace of my life to resemble our crawl through the Tapeats. My yearnings are as ordinary and predictable as the decay of potassium-40 atoms, but I want to stomp hard on time's brakes, reduce my temporal velocity to zero, maybe even throw it into reverse. I want the fletching of time's arrow to fail, watch as its path suddenly veers from a fleet horizontal vector into a plunging parabola. I yearn for my pre-marathon, pre-Outward Bound knees, for ten easy and fluid miles on a run. I want to shed my sins, the nagging sense that isotopic decay is an allegory for my life's trajectory. And much as I love seeing Liza mature into an independent young woman, there are moments when I want to reclaim her early years, to once again support her whole length with my hand and forearm, and replay her childhood tape.

This desire to slow the passage of time is one thing that draws me, so passionately, to the far North. Normally, I prefer to go to bed early, rise before dawn, and so claim some of morning's stillness. But when I am fortunate enough to spend part of my summer in the Arctic I undergo a phase shift, and stay up to well past midnight. It's not a matter of sensitivity to light, as I sleep well and hard north of the sixtieth parallel—rather, it's a desire for those late, luminous evenings, the way in which the lingering light plays across the tundra, catches the roll of gentle chop on some northern lake. It's a love of the first whistled song of a Harris's sparrow rising into the air at one in the morning, the slide of one day into the next without an intervening bout of darkness. The days roll into one long, continuous song, and time is spun more slowly into the fabric of my days than it is "down south." There's an illusion that the days, weeks, and months will not pass, that I will not grow older—or if I must, that it will happen more slowly and gently. I step out of a cabin at midnight, look out over the Bering Sea or a river curving toward Hudson Bay, and in the late and burnished light, time loses some of its insistence.

Once beyond the Tapeats, the mostly vertical world of the Canyon goes horizontal as we climb onto the Tonto Platform. The views open up to the north and west as we ascend the grayish-green slopes of Bright Angel Shale, and I no longer feel as though I am held so deeply below the earth's horizon. The rock here is soft and easily eroded, hence the broad expanse of the platform, which on the south side of the Canyon runs west from the Little Colorado River for about fifty river miles, to just past Bass Rapids. But it's over twice as far to follow the Tonto Trail along the same stretch of river. For much of its hundred and fifteen miles, the trail wanders in and out of the numerous side canyons that drain from the South Rim, tracing each back to a crossing above the cliffy Tapeats Sandstone, then heading toward the river to round each promontory of Redwall Limestone. I love hiking along the Tonto because of the expansive views and easy rhythm that comes to my walking: in and out of each side canyon, a rolling stroll through fields of blackbrush and Mormon tea, perhaps the grace of a small stream above the Tapeats, where percolating groundwater has been blocked by the impermeable mudstones of Bright Angel Shale. But for us the walking isn't so easy, as we're cutting across the grain of the Tonto Platform, through Cambrian sediments — once a world of trilobites and "inarticulate brachiopods," a name that I love. "Inarticulate" refers to the manner in which the two shells of the brachiopod were held together by muscles rather than a hinge-like joint, but the term makes me imagine garbled mutterings of fossil invertebrates across 500 million years of time, the lost languages of lost species.

Above the Bright Angle Shale, the trail works through thin, gray beds of Muav Limestone ("Muav-e-lous," I say to Liza, who appreciates a good pun), the last Cambrian rocks of the Tonto Group, and crosses another big unconformity, this one spanning about 165 million years. We have moved, steeply, into the spectacular Redwall Limestone, which forms massive, vertical cliffs four hundred to eight hundred feet high. The name comes from the iron oxides that have washed down from the overlying red beds of the Supai Formation and in many places stained the gray limestone. Along the human time line of this walk, a few steps have pushed us through another two years of Liza's life, and seven years of mine. We have also jumped through the Ordovician, Silurian, and Devonian periods and landed in the Mississippian, a sedimentary world roughly 340 million years old. During the Mississippian, terrestrial animals such as insects, amphibious fish, amphibians, and groups closely related to reptiles diversified, but at that time the area we are walking through was a shallow sea, the province of marine brachiopods, corals, crinoids, bivalves, snails, nautiloids, and fish. As we work higher into the Redwall, the sun breaks above the cliffs and morning's coolness evaporates. Louis Boucher's trail seeks a narrow slot, angles steeply upward over broken limestone, cuts through a tangle of shrubs, and suddenly I've topped out above the Redwall, two thousand feet above the river, and about the same distance shy of the rim.

I slip off my pack and flop down to wait for Liza, who has lagged a few minutes behind. To the north is Whites Butte, in back of me the South Rim, but everywhere else there is glorious space, oceans of it, and the expanse is exhilarating. I take a small drink of water, mindful that we will make a dry camp tonight, close my eyes and doze for a few minutes. Chattering white-throated swifts, which look like cigars with narrow, sickle-shaped wings, cavort above me. There is a burst of twittering, swirling bodies, a flurry of rapid wingbeats, and then the flock tumbles over the edge of the Redwall and is gone. Swifts are masterful fliers, and land only to roost and nest. The rest of their lives they are airborne, scooping up insects on the wing and even copulating in mid-air, which seems like quite a trick, and I've read that their European cousins fly up to six hundred miles in a day. That is traveling, and a bit faster than my estimated one mile per hour in the steepest section of the Redwall. Still, I am feeling pretty fit, which for a few moments serves as a partial antidote to my nagging concerns about aging. But then I glance down at my leg, stretch and flex a tight muscle in my left calf, and see something that I've never noticed before: a skim of tiny wrinkles, etched in a layer of trail dust. My body has just served notice that I soon will pay for all the years that I disdained sun protection, and I am thrown forward ten years or more, into an era of thinning skin and liver spots. But then comes another one of those time warps that are such a part of this hike, and just as quickly I slip backward across decades. I look down the trail, after Liza, and see the sliver of shade where my first true girlfriend and I ate lunch, back in 1971. We were headed down the Boucher Trail on a hot April day, and found that small, sheltered alcove just above the steep descent through the Redwall. Somewhere I still have a picture of her, taken from very near to where I now sit: she looks up at me, smiling from beneath a large, floppy sun hat, the sun-blasted trail falling away toward the Tonto Platform. I haven't looked at the photo for twenty years or more, but I know this spot, and that trip from thirty-four years ago slips into my present. It is never possible to fully inhabit a moment again, but April 1971 seems close at hand, and I feel like Billy Pilgrim in Vonnegut's *Slaughterhouse-Five*. I have no idea where she is now; we split up six months after our Boucher trip, and I last saw her in 1976. I heard that she married a park service ranger, had lots of kids, and lived for awhile in Yellowstone, but that's it. Our separation was awkward, painful, and bitter, but there's this sweetness in the air, and memory, as false as it sometimes is, whispers to me of youthful adventure and innocence, of honorable intentions, of a time when the possibilities of the world opened before me like the spread of the Canyon in this sun-dazzled space.

Liza, who is nearly the same age as my girlfriend was in 1971 — Good Lord! — pops up over the edge of the Redwall, sweaty and breathing hard. I congratulate her on finishing the climb, and offer her the water bottle and a spot on the ground beside me. The white-throated swifts are back, and right now fifty-four feels pretty damned good.

We walk almost due south, above massive cliffs of Redwall that plummet into the narrow slot of Travertine Canyon. A black-throated sparrow sings, laying claim to a small tract of blackbrush and chipped limestone, then quiets. His territorial display seems a little early, as it is only mid-March and a late storm could still bring a touch of snow to this country. The French composer Olivier Messiaen, whose work was influenced by his appreciation of birdsong, once said that "birds are the opposite of time." According to David Rothenberg, Messiaen, who composed "Quartet for the End of Time," meant that birdsong connects us to the Eternal, which is beyond time. Whatever the "Eternal" and our relation to it might be, I would argue just the opposite — that "birds are the measure of time." They are fully immersed in it, more so than humans. For birds that breed in high-latitude and temperate habitats, the substance of their lives — the flux of hormones in their blood; the cycles of weight and fat, song and nest; their migrations and matings—is driven by the periodicity of the earth's orbit around the sun, and waxing and waning photoperiods. If I hike the Canyon in any year from mid-March into May, I'll hear black-throated sparrows singing in the blackbrush scrub. Although annual differences in weather or resources might affect initiation of breeding by a few days, birds like the black-throated sparrow remain bound to time and oscillations of light. Humans may hope to deny time's passage, but black-throated sparrows cannot.

We cross the dry wash of Travertine Canyon, wind through a jumble of boulders, and climb into the Supai Group, a series of mostly red beds stacked in alternating layers of shales, mudstones, siltstones, sandstones, limestones, conglomerates, and gypsum. The Supai and overlying Hermit Shale, which also consists of red beds, span some 45 million years, from the beginning of the Pennsylvanian Period to the early Permian. These sedimentary rocks were deposited in continental, shoreline, and shallow-marine environments, and form a complex series of vertical units of resistant rock interspersed with more erodible material. There are many small unconformities, or diastems, between units in these formations, some of which are obscure—hence the delightfully named "hiatus problem"—something, I think, that in a different form bedevils many of us.

We need to gain eight hundred feet to reach the top of the Supai Group, through strata that are stunningly different in texture, composition, and essence from the Redwall Limestone below. We're somewhere around 320 million years back in geologic time—or in the other scale of temporal measurement that I'm using, only seven Liza-months ago, when she was seventeen-and-one-half and ready to start her senior year at Westover School, a private all-girl's school in Connecticut. Although we were reluctant to send her away to high school, Melissa and I had worked at Westover from 1983 until 1988, and loved the community. Liza was born while we worked there, her godparents were still on the faculty, and we knew that the learning and social environment would suit her. So we offered her the opportunity to attend Westover and she decided to go. Now she's a senior, and seems happy. She's found her educational niche, has made good friends, and loves many of her teachers and courses, although she's ready to move on to college.

After we dropped Liza off at Westover for the first time, our house seemed empty, even though Martin was home and we were renting two rooms to college students. Her absence assumed a melancholy presence, palpable and sharp, and whenever one of us walked into her bedroom there was a momentary stab of sadness, a reminder that she was 325 miles away. Liza, though, appeared to adjust easily to Westover; she quickly found companions, enjoyed her courses, and revealed—at least to us—no sign of homesickness. When we visited Westover six weeks later, she seemed happy and settled. She was pleased to see us, and fully present, but it was obvious that she had her own life, and that she was comfortable in it. She's always had a sense of independence about her. When she was two-and-one-half years old and in day care at the University of Kansas, she sometimes cried if we came to pick her up when she was playing—which made us feel both like dirt (she wasn't particularly interested in seeing us) and pleased (she was happy). Later, when she learned to read on her own, she would retreat to her room for hours and immerse herself in piles of books, surfacing only to eat and take care of necessary bodily functions. And when she was seventeen she traveled to Australia without us, to see her grandparents and visit friends she'd made when I was on sabbatical there. She flew from the United States with a family friend, as Melissa and I were too nervous to let her go on her own, but she later traveled by herself to Perth, a continent away from her grandparents, and we had the sense that she would have been comfortable doing the entire journey to and from Australia without adult accompaniment.

I recall how Liza was at two-and-one-half, at fifteen, and how she is now, and I wonder—the perennial parental question—about the extent to which her basic personality traits were fixed at an early age, through some complex chemistry of genetic and environmental reactants. From a very early age, for example, she was passionate about reading. One of her first seven words, along with "Ma-ma" and "Da," was "Buh," for book, and by the time she was ten months old, she was in love with board-book classics like *Tickle, Tickle* and *Moo Moo, Peek-a-Boo*, which she demanded be read to her over and over and over, until they "accidentally" went missing. And one of her favorite games of the time was to crawl, as rapidly as she could, back into our study, pull herself up on the built-in bookshelves, and throw every accessible book onto the floor. On most nights either Melissa or I

would doze off, book in hand, as Liza requested that we pay attention, please, and stop reading the same sentence again and again. This
stage lasted until Liza was about six. One day she was watching Melissa read to herself, and the following conversation ensued:

Liza: "Mom, what are you doing?"
Melissa: "Reading, Liza."
Liza: "No, you're not. You aren't saying any words."
Melissa: "Yes, I am reading. I'm just saying the words in my head."

At this point, Melissa says that Liza experienced an epiphany. Suddenly
she understood how silent reading worked, and after that flash of understanding spread across her face, she was gone. She grew intolerant
of being read to by her parents—far too slow—and by second grade
she was deep into novels like *The Hobbit* and *The Lion, the Witch, and the
Wardrobe*. By eight, she was reading late into the night, and protesting
parental admonitions about lights off: "I can't sleep unless I find out
what happens!" She carried her love of books through adolescence
and into young adulthood; when she flew into Rochester after her
2005 Australian trip, hammered by jet lag and without sleep for more
than twenty-four hours, she insisted on dropping by the library and
checking out a stack of books, just so she would be able to wake after
a long sleep, read for awhile, and doze off again. I am certain that her
love of books will be with her always, just as she will always love spicy
foods, and fruits and vegetables.

Liza was an adventurous eater from her earliest years. When she
was about two, Melissa and I took her to a Mexican restaurant and
let her try medium-hot salsa with corn chips. She inhaled the salsa,
and when we cut her off, she cried. When she was almost five, she re-
solved to become a vegetarian. Perhaps she was influenced by several
of her friends and her preschool teacher, none of whom ate meat, but
it was her decision, one which she held to for several months. She disdained McDonald's, and requested cranberry küchen for her birthday
instead of a regular layer cake. Her tastes turned to tofu and tempeh,
Indian curries and mango ice cream, banana smoothies and pungent
hot sauces, and that's where they've remained.

Or take order. In most aspects of her life, Liza seems firmly opposed to it; she has always been a devoted fan of the Second Law
of Thermodynamics. At preschool, she consistently refused to pick

up her toys at the end of the day, and she fought the same battle at home. Throughout her New York years, from first grade until she went away to Westover, the entropic clutter of her room was a source of great contention. Melissa and I would demand, over and over, that Liza clean her room. She would engage in civil disobedience until compelled to do *something*. She then would spend hours engaged in a lethargic and futile attempt to reshelve her books, separate dirty and clean clothes, and tidy her bed. Eventually, Melissa and I would surrender and divert a local river to clean up the Augean stables on our own, a task that could consume almost an entire day—only to watch as disorder immediately reclaimed her room. Out of frustration I eventually gave up playing Sisyphus, although Melissa persisted for several more years. We just never got it—at least not until Liza came home one vacation, deposited her duffel bags in the middle of the bedroom floor, and let the jumbled mass inside ooze out into her immaculate room, like the pestilent blob in the 1958 Steve McQueen science fiction movie. When we asked her how she could live with such a mess, she said, "It feels cozy." And there it was. It wasn't so much laziness or the imperative of her will that prevented her from cleaning her room, as an innate preference for clutter. Liza was, and still seems, content to live in the kind of mess that makes me more anxious than a cat in a room full of Rottweilers.

Independence, emotional reserve, books, messiness, the natural world, spicy foods—I could build a longer list, overwhelm the reader with a parent's encyclopedic knowledge of their child's attributes and development. The point is that many of Liza's basic traits seem to have been settled early in her life, and I wonder if this is true for most of us. Does the essence of a young child predict the adult they will become? The Jesuits declared, "Give me the child until he is seven, and I will give you the man." If this maxim is correct, then much about a person's nature is determined in their first few years of life—a frightening prospect, both as a parent and for personal reasons. Sure, a serious accident, a divorce, the death of a parent, or the wrong stepfather at the wrong time might deflect a person's behavioral vector, but there seems to be so much developmental inertia. It takes a tremendous amount of will, dedication, and energy to quiet or divert our fundamental impulses, drives, and desires. Our fault lines run deep, and they remain active. As a parent I worry that my child-rearing errors will have long-lasting effects on Liza and Martin. And for myself I worry that I will never be able to change what I need to change in myself. It is, I sometimes fear, as Bernhard Schlink writes: "The tectonic layers of our lives rest so tightly one on top of the other that we always come up against earlier events in later ones, not as matter that has been fully formed and pushed aside, but absolutely present and alive."

In contrast, I wonder what one point in time can predict about the character of the earth millions of years later. To what extent did the Vishnu Schist—its texture and composition—prophesy the Tapeats Sandstone? Could an imaginary Paleozoic geologist have studied the Redwall Limestone, circa 340 million years old, and predicted the Supai Group's sandstones and mudstones some twenty or thirty million years later? Perhaps a professional geologist would disagree with me, but the earth's history—and life's history—seems more contingent than does personal history. Sure, an active fault line suggests an earthquake, a restless volcano predicts an eruption, a subduction zone says something about the fate of a continental margin. Perhaps the start of the Laramide orogeny some seventy to eighty million years ago demanded the extent, height, and texture of the Rocky Mountains. Perhaps the northward drift of the Indian plate, which began about 125 million years ago, guaranteed the Himalayas, but I doubt it. There is the imperative of cause and effect, and it is easy to look backward in time and think, "This is the only way things could have developed," but there always were, and are, countless other possible paths. Push back the seas, and the depositional environment of the Redwall Limestone could have been transformed instead into one that produced the Supai Group—rocks so very different in their character, and in the remains of the creatures that inhabited their worlds. Spew out enough basalt lava at the end of the Permian, some 251 million years ago—two million cubic kilometers of the stuff, which covered 1.6 million square kilometers of eastern Russia with an igneous blanket anywhere from four hundred to thirty-five hundred meters thick—and bring life perilously close to complete annihilation. Cool down and dry the East African climate some ten million to five million years ago, break up the tropical forests and spread the savannahs—an environment favoring increased terrestrialism in hominids—and perhaps the stage is set for the evolution of an upright, bipedal, tool-using great ape. These things happened—but what if the great sieve of extinctions at the Permian/Triassic boundary had not occurred? What if the Miocene tropical forests of East Africa had not retreated in response to climate change? What if a great period of mountain-building and metamorphism had transformed the limestone of the Redwall into something other than what it became?

Whatever the Supai Group might have to say about the layers above, it is a long ascent through its complicated units. Liza and I stop for lunch, then continue upward. Along the way we are pestered by the insistent and persistent thump of helicopters as they ferry tourists to and from the nearby airport at Tusayan. I hate, passionately, these "scenic flights" through what the Park Service calls the "Dragon Flight Corridor." They devour silence and vomit noise, and are as antithetical to the spirit of the Canyon as an Andy Warhol painting would be in the Sistine Chapel. When the helicopters are whumping above us, my jaw muscles tighten and I begin channeling the fulminations of Ed Abbey. Each flight is an invasion; the tourist helicopters don't belong here, any more than a Las Vegas casino belongs perched on the South Rim. In 1987, Congress passed an Overflights Act mandating control of helicopter and fixed-wing aircraft in the Grand Canyon, and "substantial restoration of the natural quiet and experience of the park," but the air tour companies have too much political juice, and the number of overflights has actually doubled. A pox on their rotors and the politics of money.

Liza and I eventually reach a spot where the trail ascends through a tall, vertical band of cross-bedded Esplanade Sandstone, the uppermost unit of the Supai Group. Erosion has destroyed much of Boucher's original trail here, and for a short stretch we climb hand-over-hand through tumbled rocks and a series of ledges, before we emerge on top of the Esplanade. As we're scrambling through the last of the Supai, some twenty-five hundred feet above where we began the day, I think of a Zen saying: "The way is without difficulty. Strive hard." We contour northeast for a mile or so, to a promontory directly below Yuma Point, then take a break amidst the pinyon pines. It's three o'clock; time to refuel and rehydrate, look around, and let a party of loud teenagers move on by. They are competing with the helicopters for the Irritating Noise Production Award, and are making us, once again, cranky. So we ditch our packs and scramble through some rocks to a point overlooking the Canyon. The Esplanade here is reddish beige and pitted with a scatter of black-rimmed pockets, six inches to a foot deep, many of which hold water from recent rains. There are streaks of raven shit here and there, and a layer of debris in many of the pockets, but the water looks good enough to filter, and a welcome addition to our supplies. As I fill our water containers, Liza plops down at the edge of the cliff and dangles her legs into space, facing east. From her perch, she can look down upon the gulf of Hermit Creek, where we began our hike, the black schists of the Inner Gorge, and a short section of the Colorado River. Beyond is the North Rim, and the mesas and buttes north of the river—Wotan's Throne, Zoroaster Temple, Brahma Temple. The sound of rapids drifts up from the river, a faint, whispered reminder of the noise that bathed us two days ago. Liza is quiet and contemplative, and so I grant her the silence and the privacy of her thoughts. She sits at the edge of the great abyss, her expression invisible, but I'm thinking that she must have a small grin on her face, for she is in one of her best places.

I finish filtering water, sit beside Liza, and look down on the Vishnu Schist. We've climbed through five major strata, across something on the order of 1.4 billion years, traveled from a world dominated by single-celled bacteria to one populated by a menagerie of invertebrate and vertebrate forms—reptiles, amphibians, fish, corals, brachiopods, bryozoans, echinoderms, cephalopods, and more, organized in complex marine and terrestrial communities. I feel like an immigrant to the past, but it's a past that I cannot fully comprehend, for how does one get hold of 1.4 billion years, when our lives are measured in decades? For all practical purposes, we might as well be dealing with infinity. It's not that we are unable to quantify such periods of time; we have the tool kit of radiometric-dating techniques that will do this, and do it well. It's that the world is so much larger and older than our lives, and thus imaginations. Paul Fraisse, an experimental psychologist, has written that "the psychology of time—which is not the same as the physics of time—is necessarily that of our experiences." And if my experiences occur on a scale of decades, and the Grand Canyon is the product of a time scale eight orders of magnitude greater, how do I see into the depth of time, grasp it in some fundamental, gut-level way? It's difficult enough to see across the span of Liza's years, to truly *get* the passage of her life. The years, the years, this continental drift of time. . . . On coming down from Mount Katahdin and thrashing through the burned-over wilds of Maine, Thoreau asked, "*Who* are we? *Where* are we?" Instead I might exclaim, "*Who* are we? *When* are we?"

I lie back against the warm Esplanade Sandstone, all 315 million gritty years of it, close my eyes and listen to a pair of ravens cawing and gurgling above us. I feel as though I'm stuck in some kind of temporal infancy, a prime example of Piaget's theory of how children develop a time concept—that I am mired in an "immature knowledge state," which reflects my set of "logical deficiencies" concerning the relationship between time, distance, and speed. I'm back to thinking about Liza's early years, and how she grew into an understanding of both the relationship between the past, present, and future, and conventional systems of time. When she was three or four and was sentenced to "time out" for some egregious transgression, we sat her on a chair in a corner and set a kitchen timer for five minutes. We told her that she could not get up until the timer rang, and as the seconds ticked away, she would weep disconsolately: her world was in ruins and she was bereft. Yet her tears ended as abruptly as the ring that announced the end of her incarceration; she would stand immediately and go about her business as if nothing unpleasant had happened. I think that she was sad, in part, because she had no concept of "five minutes." Her grief was as limitless as the sentence that stretched before her into the unknowable future, as wide as the Great Plains we often drove across, through an endless progression of wheat, corn, and pasture. Eventually, though, Liza stopped crying when she was placed in "time out," at least after her initial upset. Perhaps she no longer cried because she was inured to the effects of temporary isolation, but I suspect that it had something to do with her developing understanding of the concepts of "future" and "five minutes." It's interesting that three-year-olds understand the term "yesterday" better than the term "tomorrow," perhaps because "yesterday" refers to events that they have already experienced, while "tomorrow" relates to the uncertain future.

Liza was using terms such as "month" and "year" by the time that she was three, although her understanding of them, which is built around cyclic patterns of order and recurrence, developed more slowly. One indication of how her sense of time developed came during her third, fourth, and fifth years. Each summer I left Lawrence for about ten weeks to work on my PhD research in the Canadian Arctic. In the first summer, when Liza was two-and-one-half, it seemed impossible for her to understand anything about the length of my absence. Melissa tells me that Liza did not want to talk about me during the first month I was gone, perhaps because she was angry and had little sense of my future return. On the first day of my second summer's absence, Liza insisted on setting a place for me at the dinner table, but when Melissa told her that I would not be back for a long time, she burst into tears; in her mind, perhaps, there was little difference between a future "day" and a future "month." But as my final summer of fieldwork approached, Liza understood that I would be gone for much longer than a day or week. In the month leading up to my departure, Liza was alternately clingy and angry with me, and as I boarded the plane that would take me away, she burst into tears and yelled, "I don't want my daddy to be a biologist!" A year later, Liza was talking about "years" in situations other than those dealing with age, although she still had little understanding of what a year represented, as illustrated by one angry question she flung at Melissa: "Do you not want me to speak to you for two years, or two days?" It was not until Liza was eight or nine, and she had experienced enough birthdays, transformations of maple leaves from green to scarlet, and January snows, that she began to develop some deeper comprehension of the cyclical structural properties of order and recurrence that characterize a child's mastery of conventional time systems.

But understanding something of the nature of one year or even a lifetime of years is far different than grasping what "deep time" really means. Four billion years, one billion years, one million years; the numbers are too far removed from the realm of human experience to make much sense. Perhaps I'll have to look elsewhere—beyond radiometric dating, beyond the temporal flow and magnitude of my life, or the realm of developmental psychology—for whatever understanding I can achieve about the great gulf of time that opens up beyond our aerie. Maybe I'll never do any better than the inarticulate, visceral reaction that seizes me whenever I step to the edge of the Grand Canyon after an absence—that involuntary inhalation of breath, a sensation in my gut like a soft touch to the solar plexus, a slight but pleasant sense of vertigo and heady euphoria. I cannot quite process the space and time that open before me, which always feels almost as new to me as Liza and Martin did when they first came crying into the world, smeared with the blood and water of their births.

Or perhaps it is death that will carry me closest to some fundamental understanding of deep time, for what is more infinite than obliteration, whether we are confronting a world without those whom we love, our own annihilation, or the disappearance of a species? I think of all the fossils held within the Grand Canyon, and elsewhere on earth, of life's great path as told by the legions of the dead. I've read that the average life expectancy for a species is one to ten million years, and that 99.9 percent of all the species that ever lived are extinct. Ghosts, speaking to us across great gulps of time, just as human deaths speak to us with their immediacy and force. As with time, we grow into an understanding of death, even if some fundamental aspect of its reality eludes us — at least until we are faced with the sweat of our own deathbeds. Liza began thinking about death at a surprisingly early age, and in September 1990 she had the following conversation with Melissa:

Liza: "I've lived a long time."
Melissa: "Yup, three-and-one-half years!"
Liza: "Will I live forever and ever?"
Melissa: "No one lives forever and ever."
Liza: "Will Sarah [her best friend] live forever and ever?"
Melissa: "No."
Liza: "Will she die?"
Melissa: "Yes."
Liza: "Will you and daddy die?"
Melissa: "Yes, someday we will die. But we will have a long, long time together."
Liza: "Why do people die?"
Melissa: "Sometimes they have accidents. That's why we need to be very careful. And some people get very old and tired, and then they go to sleep."
Liza: "And do they die? Is that why Papa Lee [my stepfather] died?"
Melissa: "Yes, partly. But also because he drank too much alcohol. And some people just get very sick and we feel very sad for them when they die."

A few months later, Liza asked, "What happens to trees when they die?" and shortly after she turned four, she was again thinking about death:

> Liza: "Where do dead bird's spirits go?"
> Me: "I'm not sure because we've always been alive."
> Liza: "Do they go to newborn birds?"
> Me: "How do you know about spirits?"
> Liza: "I was just thinking."

Perhaps Liza's questions about the spirits of dead birds grew out of the recent deaths of our two zebra finches, which had moved her to tears, as well as her developing sense of time—although her thoughts about death seem more sophisticated than her contemporaneous understanding of time. The two concepts are, of course, related. In *Children's Conceptions of Death*, Richard Lonetto writes,

> There is hardly what one would call widespread agreement as to the precise age at which the child understands the passage of time and death; however, there is an almost overwhelming feeling this understanding emerges in the period extending from late childhood into early adolescence. Coexisting with this feeling is the view that the young child cannot conceive of futurity and death in adult terms.

"The young child cannot conceive of futurity and death in adult terms." Perhaps, but I'm not sure how much closer I've come to understanding death than Liza had when she was five. Like Liza, my basic question still is, "Where do creatures go when they die?"—although the implications of the issue are more immediate for my middle-aged body and mind. I've also had more experience with death than Liza had when she was young, and the deaths of friends, my stepfather, and even a high school classmate of mine whom I had not seen for more than thirty years have thrown me into emotional cauldrons composed of various mixtures of grief, recognition of my own mortality, examinations of personal history, and questions about the nature of death. And when I am banding birds, and one suddenly goes still in my hands, as occasionally happens, and I no longer feel the insistent flutter of its tiny heart against my fingers, I, too, wonder about the spirit of dead birds. Or perhaps it is a wonderful spring day and I have just come up through the Redwall, with my daughter close behind. I stoop to pick up a fossil brachiopod from a scatter of limestone debris, and death's terrible beauty is suddenly before me—the warp and weft of extinction and speciation, the extent to which death and time have crafted the cloth of this living world. I run my fingers along the fan of radiating ridges, imagine the creature's Carboniferous seas, and in this moment I come as close to deep time as I ever will. It's like the gleam of a faint star, seen dimly from the corner of my eye, an act of retinal rods more than cones. For a moment deep time flickers before me, and I gaze across 320 million years, glimpse something of its essence. And then Liza is beside me. I show her the brachiopod, then gently place it on the ground, and we go on.

The teenagers resume hiking, and tourist helicopters obey their late-afternoon curfew. Blessed quiet returns to the Boucher Trail; Liza and I load our packs with full water bottles, then contour south along the top of the Esplanade, deeper into Hermit Creek Canyon. We walk on for an hour or so, then find a good, level camp spot amidst scattered pinyon pines. We pitch our tent on the fine red sediments of the Hermit Shale, which erodes easily in most places and forms a sloping layer below the massive, cross-bedded cliffs of Coconino Sandstone. Tonight we'll sleep upon a bed of finely fractured mudstone, only four miles, twelve hundred feet—and ten or fifteen million years—shy of the rim. As Liza and I heat refried beans and tortillas, a small pinyon mouse scuttles between our legs, exploring the rocks around our cooking spot. It seems almost fearless, and with its huge ears, large dark eyes, and lustrous fur, is extraordinarily cute. We curry favor with our companion by offering up tortilla morsels, which the mouse accepts, then shift our attention toward the Canyon, watching as night colonizes the massive cliffs and crenellated bays of that great space. The silence of the place fills me up, and in that silence the possibilities of the world open before me like the endless skein of years that spreads outward from the Vishnu Schist, three thousand feet and 1.4 billion years below us. Time is a beautiful, but fierce and fearsome, deity. As Lord Krishna says, "I am come as Time, the waster of the peoples, ready for the hour that ripens to their ruin." Time—waster of peoples and species, yet also crafter of the world's story, of mine and Liza's. As I sink into my middle-aged body, Liza climbs into the ascendancy of young adulthood. The years spall away from us, from the trilobites and brachiopods, from the australopithecenes who once walked upright through the Pliocene savannahs of the Great Rift Valley. In this extraordinary place, in coming out of the Canyon, I have seen time as something more than the linear progression of seconds, minutes, months, and years. Here I can cup time in my hands, much as I might scoop water from a spring in the Bright Angel Shale, and feel its substance spill through my fingers.

This country is built not on the scale of our individual lives, or even human history, but on the scale of our genes, which carry the memory of the first living cells deep within their helical necklaces of DNA. As Anne Michaels has it, "our blood is time," and in the memory of our blood, and in the blood of our ancestors, is the fullness of time. Rebecca Solnit argues that the technologies that developed during the nineteenth century—photography, railroads, the telegraph—began the technological cascade that has "annihilated time and space" by changing the pace at which people move, live, and perceive the world. But science, through technologies such as radiometric dating and the Large Hadron Collider, have also expanded time's horizon and shoved us into a temporal landscape that verges on the infinite. We now can witness a history that ranges from picoseconds to billions of years, from Precambrian rocks rising out of the basement of time and the segments of bacterial DNA we carry in our blood, to bottom quarks whose life is measured in trillionths of a second. At most, we live for little more than one hundred years. We can fully grasp only the smallest portion of time's spectrum, that which we best feel and understand, but we still can know that time, in all of its glory and magnitude, is *out there* and in us, and in all that lives and breathes, and in all that does not live and breathe.

In the Grand Canyon, time and the great silence—this view from below Yuma Point—are antidotes to the clatter and rush of our lives. Like most of us, I inhabit a world that cultivates maximum velocity. One currency of this world is time, and the rate at which I spend it is a validation of what I do and who I am. How often in a normal week do I complain of my lack of time, and being too damned busy? How many of us, when asked about our lives—particularly our work—will say, "Things are great. I have plenty of time to do what I must, and I feel pretty relaxed"? What validation is there in *that*? I rarely find the time to just stop; instead, I practice my very best imitation of a hyperactive hamster and keep my exercise wheel constantly spinning.

Most nights I sleep less than six hours. I feel the onset of a twitch in my right eyelid as the academic year progresses, begin to curse more and more under my breath, and find decompression mostly in physical exertion. The pace of my life accelerates and I operate in a world with an ever-decreasing window between desire and satisfaction. I can travel from the village of Brockport in western New York to the Alaskan tundra in less than twenty-four hours, or open a catalog and spot a shirt that I really must have, then electronically slap down that piece of plastic and order it with the click of a mouse. And in this decreasing gap between desire and fulfillment lies satiation, impatience, and dissatisfaction. We are conditioned to accept and demand convenience and immediacy, and are less content with what we have; our unrequited desires and impatience metastasize. In the daily rush of our lives, time collapses, or has the appearance of doing so, regardless of Lord Krishna's admonition. But out here, on this pilgrimage from Boucher Rapids to the South Rim, I can negotiate with the small piece of Vishnu Schist in my pocket, consult with the view from our camp, and rediscover some measure of slowness.

The darkness gathers around us, and the stars come on. The wind is up, and stirs the scraggly branches of the pinyons. Liza says she is cold, bids me goodnight, and makes for the tent. I zip my fleece jacket, watch the day's last light fade from the North Rim. To the east, a solitary light winks on at Hermit's Rest, where in the morning Liza and I will end our hike. It is all here, I think, the history of the world, or at least several billion years of it, give or take a few hundred million years. And it is incredible to me that there are people who would look at this same view and see a world that is fundamentally different. According to Tom Vail and other authors of *The Grand Canyon: A Different View*, which is available at the Grand Canyon Bookstore (although thankfully no longer displayed among the science books):

> God created the heavens and earth, and everything in them in six literal days. Based on the lineages laid out in the Bible and other historical documents, this occurred about 6,000 years ago. The vast majority of the sedimentary layers we see in the Grand Canyon . . . were deposited as a result of a global flood that occurred after, and ultimately as a result of, the initial sin that

took place in the Garden of Eden. And the fossils found in the rock layers are remains of the plants and animals that perished in the Flood.

The authors of *The Grand Canyon: A Different View* see Liza and me as having climbed through a world built on a time scale six orders of magnitude less than what we consider to be true, and their view from our camp would be—is—stunningly different than ours. That bit of Vishnu Schist in my pocket is roughly six thousand years old; the deep gash of Hermit Creek Canyon, the five-hundred-foot-tall battlements of Redwall Limestone, the massive, cross-bedded cliffs of Coconino Sandstone—everything in the length and width and depth of the Canyon—was formed during a year-long Noachian Flood, and "not much happened geologically in the roughly 4,500-year period since." In *The Grand Canyon: A Different View* time has collapsed and radiometric "dating methods utilizing long half-life radioisotopes give an earth age that is incorrect by orders of magnitude," because "God intervened in the natural order during creation and during the Flood. . . . [and] this intervention included very high rates of nuclear decay relative to what we observe today."

In the darkening chasm I touch, as always, the great antiquity of the Canyon, the forces of wind and water, faulting, and metamorphism that have shaped it, and continue to shape it, and marvel that some people could look out over the same vastness and see something equally beautiful, but formed only forty-five-hundred years ago, during a great deluge. To me the world is larger and older and more magnificent than our imaginations can fully grasp, and perhaps this is part of the problem for "young-earth" creationists—a failure of the imagination, an inability to see much beyond a few generations of human lives. As Richard Lonetto observes, "There is [in children] a seeming inability to conceive of time as separate from one's existence; to accept the occurrence of events when one was not there to witness them. This inability, however, is not restricted to children."

But I am in a gracious mood this evening. My belly is full of food, our camp is wonderful, and the hike has been excellent. So I allow that, maybe, by some astonishing fluke, young-earth creationists are right (but for heaven's and honesty's sake, do not quote me out of context). If so, such rightness would have absolutely nothing to do with science and what we know of the natural world. It would be a religious reality, the ultimate miracle contravening every solid fact and good scientific theory that we have. And even though I'm trying to be open-minded, I must admit that I don't "get" a six thousand-year-old earth, or a year-long flood that washed over the earth forty-five-hundred years ago and formed most everything we see in the Canyon. By "not getting it," I don't mean in the sense that I am puzzled by the QVC shopping channel or professional wrestling. I mean that profoundly, completely, and utterly, in the core of my being, I do not understand the mindset that allows Tom Vail and his fellow travelers to approach the world with such absolute and terrifying certainty. Their beliefs reject both the practice of science and its knowledge, for to insist upon a six thousand-year-old earth is to dismiss everything we understand about geomorphology, petrology, and the structure and behavior of radioactive isotopes. It's as if the young-earth creationists are denying some crucial essence of the Canyon itself, the patient and unpredictable processes that created this astounding place. But in their certainty they are rejecting far more than just the Grand Canyon — for to deny the Cambrian and the Carboniferous is to deny the human species' fundamental relationship to the past, to when and where we are from.

I scratch my head (figuratively, although I have not washed my hair for a week, and my scalp is itching), take a pull from my water bottle, look around. The Canyon is climbing, once again into light, only now it is the light of a waxing half-moon. The sheer face of the Coconino Sandstone is a glowing study in silver, a vertical garden of luminous stone and deep shadow. I recall that in sandstone something like this, in north-central Afghanistan, there once stood two three-hundred-foot-tall statues of the Buddha, carved out of solid rock. The Bamiyan Buddhas were about fifteen-hundred years old, expressions of our deep need for a spiritual connection to the world. They were as beautiful and meaningful as anything that humans have created, and they were destroyed in March 2001 by Taliban dynamite, by those who justified their actions through their absolute certainty about the Word of God, actions that foreshadowed the jets that crashed into the World Trade Center only four months later. Both acts were committed by men who were convinced that they were absolutely right, and that their desired ends justified their chosen means. These people lacked many things, including compassion and love for their fellow humans, but most of all, they lacked enough humility to concede that they could be wrong. Standing in opposition to this bitter arrogance is the fundamental message of science: that we must be humble in the face of the natural world, for our knowledge of it is provisional and uncertain. We do not know everything that we desire to know about the Grand Canyon—and what we do know may change, as geologists accumulate more and better data. We may know, as well as we will ever know anything about antiquity, that the Vishnu Schist is approximately 1.7 billion years old, yet we do not know for certain the exact sequence of events that led to the Grand Canyon's current configuration. Beginning with John Wesley Powell, there have been many hypotheses about how and when the Canyon was formed; many have been discarded in the last 130 years, but there still are conflicting data and multiple, testable explanations for the origin of the "world's most famous erosional surface." At present there is no scientific consensus on the route of the ancestral Colorado River and the time at which the present canyon began to form, although this probably happened around six million years ago. But I have faith. Ultimately, the data will decide; geologists will find the evidence that they need, and the best theory will emerge.

All in good time, I think.

In the morning Liza and I will forgo breakfast and break camp before sunrise. In less than an hour we will meet the well-traveled trail to Dripping Springs, turn east, and climb through the last of the Hermit Shale and into the Coconino Sandstone. Above the Coconino are the last two series of Grand Canyon strata, the Toroweap Formation and Kaibab Limestone, which are from a time before the great end-of-Permian extinction. In the few hours that it will take us to hike from our camp to the South Rim, we will climb through twelve hundred feet of marine and freshwater sediments, material that was deposited over a period of roughly ten to fifteen million years, but in Liza units we will be traveling through the most recent month of her young life. We will walk our last few miles and Permian millennia and Liza days mostly in silence, enjoying the quiet before hikers bound for Dripping Springs or Hermit Creek begin their descent. In the coolness of the morning, I will feel blessed by our walk, by the week with my daughter, and the deep time of the Grand Canyon. At the rim we will step off of the trail and onto pavement, throw our packs into the rental car, and drive south to Phoenix. In the evening we will eat a meal of burritos and enchiladas, grab a few hours of sleep, then catch an early flight east. The present will rise up before us like a huge gate, and we will hurtle through its opening and into the daily rush of our lives. We will live, once again, in a cascade of seconds, minutes, hours, and days, each one lost in the succeeding one. And in this rush I will continue my slide into senescence, watch as Liza and Martin ascend into adulthood. But every so often I will look up from my computer, or pause while mowing the lawn, and recall the long view from above Hermit Creek. Suddenly the years will once again flow away from me, across the eons, through the great strata of rock and great unconformities of time, across the legions of the dead and living, through all the lost species of all the vanished worlds. In the memory of this view, and in the full presence of time and my waning years, I will take some comfort.

And Then I Was Home

Martin and I slip out of Brockport in the pre-dawn light of a beautifully cool, early-summer morning: south on New York 19, through drowsing Bergen, and then onto the deserted New York state thruway, I-90, headed west. The morning gathers its light, dawn strung with tendrils of gray and then orange clouds streaming toward the flat horizon, like the Nebraska sky in a Keith Jacobshagen painting, *In the Evening I Dreamed of Rain and Cicadas.* South of Buffalo, vineyards and freshly cut fields, scent of newly mown hay in the air. Along the thruway margin, crows gather like gangs of unruly street urchins, fossicking among the weeds and haggling over road-kill treasures. Martin is awake—he stayed up all night, packing—and so we talk about the drive, his hopes for a summer's worth of kayaking in Montana and British Columbia. Once he crashes, though, I switch to some soft and gentle morning music, mostly instrumental pieces: Pat Metheny, Lanterna, Six Parts Seven, which at times verge on the vapid and monotonous, but remain pensive and rhythmic, 2/4 time in love with our motion.

Since 1984 I've made this summer drive at least a dozen times—out of the humid heartland and eastern forests, across the Mississippi River, and then beyond the hundredth meridian and into the West—sometimes with Melissa, at other times with the full family or just Martin and Liza, occasionally on my own. Each day of driving brings the slap of tires on concrete and asphalt for six hundred miles or more, iterations of atlas maps, vectors pointed toward imagined mountains. On this particular westward roll I am happy to have my sixteen-year-old son along for the westward progression that I love so much. Martin and I travel well together; he's relaxed and comfortable with long days, and the silences that such driving inevitably brings.

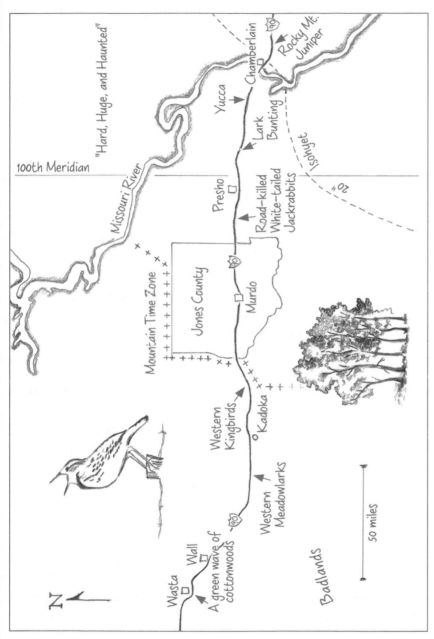

Across the Hundredth Meridian in South Dakota.

Across the tip of Pennsylvania, leaving the vineyards and orchards behind as I-90 climbs the escarpment north of Erie, the lake spreading huge and calm to the west, my heart as big as the sky. The heavy traffic east of Cleveland continues along the Ohio Turnpike to Toledo and beyond. I lose the easy rhythm of the early-morning drive, find mostly staccato-like movement among the hectic migration of semis, minivans, and RVs. I unconsciously increase my speed among the herds of vehicles, perhaps because I am pulled along by other drivers, their velocity more contagious than last winter's flu. Martin dozes through much of the congestion, magnificent in his adolescent male's ability to sleep anywhere, anytime, for hour after hour; if there were an Olympic sleeping team, he would be their man. The musical score is now, appropriately, "Boogieing with the Buckeyes," a mix of Ohio songs that I assembled for the drive—the industrial decline of Springsteen's "Youngstown," the upbeat rhythm of the Jayhawks' "Somewhere in Ohio."

Along I-90 western Ohio lies flat, like the lowlands south of Lake Ontario, but it's more expansive, with a gathering sense of the midwestern prairie. We hurtle toward the Great Plains and into the building heat, beneath a hazy sky the color of dirty gauze. Now only the faint shapes of cumulonimbus clouds are visible through the viscous air, but summer is a frenzy of green, and its hues decorate the earth: the brownish-green of grasses, where the heads have gone to flower; the dark yellowish-green of cornfields; the variegated-green of riparian foliage, dark-green oaks and lighter shades of ash and hickory. Away from the muddy, sluggish streams, which drift north, the trees have mostly been annihilated, replaced by acre after acre of agricultural fields. The occasional, lonely oak rising from the industrial corn ocean seems like a barber's mistake: "Hey, right here—you missed a spot." In Indiana and Illinois, American flags are as ubiquitous as the cornfields—on cars, poles in front of homes, decorations at RV campsites. Roadside billboards: "Jesus is Real," and a "Guns Save Lives" set, modeled after the old Burma-Shave signs: "Every Year / Two Million Times / Armed Citizens / Prevent Crimes." The RV Hall of Fame. The Heartland, or at least one of its permutations.

We stop only for gas and bathroom breaks, and I pull at least three-hour stints behind the wheel. The music shifts to Martin's sphere—Linkin Park and hip-hop. Our agreement is that we alternate CDs, although I retain the right to an executive veto on excessive noise-to-melody ratios. We eschew Big Macs for carrots, muffins, and sandwiches from the cooler, which trump the homogenous, franchised fare that makes me feel sluggish and congested. As the interstate highways have spread, depositing spoor from the fast-food industry at each major off-ramp and service plaza, regional cooking, at least the kind available in roadside diners, has become difficult to find. Now it's hard to tell where the home fries used to end, and the hashed-brown potatoes began. The interstates, with their broad concrete swaths, fenced margins, and routes that swing around the edges of towns, past clusters of service stations, mini-marts, motels, and drive-through restaurants, insulate and isolate us from cultural and physical landscapes — or perhaps they have created their own, monocultural landscape. The décor of a freeway exit in Indiana, with its Days Inn, Super 8, Mobil station, and Taco Bell, is mostly indistinguishable from that of an exit in Oregon or Texas. We have sacrificed the local for speed and utility, and I'm a partial participant in the rite. In the past, I have sometimes taken to what William Least Heat Moon called the "blue highways," those secondary roads often shown in blue on the old road maps, such as my 1960 Chevron Colorado edition. In 1984, after reading *Blue Highways*, Melissa and I tracked secondary roads westward from Ohio all the way to Wyoming. It was a wonderful drive, which took us almost twice as long as it would have on the interstates. But now the "blue highways" have become "red highways" or "gray highways" on most road maps, and I am too hurried for leisurely driving. The pace of my work has invaded all facets of my life, and I am willing to make a Faustian bargain with the interstates most every summer: I want the West, and on this trip I anticipate that Martin and I will see it tomorrow, in the late afternoon, if we push hard.

I take my regional sense from the topography, the ebb and flow of vegetation, the ecological transitions that I know are there, beyond the road margins and agricultural fields, but I also search for other signs of westward progression, such as in barn-roof styles. In western New York and through much of Ohio, I note many gambrel-type barn roofs, with a double slope on each side, the lower slope having the steeper pitch. The gambrel roof became the standard for the Midwest dairy industry by the beginning of the twentieth century, as it provided more storage space in the loft than third- or half-pitch gable roofs. Near the Ohio/Indiana border, gambrel roofs appear to yield to single-pitch gable roofs; further to the north and west, in Wisconsin, we'll see more gothic barns, with their rounded roofs. Perfected in the 1920s, this style provided even more storage space than the gambrel roof. An ecological cline is a gradual change in an organism across its distributional range, and I believe that I can detect an architectural cline in barn styles, perhaps reflective of the combined influences of settlement patterns (Dutch? German? English?), economics, and type of farming, but it's possible that the patterns I perceive are simply sampling error introduced by our interstate velocity. One pattern does seem to hold, though — the larger, more elaborate and elegant barn designs of the late-nineteenth and early-twentieth century are giving way, throughout their range, to prefabricated, metal-sheathed buildings, which are cheaper, easier to erect, and designed for specific functions, such as storing large combines and other farm equipment. As economic imperatives lead to the demise of older, traditional barn styles and the spread of prefabricated structures, there is homogenization in agricultural architecture as well as freeway food.

I've done this drive enough to know how long each state should take on this first day, if I can stay rooted behind the wheel and there isn't too much road construction: about three hours for New York and Pennsylvania, four hours for Ohio, five hours for Indiana and Illinois combined, with an hour gained when we cross into the Central Time Zone in western Indiana, and a few minutes lost whenever Martin and I stop at a rest area to loosen up and play a little Frisbee. I'm also familiar enough with the entire route to drive it without a map, although I still refer to the state highway maps that we pick up along the way, just to mark our progress: I-90 all the way from Brockport to just south of Chicago, where we avoid the nightmare of the I-294/ I-290/I-90 hypotenuse to Rockford, with its clotted traffic and endless succession of toll booths, for the longer sides of the triangle that take us west on I-80 for eighty miles, and then on to I-39 North. What we lose in miles (a bit) and time (not much), I gain through more-relaxed driving and lower titers of circulating adrenalin. As the miles slip by I track our route on the maps, and occasionally consult one for an alternative route to avoid thick traffic or construction, but I refuse to use one of those infernal, talking GPS navigation devices that are now standard equipment in many vehicles. I hate the damned things. Although I use GPS technology in my research, to map study sites and locate unmarked bird count stations, I'd prefer to banish it from automobiles. Partly this is an expression of my Luddite-like tendencies (okay, prejudices), but there are other more-legitimate reasons for my curmudgeonly attitude. To begin with, I detest the mantra-like intonations that announce an approaching intersection: "Bear right onto Route 31 in one-half mile. Bear right onto Route 31 in one-quarter mile. Bear right onto Route 31 in two hundred yards. Bear right onto Route 31 in one hundred yards."

"Shut up and leave me alone!"

More important, though, GPS tour guides train people to function as automatons incapable of route-finding and thinking for themselves. I've noticed that drivers who habitually use navigation systems have difficulty reading maps or identifying cardinal directions—or even understanding the nature, direction, and length of a route that they've just driven, directed as they've been by the figurative arm of the GPS, with its firm grip on the driver's mental nose ring. They have little sense of where they are or where they've been. Once I asked someone who'd driven from New Jersey to Brockport about the route he had taken. He replied, "I don't really know. I just let the GPS tell me where to go." We are training generations of spatial and geographical incompetents, and what if the satellite signals are lost and the GPS units fail?

And then there's the unnerving quality of many units' narrating voice, which reminds me of HAL, the rogue computer in *2001: A Space Odyssey*. As an experiment, I have taken a portable GPS unit, programmed it to find a location, and then purposefully made a wrong turn. The unit, of course, informs me in an emotionless voice that I have made a mistake (idiot), and that it must recalculate the route. I half expect it to offer up some sort of *Space Odyssey* dialogue, before it takes whatever steps are necessary to correct my threatening behavior: "Just what do you think you're doing, Chris? Chris, I really think I'm entitled to an answer to that question. I want to help you." But the GPS simply recalculates the route, before squawking again when I cheerfully make another incorrect turn. It goes blessedly quiet, though, when I punch the off button. I want to say that I'm done messing with its mind, but realize how spooky this sounds. Instead, I remind myself that my silenced GPS unit is not HAL, and that I have control. For the moment.

Once we've turned north on I-39, the traffic thins and the land begins to undulate more. I grab a quick glance at the official Illinois highway map, which unaccountably bears no photo of Governor Rod Blagojevich. Most state road maps function as a free political advertisement for the governor *du jour*, with a prominent cover display of the first family, but in 2005–2006 "Blago" was being uncharacteristically coy. The hills gather and forests spread as the highway climbs, gradually, out of the agricultural plains. Clouds coalesce and the late afternoon turns to light rain, bringing with it the delightful smell of water on hot pavement. Wind farms proliferate, the march of huge, white, three-bladed towers like huge flocks of giant storks foraging amidst the fields. Like the wind, the slow revolution of the immense blades adds an element of motion to the prairie. It's nice to have lighter traffic for awhile and I relax, rediscover the rhythm that I lost somewhere back in western Ohio. I turn off the music, a water/kayaking mix I put together in honor of Martin's whitewater obsession — from the Talking Heads's "Take Me to the River" to Jimmy Cliff's "Many Rivers to Cross" — and collect the quiet around me, happy in the motion. But then we meet I-90 and heavy traffic heading north out of Chicago, and the route past Madison and the Wisconsin Dells is clogged with vehicles. Once again we're enveloped by the waves of kinetic energy that we first encountered near Cleveland — but there's a difference, as this will be the last dense traffic of the drive. We are almost free of the noxious pulse of vehicles, the pounding rush of noise and thick fug of exhaust fumes, the incessant jockeying for position, with huge semis always hemming us in and forcing me into the frenetic style of driving that I detest.

North of Madison I see the first and last paper birch of the trip, as I-90's tangent brushes the southern edge of the great continental sweep of boreal forest before it swings west toward the plains. We pass consecutive exits for John Muir's boyhood home north of Portage and Aldo Leopold's Sand County shack near Baraboo. These shrines for two of my conservation heroes lie only about twenty miles apart, but although I've driven the I-90 route through Wisconsin seven times, I've never visited either of them. I've always been in a hurry, and drawn westward. Near the highway are several tourist magnets of the Wisconsin Dells, rich in the unintended irony of their names, and their proximity to the ghosts of Muir and Leopold: the Kalahari Resort Waterpark ("authentic African-themed resort" and "Wisconsin's largest indoor waterpark"), Great Wolf Lodge ("where the waterpark stops, the fun keeps going"), Noah's Ark Waterpark ("America's largest waterpark"), and Wilderness Hotel and Golf Resort ("America's largest waterpark resort"). The Kalahari, Noah's Ark, and Wilderness resorts are going mano a mano for rights to the mantle of "largest" (World's? America's? Wisconsin's? Indoor? Resort?) waterpark. The Kalahari gets double credit for being named after a desert, but the Wilderness Hotel and Golf Resort, with its "12 football fields of waterpark fun," "OK Corral Lazer Tag," and "Cosmic Go-Karts and Kiddy Karts" comes on strong with its lexical dissonance. Aldo Leopold, whose shack was less than ten miles from the Wilderness Hotel and Golf Resort, once wrote that "wilderness is the raw material out of which man has hammered the artifact called civilization," and it beggars the mind to consider what artifacts of civilization might be hammered out of "Cosmic Go-Karts."

Even though the topography and vegetation of the Wisconsin Dells situates the region at the southern edge of the boreal forest, its tourism laden ambience, and the heavy surge of traffic on I-90, makes it feel like an outlier of Chicago. It's not until the I-90/I-94 split, ninety miles north of Madison, that I declare the first section of our drive complete, some fourteen hours and 850 miles out of Brockport. Most of the traffic veers north toward Minneapolis on I-94, and I-90 is suddenly quiet. My jaw muscles relax and I breathe deeply, force my diaphragm down and into my belly: air, the quiet road, and the verdant country around me, the sinuous flux of its terrain, dairy farms and gothic-roofed barns nestled against oak- and hickory-covered hills, everything awash in the emerald pulse of photosynthesis. What would refugees from some drought-stricken country on the Horn of Africa think of western Wisconsin, with its lushness and neatly ordered farms?

Less than an hour later we pull into La Crosse. We find our friends' house, eat a late dinner and visit over a glass of wine, then walk with them through the neighborhood, happy for companionship and release from the car for a few hours. I fall into an exhausted sleep, and in the early morning wake to a cool breeze drifting through the open window, and the backyard birdsongs of cardinals, robins, and black-capped chickadees — the same summer music that graces my Brock-port home. I know, too, that if I were to step into a local woodland, many of the tree species also would be the same: although American beech dropped out in eastern Wisconsin, I still would find sugar maple, hop-hornbeam, basswood, white oak, shagbark hickory, and American ash. I have traveled nine hundred miles from western New York, across almost a third of the North American continent, but as Led Zeppelin sings, the song (and the forest) remains the same. To-day, though, in the long shot across Minnesota and South Dakota, the music will change.

Martin and I bid good-bye to our friends and are on the road by seven. We cross the Mississippi River, parallel the limestone cliffs that line its valley, then climb onto the higher ground of eastern Minne-sota, which at first is mostly rolling hills and caprock country. But near exit 175, just west of Rochester, there's a sudden shift in the tenor of the earth. The land flattens and trees begin retreating into swales and the margins of farmsteads. Each farm is an island in a sea of wheat and corn; each island in the archipelago is ringed by a garland of trees, which shelters a white farmhouse and barn (gothic to the east, tend-ing gable to the west, with some gambrels thrown into the mix), and a collection of short, conical grain silos.

West of Rochester, I yield the wheel to Martin, who has his license and has been agitating to drive ever since Ohio. Yesterday, the heavy traffic made me too nervous to grant him his wish, but I promised that once we crossed the Mississippi River, he would have his oppor-tunity. I ask him to stay well below the speed limit and let him drive for only an hour, but soon he will be cruising along at seventy miles per hour and going for two to three hours at a stretch. Martin's a care-ful driver, but during his first stint I am a little tense, especially when he's passing a semi. Having him in the driver's seat is quite a transition for both of us, after all of those earlier cross-country drives when he was just a passenger who sat and watched. But now, by sharing the driving, he's suddenly become more of a participant and companion, and I like the feeling. Besides, it gives me more opportunity to study the maps and the country, which collects its space as the sky expands. Everything feels more exposed, and there is nowhere to hide. It's easy to imagine the slashing winter wind, the sense of isolation that must come with the snows and thinning population, which declines toward less than ten people per square mile in the southwestern part of the state. And at a rest area along our route I see an embossed, red promise (hope against hope) set in the concrete base of a newspaper stand cradling copies of *Country Singles*: NO NEED TO BE LONELY.

Out here, the land can be intimidating; human enterprise is made punier by the scale of the Great Plains and its emptiness. Thus, perhaps, the midwestern fascination with roadside "Big Things." Now, Big Things are a common human preoccupation and they are found everywhere. Yet they seem most common in the western reaches of the Great Plains: the sixty-foot-tall statue of the Jolly Green Giant (Blue Earth, Minnesota); The World's Biggest Bull's Head (Montrose, South Dakota); The World's Largest Sandhill Crane (Steele, North Dakota); The World's Largest Metal Sculpture (Belfield, North Dakota); The World's Largest Holstein Cow (New Salem, North Dakota); The World's Largest Ball of Twine (Cawker City, Kansas); The World's Largest Prairie Dog (Oakley, Kansas). Whether claims attached to these Big Things are correct is beside the point. What's important is the human desire for significance, and to create the memorable, as an antidote to a landscape that makes people feel small, vulnerable, and lonely. In the face of emptiness and wind, and the great arc of sky, in a land where distance devours human connection, we will erect The World's Largest.

Take that, Great Plains.

Western Minnesota opens up, and its general expansiveness carries an intimation of the West. But around eleven, when I step from the car at a rest area near Luverne, the air is still dense and moist, and the sky lacks clarity. As Martin and I toss the Frisbee back and forth, I notice an eastern kingbird hunting from a nearby tree. It sallies out from its perch, grabs an insect, and makes for its nest, where there's a squawk from the hungry nestlings. The mean annual precipitation in this part of Minnesota is around twenty-seven inches per year; it's enough to keep the eastern kingbirds happy and maintain the humidity and haze that gives the atmosphere an eastern ambience, even though we're close to the South Dakota border. I know, however, that over the next four hours, as we approach and cross the hun-

dredth meridian, the sense of the land will change dramatically, more
than it has during our previous nineteen hours and eleven hundred
miles on the road.

Across eastern South Dakota, the sky surges as the forest continues its retreat into sheltered, well-watered valleys. Eastern meadow-
larks, which dropped out in eastern Minnesota, have been replaced
by their western relatives, and the flycatcher balance at rest areas has
shifted from eastern to western kingbirds. I begin seeing lark bun-
tings, a classic prairie bird, and more road-killed white-tailed jackrab-
bits decorate the highway. Plants characteristic of the West gather on
dry, rocky soils—yucca and plains prickly pear, and the first Rocky
Mountain junipers appear just east of the Missouri River. The prairie, as trashed as it is by overgrazing, row crops, and introduced
species, moves from taller, sod-forming grasses in the east, to the
shorter, more drought-resistant bunch grasses in the west. Bare soil
spreads. All of these transitions form, as Merrill Gilfillan observes, a
"satisfying transcontinental dovetail." Windmills become more common as the aridity and windiness increase; grain silos, like giant gray
rolls of stacked coins, blossom. The air empties out as the average
annual precipitation falls toward twenty inches—the minimum, as
John Wesley Powell observed in his *Report on the Lands of the Arid Region of the United States*, to support agriculture without irrigation. The
prairie grasses wave green near Sioux Falls, but one hundred miles
to the west, July's prairie palette trends to brown. As the grass dries,
the people thin. Around Sioux Falls, the population density runs
from about twenty-five to one hundred people per square mile, but
out west, away from the Black Hills, it may fall to less than one person per square mile. Not enough water to support many people, and
as Powell argued—to the detriment of his fortunes as head of the
U.S. Geological Survey—completely inadequate to maintain a family on the idealized agrarian allotment of 160 acres, born out of the
country's eastern experience and enshrined in the Homestead Act of
1862. As the historian Walter Prescott Webb observed in the 1930s,
the basic "land unit" on the High Plains was more like four thousand
acres—far too big to be successfully farmed using dryland technology of the late-nineteenth century, although acceptable for raising
livestock. Somewhere between 40 and 66 percent of the settlers in the
western Great Plains who tried to "prove up" under the Homestead

Act failed, and scattered along I-90 are the weather-beaten remnants of their shacks and barns, perhaps decorated by an iconic windmill and a few skeletonized trees, the entire gray enterprise collapsing into overgrazed shortgrass prairie.

We drive on, past the turnoff for Mitchell and its Corn Palace, descend to the Missouri River at Chamberlain. Here, Lewis and Clark's pathway is a reservoir, choked with speedboats and Jet Skis. Beyond the Missouri, we climb onto a high plateau and roll toward the hundredth meridian, which lies near mile marker 228, just east of the tiny settlement of Presho, population 588. Above us is a Salvador Dali sky, with a scatter of white, fluffy cumulus clouds etched against a background of electric, Dali-like robin's-egg blue. There's a verticality to the clouds, an ascending spatial expanse that I rarely see in the East. I pop a CD into the player, select the music for the moment, The Tragically Hip's "At the Hundredth Meridian"—"Left alone to get gigantic / Hard, huge, and haunted." And what haunts this land, and the ghosts of the immigrants who went bust out here, is aridity—for somewhere on the high prairie, near this imaginary line, lies another line that wanders from decade to decade, but is absolute in its imperative—the twenty-inch precipitation isohyet. The aridity marked by this line destroyed the wishful thinking that "rain follows the plow." It laid waste to the unwarranted optimism and hucksterism of boosters like William Gilpin, the first territorial governor of Colorado, who proclaimed that "the *untransacted* destiny of the American people is to subdue the continent," much like it will eventually dismiss the center-pivot delusions of those who now mine the Ogallala Aquifer to supply an unsupportable agriculture.

The insistent reality of the twenty-inch isohyet drives the rural flight that plagues the High Plains. Between 1969 and 2007, Jones County, which lies just west of Presho, lost 46 percent of its population, while South Dakota's overall population increased by 19 percent. Harding County, in the extreme northwest corner of the state, lost 39 percent of its population during the same period, a pattern repeated across the region, except in the Rapid City area. Emigration from rural South Dakota counties is disproportionately weighted toward the young; in Jones County, 21.7 percent of the population is sixty-five or older, compared to the national rate of 12.8 percent. And Jones County residents, as in other rural parts of the High Plains, are not reproducing much: between 1990 and 2000, the county recorded only two more births than deaths. North Dakota is doing even worse than South Dakota. Although South Dakota's population has continued to grow, albeit more slowly than the national average, North Dakota has experienced a net decrease in population. In 1920, the state's population was greater than in 2000, a trend mirrored by the decline of its congressional delegation, from three in 1910–1920 to one currently.

According to the National Atlas, the twenty-inch isohyet in this part of South Dakota bisects the Missouri River where I-90 crosses, and beyond the river I recognize the West. There are the spatials of the land, the topology of sky and horizon, the sinuous sway of cottonwood-lined streams, soft undulations of prairie earth. Aridity claims its presence as humidity drains from the air and the atmospheric haze of the eastern summer vanishes. Huge cumulonimbi billow into the sky, John Muir's "cloud mountains," some anvil-shaped and flowing horizontal, others metamorphosing into vertical pillars, each a shape-shifting chrysalis. Brilliant white columns abutting a charcoal-gray wall of rain clouds, broken here and there by lightning, and at the edge of the wall, torn shreds of virga, hanging like ragged curtains from the endless sky: a symbol for all my longing, for all the undelivered promises of this motion, this continental highway vector. Off to the southwest the jagged spines and buttes of the Badlands rise from the dip and sway of the shortgrass plains, shining in the afternoon light, then disappearing behind a wall of water. The distant track of the Badlands adds perspective to this country, enhances the sense of space, the distant view, the endless spread of light across the land, which opens and empties my heart: "Beautiful my desire, and the place of my desire."

In *The Conversations at Curlow Creek*, David Malouf describes the Australian Outback:

> So much space, so much distance under the dry air, had opened his eyes to the long view . . . a high, wide emptiness that drew you into an opening distance in yourself in which the questions that posed themselves had no easy sociable answers, concerned only yourself and what there was at last, or might be, between you and the harsh, unchanged and unchanging earth.

Malouf's character, Adair, worries that his reaction to the sprawl of the Outback is an expression of "some darker wish to annihilate the self with distance," but for me it is the opposite: to affirm the self with distance. Out on the shortgrass prairie, all my neurons are firing and I can sense the edge of this affirmation, but it's an elusive thing. I cannot keep up. I cannot quite grasp, and hold close to my heart, the sensuous intensity of the earth. I do not want to romanticize this country, the hard edge of the land that drives the winter winds, the droughts, the poverty and outmigration, the isolation. John Martin Campbell's book on the western homestead era is titled *Magnificent Failure*, but it also could have been called *Miserable Failure*. I'm sure that there's as much memory of human struggle and misery held within the ruins of the abandoned farmsteads along the highway, as there is grain in the giant silos that rise out of the South Dakota prairie. The High Plains would be a difficult place to live, and I doubt that I'd be up to the task. Yet the essence of this country is like the virga that grace the afternoon sky: numinous and beautiful, but also representing an unrequited promise—of deliverance from drought, or from a hardened heart that prevents me from feeling, fully, the intensity of the land. I reach out for something like an epiphany, but cannot take hold of it. What I am left with, beyond my longing, are the curtains of rain that hang there, suspended in space, evaporating in the arid reality beyond the hundredth meridian.

I've driven all the major east-west routes from Texas to North Dakota, and on each one there's Gilfillan's "satisfying transcontinental dovetail" as the West gathers its presence. There's a pleasing gradient as the sky, the land, and the plants and animals are transformed by the aridity, and as this change progresses, there is a point—which I can often identify precisely—where I recognize my place and feel as though I am home. This moment of arrival is like a chemical titration: you add a reagent, drop by drop, to a solution, until the endpoint of the reaction occurs. The transition is often extremely sharp, and during a titration a single drop of the reactant just before the endpoint can lead to an immediate color change in an indicator. In South Dakota, my aesthetic reaction occurs where I-90 crosses the Missouri at Chamberlain, about thirty-two miles east of the hundredth meridian. In Nebraska, along U.S. Highway 26, my aesthetic titration reaches its western endpoint near the 102nd meridian. There, in Ash Hollow State Park, the highway slides off a high plain, cuts through eroded breaks, bunchgrass, and scattered juniper, to cross the North

Platte near tiny Lewellen. In Texas, west of Amarillo, there's a similar place—I can't recall exactly where, and my journal is silent on the subject—where 1-40 dives off the tableland of the Llano Estacado and falls through an escarpment into a realm of caprock buttes and blood-red earth. Along 1-70 in Kansas, the endpoint is less precise, and comes a little to the west of the hundredth meridian, somewhere between Oakley and Colby. And the last time that I drove 1-94 across North Dakota, I felt that I should have sensed the West sooner than I did. But it wasn't until near the 103rd meridian, where Martin and I camped beneath beige bluffs at Sully's Creek Primitive State Park in the Badlands, at the edge of a thicket of ash and juniper, with the wind a rustle in cottonwood leaves, and nighthawks plunging through the arid evening air, that I understood I had arrived. In all of these places, on all of the occasions when I've crossed into the West and become alive to the country, I've entered into Nabokov's "momentary vacuum into which rushes all that I love."

As a scientist, I desire a precise definition of the West, something as clean and distinct as the hundredth meridian or the twenty-inch isohyet of precipitation, or even as complex as a highly predictive multivariate model built with parameters of aridity, space, topographic relief, cloud development, vegetation, and birds. I want to know exactly when, and why, that quivering, joyful recognition rises up in my mind and heart. But this quantitative desire is futile. It's like the discussion I once had with Dick Johnson, my major advisor while I was a master's student at Washington State University. Dick's passion is alpine ecology, and I recall a long, rambling conversation we once had, about what exactly defines the alpine. Was it the lack of trees? But there are treeless landscapes (desert, high plains, the Arctic) that aren't alpine, and there are areas with small, wind- and ice-sculpted pines, spruce, and fir that are clearly alpine. And up north, say in the Brooks Range, are those treeless landscapes alpine or arctic? Or what about mountain ranges in the Great Basin that are too arid to support subalpine forest? Surely there's alpine habitat above 10,000 feet in the xeric Sweetwater Mountains, where big sagebrush, *Artemesia tridentata*, grades into low sagebrush, *Artemesia arbuscula*. But in some places, low sagebrush extends downslope, well into the *Artemesia tridentata* zone. On and on we went, arguing, circling around this notion of "alpine," which we both recognized but could not quite define to our mutual satisfaction. We were struggling with something intractable, as Dick—one of the most precise and quantitative people I know—finally recognized when he shrugged his shoulders and said, "I give up! The alpine is where I feel good." And that's it. The alpine is where Dick feels as though he belongs, where he is at home. I, too, feel at home in the alpine, but in a more general way, in the West. Its particular chemistry of light and air and space and life is where I feel good—and I feel particularly good right now.

Martin and I skirt the Badlands and the rain, pass the exits for Murdo (population 612), Kadoka (population 706), and Wall (population 818), home of Wall Drug, a tourist attraction whose billboard spoor decorate the I-90 corridor across South Dakota. (Oh for a legion of hearty sawyers, with well-oiled chainsaws!) Just beyond the 101st meridian, at the western edge of Jones County, we cross into the Mountain Time Zone, which adds nicely to the accumulating evidence of the West. At tiny Wasta (population 75), where the interstate crosses the Cheyenne River, there's a graceful green wave of cottonwoods along the stream, before I-90 resumes its climb toward the Black Hills. Martin is mostly quiet, listening to music and gazing out the window. I want him to know how much this empty, spectacular sprawl of space means to me, but I don't say much—as if the telling will diminish the intensity of my feelings. Or perhaps I'm worried that I cannot articulate the nature of my longing for this country, that such immensity and intensity will render me mute; I want words when none seem adequate. But there's another possibility—that my silence is protective, that what motivates me here is the worry that if I do express my feelings (for this country, for a poem, for a song, for anything of beauty), they will not be reciprocated. There's a risk in talking about what I hold closest to my heart, as if the exposure will render me too vulnerable—for if my emotions are not reciprocated, I will feel more isolated and alone. Fool. I should talk about what most moves me, but even more importantly, I should never expect anyone to function as a mirror for my emotions. It's an unfair burden to place on anyone, especially my sixteen-year-old son. I sort through these notions as we slip through the High Plains, and stay mostly quiet. It's best now, in my confusion, to let the country speak for itself, in the language of light and cloud, with the beautiful signature of its emptiness.

We enter the populated corridor between Rapid City (Reptile Gardens, Ellsworth Airforce Base, the road to Mount Rushmore), Sturgis (annual motorcycle rally), and Spearfish (passion play), and swing north around the Black Hills. Unlike most of South Dakota, the Black Hills region is growing. Meade County's population expanded by 41 percent between 1969 and 2007, while Lawrence County grew by 33 percent during the same period. The surge of traffic and the sprawling clusters of condominiums and subdivisions tell the story—none of this feels like 1-90 across most of the state. But once we're beyond Spearfish, the country empties out again. Just west of the Wyoming border, in the aftermath of a gentle shower, there's the odor of cut grass and rain in the air, and a long view to the south. My eye floats over hayfields and a meandering, willow-lined creek, seeks the horizon beyond the western slopes of the Black Hills, where cumulonimbus clouds rise, once again, into a luminous sky. The map tells me that I'm looking toward Inyan Kara Mountain, a name that is as evocative as the scene before me. We push on late into the night: west through the Powder River Basin, a focal point for America's hydrocarbon addiction (coalbed methane development, an open-pit coal mine, scattered oil wells), then north past the rugged scarp of the Bighorn Mountains, a backlit panorama of foreshortened ridges piled against one another, the grass-covered hills to the east of 1-90 falling into gentle shadow. Gas in Sheridan, then on into the dark, my son wanting the pleasure of late-night driving, and to push deep into Montana. We switch drivers every few hours, and I like the way that Martin settles behind the wheel, his quiet delight in the long skein of miles that we have unwound from Brockport: two thousand one hundred in less than forty-eight hours, over one thousand since La Crosse. I think of Martin's early years, of "ouside" and his toddler's walks in Lawrence, of diapers and conflagrations with his "sisser." He's a long way from all of that, but he still has that same infectious grin, and innate, boyish gentleness. Right now I'd like to reach over and tousle his hair, but I let him have his space, and maturity. The instrument panel glows a soft and lovely red, and outside of our small vessel of light, the grasslands are dark and empty. East of Billings are giant flashes of lighting, streaking across the high plains. We are road-weary but easy in the motion and our companionship. We talk quietly of the drive, of the West and the country we've seen, of music and the summer to come, of the merits of various styles and makes of whitewater kayaks. There is a firm peace about us, as we roll

> on through the deep sleep of small towns
> strewn along the highway, the odd light of a house
> like a single unshut eye somewhere on the edge,
> the silence of the high plains huge yet imminent,
> like the earth's held breath.

Around 1:30 in the morning we pull off the interstate and find a place beside the Stillwater River to throw our sleeping bags. Martin is asleep almost immediately, and for awhile I listen to the quiet rhythm of his breathing, the tumble of the river across a field of boulders. The sweet riparian smell rises into the night; above us are cottonwoods and an ocean of western stars. I muse about where we have been, and the maps of my longing: to love this land, and my people.

There is, finally, no need to be lonely.

Without a Map

ate on the second day of our two-week trip through the Pasayten Wilderness, Paul and I laid down our packs and climbed a ridge west of camp. Since leaving the trailhead we had traveled mostly through lowlands, and on this cloudless, luminous afternoon we desired nothing so much as a view of the high country and a better sense of the terrain. We followed the trail to a pass, then climbed through slippery heather and stunted subalpine larch to where we could scramble along a rocky ridge to a small summit, one too insignificant to merit a cairn. Although the peak was a minor one, the prospect was magnificent. To the west, perhaps twenty miles distant, was the crest of the North Cascades, a jumbled mass of black, jagged peaks and brilliant snow-fields, backlit by the afternoon sun; in the foreground, deep valleys sinking into shadow, dark green and violet, filled with smoky haze. To the north were rolling parklands—verdant green meadows ringed by garlands of late-lying snow, a patchwork quilt of subalpine forest and tundra flowing toward the Canadian border. Eastward, the country was more arid and nearly snow free, but still spectacular—serrated, brownish-orange summits, steep-sided valleys, swathed in a complex mosaic of old-growth forests and burnt-over woodlands. Finally, to the south was the way that we had come, our route obscured by broken terrain. The country opened before us, like giant hands spread in supplication, and the mountains were spectacular—an endless iteration of peaks and valleys, ridges and tablelands spreading outward in all directions, vanishing into a guess of blue against lost horizons.

For all of its beauty, the view was familiar, because we had stood on similar summits, looked out over similar mountain reaches many times before. Yet on that expansive afternoon the essence of our view was profoundly different, for we were traveling without maps. We were walking into a wilderness landscape that we would encounter in ways fundamentally different from our usual practice. We would not christen each pass, summit, trail junction, and camp by unfolding a map and planting ourselves firmly in a place, the route behind us known, the course before us anticipated. On that small peak we beheld a country without names, without imposed reference points, degrees of latitude and longitude, or elevations. There were no political or administrative boundaries, no public or private lands. There were trails; we had been hiking on one for two days, but although we understood our trail's general orientation, we knew nothing of its ultimate destination. Somewhere there were paper maps of the area—USGS quadrangles, U.S. Forest Service administrative maps, state maps—filed in metal drawers in libraries, offices, and stores. Undoubtedly there were digital maps and satellite images of the area, available for download. But Paul and I had left the maps behind, guidebooks unopened, web pages unbrowsed. We carried no GPS, cell phone, or satellite phone. For two weeks we would live without the comfort and security of maps, or the expectations they generate. We would have to find the right direction on our own, as we navigated through an unfamiliar landscape, without any certain destination. And so, on that spectacular afternoon, and in spite of their etched relief, the mountains lacked a certain definition—but at the same time, I sensed a different sort of clarity and way of dealing with the world. And still there was the wonderful sky, the endless hills and valleys, the world that we might create, and which might create us.

I'd taken mapless backcountry trips before our Pasayten hike, had my share of fecklessness and folly, been lost a few times, confounded more often. One mapless misadventure had been particularly illuminating, although it was neither very long, nor very far from a road. I was visiting my family in Portland, Oregon, and after a week of inactivity I grew restless and asked a friend if she wanted to go on a day hike up the Columbia River Gorge. I told my mom that "I wouldn't be back late," then drove east on I-84. It was a crystalline winter day and unusually cold for Portland; there had been a recent snowstorm and temperatures were in the low twenties. I didn't bother with a topographic map, figuring that trails along the gorge would be clearly marked. Pat and I found a trail east of Multnomah Falls and began hiking into higher country, climbing through dark basalt cliffs, cedar and fir, brittle crystals of light glittering in the fresh snow, the air cold enough so that I could feel its sharpness each time I inhaled. At first route-finding was easy. Blazes and the shallow, symmetrical trough of snow blanketing the trailbed showed the way—but eventually our route wandered into a maze of logging roads and small clear-cuts. We lost the now indistinct route and regained it, lost it again, inscribed figure-of-eights in the snow, finally broke out of cutover country and picked up a clear trail again. We worked our way north toward the gorge, past a cabin partly hidden in the trees, before deciding that, rather than backtracking, we would return to the car via a trail marked with a small sign: "Fire Escape Route to River." Easy enough. We could see the bottom of the gorge and the highway, far below, and assumed that all that remained of our walk was a steep but manageable, switchbacking descent to the river, which we would reach by dark. But the "trail" dove straight down a narrow, icy chute, toward a vertical cliff. The footing was precarious and almost immediately we were skidding downhill, barely in control, scrambling to grab trees to prevent cartwheeling into oblivion. To continue without ice axes and crampons was madness, and so we retreated toward the maze of logging roads, into the gathering dark and bitter cold—without flashlights or matches, or much in the way of warm clothes.

It wasn't that we were lost, at least not technically. We knew where we were and our relation to the trailhead, but in the dark we couldn't retrace our inbound footprints, which we lost in the logged-over area and the tangled skein of our tracks. We were, euphemistically speaking, "mislaid," and like the recalcitrant teenager who slowly concludes that he is in big trouble, this time, I gradually and grudgingly accepted the ugly possibility of a long, miserable night outside, with temperatures well below twenty degrees, and neither shelter nor fire. I figured that I could survive, as uncomfortable and hypothermic as I would be, but I was concerned about Pat—she had fewer clothes and less experience with outdoor misery. I tried to retain a veneer of calm as we discussed our options, but inwardly I was seething, and worried about getting through the night.

The only alternative to a wretched bivouac was locating the cabin that we had passed on the way in, and after thirty minutes of anxious searching, its cold shadow rose out of the gloom. My adrenal glands immediately calmed: such a relief to know that the night would be easier. The cabin was locked, but we gained access by breaking a small window, and groped around until we found matches, a candle, and firewood. We started a blaze in the large fireplace, then spent a sleepless and hungry night huddled together on a bench, feeding the fire and waiting for dawn. In the morning my water bottle was frozen solid, but at least we weren't. We left the cabin at first light and had no trouble finding our way back to the trailhead, which we reached just as a search-and-rescue team arrived. Later, I thought about what had happened in the country above the Columbia River. The problem wasn't so much that I had neglected to bring a map. I'd been foolish in leaving behind matches, a flashlight, and extra clothes, but I could have done without the map if I'd focused on keeping my bearings and been more conservative in dealing with the short day and confused tangle of trail, clear-cuts, and logging roads. The real problem was my mindset. I had traveled without a map, but I'd carried the attitudes and behaviors of someone who had one tucked away in his pack. I'd had my expectations and hubris, and as in the Greek tragedies, excessive pride is always a harbinger of trouble.

The mapless trip in the Pasayten Wilderness—this time, intentional—was my idea. Always when I travel, whether on highways or in the wilderness, I fuss over maps, noting where I've been, where I have yet to go. Sometimes I teeter on the edge of compulsion and think obsessively about distances, routes, and destinations. I measure my progress in miles and elapsed time. If I'm in the passenger seat on a road trip I thumb incessantly through my road atlas, and repeatedly unfold the state highway maps that I grab from information desks at rest areas. My hope for the Pasayten trip was that by traveling without maps, I might understand more about their utility, as well as their shortcomings—how they affect the ways in which I perceive the world, and how I find my way through it. By dispensing with maps, I sought to grasp something of their essential paradox—how they bestow placement and certainty, but simultaneously, disconnection. I wanted to shed a layer of insulating information, confront the environment in unanticipated ways, and abandon a measure of security.

I think, too, that I desired metaphor. There were no hippogriffs or unicorns lurking amongst the lodgepole pine-shrouded slopes of the Pasayten Wilderness, but in my fifty-fifth year a mapless journey meant discarding the familiar and finding my direction without the habits, preconceptions, and attitudes of a lifetime. I wanted a symbolic quest, in which

All maps are useless now.
These final steps must be taken alone, like the ragged first footfalls
of some yolk and caul hatchling along a wild river,
in the woods, at the foot of the mountains, in a valley of stars,
beyond vehicle of the familiar, language or skin,
in the darkness without and the darkness within.

The most profound difference that I anticipated between a mapped and mapless trip was an absence of expectations about the country I would travel through. In *Arctic Dreams*, Barry Lopez quotes the geographer John L. Allen: "No exploratory adventure begins without objectives based on the imagined nature and content of the lands to be explored." Maps shape our imaginations, explorations, objectives, and perceptions in fundamental ways. Although a map is a useful and often necessary tool, it also "creates a false sense of space; it achieves simplicity and compression . . . with an enforced perspective." I wanted to confront the land without "enforced perspectives" and the preconceptions engendered by maps. I hoped that the prospect from every peak that we might climb, every pass that we might cross, every ridge that we might traverse, would be fresh and direct. And although Peter Turchi argues that, "if we have no expectations, there are no surprises; that's why it's hard to tell jokes to dogs," I planned on being the dog that got the joke, and was thus surprised.

I also knew that I could not get lazy. In abandoning maps, I would need to attend to the details of the land—as on one winter day in the Canadian Arctic, when a friend and I were traveling by dog team across a level, almost featureless landscape. John and I were forty miles from our base camp, moving beneath a cover of low clouds, through treeless terrain, on a day when the temperature hovered near twenty below zero. There was not even a slip of wind, and no animals were about; we were the only thing moving through all the stillness and emptiness. The light was diffuse and threw no shadows, the clouds and snow were the color of weathered ivory. Nothing in that flat, monochromatic world had any dimension or scale that would have helped us find our way. We carried maps, but on that day they were almost useless. Our route took us south, along the edge of a twenty-mile-long lake, but the light and terrain were such that it was difficult to discern where the land ended and the lake began. We were following a compass bearing, but the magnitude of declination in the area, roughly twenty-seven degrees east, made us nervous. Every fifteen minutes or so, we would stop the dogs and walk carefully across the frozen land, and gather our bearings from the details of winter—the shape of the hardened, wind-sculpted waves of snow oriented in the direction of the prevailing winds; the accumulated drifts of softer snow in the lee of any obstruction; the subtle inflection of the terrain where the lake ice met the shore.

On and on we ran, following the evidence of snow and ice through an empty world, the only sounds the crunch of snow beneath our mukluks and the rhythmic jingle of the dogs' harness bells. We traveled without maps for hours, until the clouds lifted and we reached an imbricated delta at the south end of the lake, where the north-flowing river broke into channels: scattered clumps of stunted spruce, steeply cut riverbanks, and the sharp vector of an esker, snaking across the tundra. We stopped for the night, but before setting up our tent and staking out the dogs, we pulled out our map. In the somber light we fixed ourselves in space, and so were comforted. But in the hours when we had traveled without maps and paid strict attention to the details of the country, the known world had fallen away. We were camped only sixty miles north of our home base, but never before had I felt so isolated, and so focused on the land—and in abandoning the security of maps in the Pasayten, I hoped for that kind of concentration, again.

Finally, although I figured that I would accommodate myself to an unfamiliar way of traveling, I hoped that by abandoning the security of maps, I would approach the wilderness with a heightened sensory and emotional awareness. You find this "edginess" in a country with grizzly bears, as opposed to one without them: the necessity of guarding your food, carefully evaluating campsites, considering the wind's direction and the drift of your scent, moving cautiously through thick brush, always anticipating a sow with cubs or a big boar feasting on a moose carcass. It is the kind of intensity you encounter while traversing rough, trailless terrain, instead of crossing a pass on a maintained trail—climbing a steep, snow-choked couloir, the feel of mittened hands on cold granite, the sharp crunch of crampons in the shadowed gully as you measure the possibility of a sudden spall of rocks from the cliffs above. It is embedded in the tension of solo travel through a land where no one speaks your language, where you confront the absence of what's familiar and safe. In these situations, writes Camus, "music finds its way more easily into the less solid heart."

In *A Field Guide to Getting Lost*, Rebecca Solnit observes that "between words is silence, around ink whiteness, behind every map's information is what's left out, the unmapped and the unmappable." I desired the "unmapped and the unmappable," yearned for an experience analogous to one Peter Turchi described for reading, itself a form of travel: "A prerequisite for finding our way through any story or novel is to be lost: the journey can't begin until we've been set down in a place somehow unfamiliar." There would be no map to surrender to, only the country itself and the stories it might tell.

Oh, yes. I wanted to have fun, too.

I needed a setting for my mapless hike—a wilderness large enough to get figuratively lost in, yet where navigational mistakes most likely would not prove fatal. If I had wanted to push the mapless concept, I might have opted for a solo canoe trip in the Barren Lands of northern Canada. There amongst endless iterations of rock and tundra and water, along the intricate shorelines of some massive arctic lake, my navigational skills would have been severely challenged. There it would have been easy to become truly lost—and perhaps never found. I did not want the tension, though, of mapless travel through a landscape built on such an intimidating scale. I sought neither Terror on the Tundra nor Machismo in the Mountains, instead aiming for contemplation as much as exertion, accommodation as much as uncertainty. So I looked to the western mountains, and in my imagination tried out the Sierra (too busy and familiar), the Oregon Cascades (not spectacular enough), and the North Cascades (too rugged for true wandering, and most likely requiring the burden of technical gear for off-trail travel). I eventually settled on the Pasayten Wilderness in north-central Washington, about seventy miles from east to west and twenty miles north to south, and sufficiently large for my project: 530,000 acres, almost twice the size of Rhode Island. (This didn't sound very impressive but, without a map, wouldn't it be possible to get confused in Kingston? Puzzled in Providence?) The western reaches of the Pasayten embraced the crest of the North Cascades. To the north was the Canadian border; to the east were the semiarid scrublands, and irrigated orchards and vineyards, of the Okanogan Valley. South of the wilderness, steep-sided canyons drained toward the Methow Valley and the nearest town, Winthrop. Most important, I was unfamiliar with the Pasayten. I had hiked the Pacific Crest Trail in the western portion of the wilderness, and many years before had done one short trip east of the Cascade crest, but all I recalled was that several rivers in the western part of the Pasayten drained north into Canada, that there were high, rolling meadows to the east, and that a trail paralleled much of the Canadian-American border.

I knew a bit about the edges of the Pasayten, but its vast center was unknown to me, and I kept it that way. I only needed to identify the trailhead where I would begin my hike, and chose one in the central part of the area almost randomly, using a Forest Service map to trace a road up Eightmile Creek to the trailhead for Billy Goat Pass, a few miles beyond road's end. But like some shy heroine from a Gothic novel who refuses to meet the enthralled gaze of her suitor, I assiduously averted my eyes from the center of the map. I opened no other maps, read no guidebooks, asked no questions of friends or Google. My image of the Pasayten was a mental analog of macular degeneration: decent peripheral vision, but a blurred, almost nonexistent, central image. Although I would be hiking through country that had been explored long ago, for me it was unmapped terrain.

Once I had a destination for my mapless quest (or conceit), I only needed a companion. I wanted someone who was experienced, steady, strong, and quiet. He would have to be capable of finding his way back to the car in an emergency, working out the best cross-country route, or stabilizing a fractured leg—someone who moved well, yet who also knew how to hold still and listen. I also did not want interpersonal stress to distract from my experience, and sought a companion with whom I felt comfortable, who could take care of himself emotionally and whose happiness was not dependent upon me, other than in ways related to basic safety. I did not want to worry about how a steep trail, heavy pack, implacable hordes of mosquitoes, or rain might affect someone's mood. And so I asked Paul Willis, a friend of almost thirty years, to come along. We'd met when we were graduate students at Washington State University; I'd seen him walking toward campus, carrying a beat-up rucksack, and figured that he must be a climber. I introduced myself, and soon Paul and I, and our wives, became friends. Over the years, Paul and I had done many mountaineering trips in the High Sierra and Washington Cascades together. I knew him as a quiet, extremely competent climber and hiker, someone who never got ruffled. He is an English professor at a liberal arts college in California, a poet and creative writer—thoughtful and articulate, with a quiet sense of humor. He carries himself quietly, and well. When I first broached the idea of a mapless trip, Paul was uncertain, but eventually decided that the trip would be an intriguing adventure. He had time during the coming summer, and he'd always wanted to hike in the Pasayten. Between us, we had about eighty years of wilderness experience, and our fifty-something bodies were still relatively sound. We would get through on our own:

> No radar, no runnin' lights, no radio
> The torches blinking on the shore tell when to come and go
> And I don't believe in the satellite, computer, GPS
> My faith is in the horizon. . . .
> My compass, my best guess.

On our final day in the Pasayten, Paul and I confirmed what we had suspected during the first hour of our trip—that we had followed our expectations into confusion. Just minutes after leaving the trailhead we'd succumbed to the overconfidence generated by maps, and became mislaid. We left the car carrying two weeks of food in packs weighing close to sixty-five pounds. Heads bent beneath our loads like weary porters, we trudged up the trail toward Billy Goat Pass, the only landmark in the Pasayten that we could name and situate with certainty on the mental maps that we began building during the drive up Eightmile Creek. Months before, when looking for a trailhead, I had noticed Billy Goat Pass on the map, and *knew* that it lay only a few miles beyond road's end. This much was true, but what didn't register was that the trail divided a few hundred yards beyond road's end, with one branch leading north toward Billy Goat Pass, and the other northwest to Eightmile Pass. Because I wasn't anticipating a trail junction early in the hike, and the weight of our packs forced our heads toward the ground, we missed the sign, which was placed high on a tree to the right of the trail. So we followed my expectations into geographical confusion where, after a gentle climb, we reached an unsigned divide and threw down our packs. There weren't any maps to examine, as was our ritual, but we were out of shape and tired (well, at least Paul was), and focused on more important things—water, a few handfuls of snack mix, and a chance to survey the scenery. Paul and I discussed the route, and our location. Easy enough. The map I'd looked at six months before told me that, sign or no sign, we must be at Billy Goat Pass. Somehow, though, the designation did not *feel* right, and the idea of Billy Goat Pass did not settle easily. My self-assurance, and the confidence that comes from being firmly placed in space, already was marbled with doubt. "Wait!" I wanted to say. "Something is not right." But I kept my silence and instead sketched the terrain to the north in the small notebook that I carried in my shirt pocket. I told myself this was "for future reference," meaning to emulate early explorers and provide myself with a little cognitive security. The problem was that my artistic impairment rendered all the sketches that eventually filled my notebook vaguely similar, and useless for identifying anything. Paul looked quietly amused as I finished my sketch, then hoisted his pack and began walking. I took a long pull from my water bottle and followed him downhill, into the Vale of Uncertainty. I was uncomfortable with the discordance between my expectations and intuitive sense of the land, but as "Billy Goat Pass" slipped uneasily into the past, I realized that, only a mile out from the trailhead, I'd already arrived at the place I'd hoped for.

Our route took us downhill for an hour, crossed a creek, and trended northeast and uphill through lodgepole pine and Engelmann spruce. By four o'clock we were ready to stop, but we'd found neither water nor a decent campsite. Here were more questions easily answered by a map: How far to water or a likely looking camp? How much longer must I push before I can dump this load? I told myself to just walk, and to abandon anticipation. About thirty minutes later the trail cut into a small drainage, and the sound of running water gathered before us. There, in a grove of lodgepole pine, we found a perfect camp. I was played out. My hips and shoulders hurt, where the straps of my pack had gouged into my flesh, their ancient, closed-cell foam having metamorphosed into wood. My thighs ached, my back was tight, my feet were sore—ah, middle age, and the knowledge that my thirty-year-old external-frame pack, which marked me as an old fart, was older than most of my students. But it was a beautiful afternoon, cloudless, with sunlight slanting through thick woods, and hermit thrushes revving up for their evening chorus. Later, after food and tea, Paul and I walked up the trail until we reached a signed trail junction: ahead, Larch Pass (8 miles); to the south and east, Billy Goat Corral (5 miles). From an earlier sign we knew that our trail led, in the opposite direction, toward Hidden Lakes, and that Three Fools Pass (but there are only two of us) lay uphill. The signs gave us names that we might link to specific places (out there, somewhere, Hidden Lakes and Larch Pass, Billy Goat Corral and Three Fools Pass), but they offered little security, for without a map the words floated free like unmoored boats drifting down some uncharted ocean current.

We reached Three Fools Pass early the next morning, set down our loads, then scrambled up a steep gully through cliffs east of the pass, in search of a view that would provide some sense of the lay of the land. Seeking the high ground reminded me of accounts from the early days of western exploration, those tales of men (mostly) settling themselves in space, like Meriwether Lewis standing on a bluff above the Three Forks of the Missouri River and working out the intersecting relationship of the Gallatin, Madison, and Jefferson rivers. This exploratory behavior was not a regular part of my hiking routine, because maps provide a substitute for good vantage points, but we would repeat the tactic often. Above Three Fools Pass, though, the view wasn't revelatory—a drainage and a ragged ridge of peaks running east to west, with an obvious route for the trail to the northeast, toward higher country. But about one mile below the pass, the trail surprised us and bent westward. I took some pleasure in this second tug at my expectations, as we contoured along a manzanita-covered slope, ascended a canyon west of our anticipated route, and climbed through dead lodgepole pine and Engelmann spruce. We had walked into what Paul described as an "apocalyptic forest," where many of the trees stood like shrouded skeletons in some dendrologist's macabre dream, raining dead needles, with great slabs of exfoliating bark peeling from their trunks, the trees' deaths gathering into a sorrowful litany. The spectral forests were a product of mountain pine beetles and spruce beetles, whose generic name, *Dendroctonus*, translates appropriately as "tree killer." Tree killers were advancing into the Pasayten, much as they were spreading through much of the West, because declining precipitation, and warming winter and summer temperatures, have helped the beetles survive in more northerly and higher-elevation forests, where, as one part of an ecological trinity—the others being drought and fire—they have dramatically altered the mountain landscape.

On that hot morning it was easy to believe in climate change and its effects on mountain forests, but we soon broke into a small subalpine meadow, resplendent with lemon-yellow cinquefoil, purple penstemon, and carmine paintbrush, wildflowers that spoke of higher country somewhere to the north. We took lunch there, clinging to pockets of shade in the gathering heat, before starting a hot slog to an early camp below what we figured was Larch Pass. It must have been little more than two miles from the meadow to our camp, but we were trail-weary by the time we set down our packs and began our second reconnaissance of the day, this time to the ridges west of Larch Pass. There, at the limit of the smallest, twisted trees, I set aside my fatigue as the world opened before us and maps no longer mattered—just as they would not matter that evening, as we sat around a small fire and the deep and gentle darkness settled around us.

We moved north toward the Canadian border, following the trail through an intricate, green fugue of alpine meadows, watered by the last of winter's melting snow—emerald green, sea green, forest green, conifer green. Stunted patches of spruce and subalpine fir bordered the meadows, each with a male white-crowned sparrow throwing out the familiar mix of whistles, buzzes, and trills that drifts across mountain parklands throughout the West. We climbed past displaying male American pipits, their territorial flights ascending arcs of song and fluttering wings, followed by a steep, descending curve. And so, when we reached a sandy divide, I named it "Pipit Pass"; here, where the country opened into a more expansive geometry, we ditched our packs and began a long ridge run, following a series of low peaks to the northwest, aiming to determine where we might go. To the west was a horseshoe-shaped basin sheltering a large, verdant-green alpine meadow; beyond, deep valleys and huge swaths of recently burnt-over country. In the distance, beyond the range of our hike, were the mountains for which we had comforting names: Silver Star, Baker, and Shuksan, the Picket Range. The day was hot and still; since the start of our hike warmth had marched further into the high country, lingering in the evening shadows, invading the morning chill. Because of the heat and the daunting prospect of hiking west through a fire-ravaged landscape, we decided to walk toward another name—Cathedral Peak—which we knew little about, except that it lay to the north and east, nestled against the Canadian border. There were several candidates on the horizon, but we disagreed as to the most likely prospect. Paul favored a rectangular-shaped peak; I argued for a serrated, pyramidal mountain more to the south.

We walked north for another day, passing several groups of hikers along the way. With each party it was difficult to not discuss geography, the common trailside language. After an initial greeting the talk invariably turned to "Where are you headed?" or "Where are you coming from?" in the same way that couples with small children always discuss diapers, body fluids, and sleep deprivation. But Paul and I wanted no information about the Pasayten's geography, other than what we gained on our own. It was difficult to talk without being exposed to route descriptions and a barrage of names; the alternative was to pass by with only a curmudgeonly grunt. So we refrained from asking passing hikers where they were coming from or headed to, instead settling on some form of "Been out long?" If someone asked us about our route, our answer was an evasive mini-version of former attorney general Alberto Gonzales's testimony before Congress on his role in firing federal attorneys, substituting "Just wandering" for "I don't recall."

Our aversion to discussing names and routes—the stuff of maps—created a distance between Paul and me, and those whom we encountered, for as Denis Wood observed, "mapping is a way of making experience of the environment *shareable*." Perhaps we should have replied that we aimed to climb Mount Analogue—the French surrealist and climber René Daumal's symbolic peak, inaccessible to "ordinary human approaches," located on a South Pacific island, beyond Port o' Monkeys. A line from Daumal's book, *Mt. Analogue*, was appropriate: "My compass went out with the prune pits." Substitute "map" for "compass" and you'd have it right. As with *Mt. Analogue*'s narrative, there was an aura of silliness to our efforts to censor offending geographical information. Yet we envisioned a trip with a certain internal integrity, and hoped to maintain its logic and character. And so, after each fumbling attempt to divert the conversation away from destinations and place names, we wished our passersby good day and resumed wandering toward Port o' Monkeys, little wiser about our route.

On our fourth day we climbed a prominent peak with a gentle, south-facing slope, slogging through glaring light and heavy heat, across brittle sedge meadows with the texture of a green kitchen scrubby. I felt baked and listless, and on the windless summit we were harassed by black flies, a first in my Cascade experience. But the views were worth it. The isolated peak lay hard up against the Canadian border, which slashed eastward through thick lodgepole pine forests, running just north of the rectangular mountain that Paul believed was Cathedral Peak. Although I had argued for a different summit, I had to yield to the border's logic and admit that he was correct; the peak was too close to Canada to be anything other than Cathedral. And so we had a point and name with which to ground us more firmly in the world.

It was comforting to have a destination, but as we descended from the peak, I was plagued by ennui and uncertainty. Perhaps it was just the heat, but Paul seemed steadier, less bothered by the temperature and flies. It was in his nature, I supposed. In the twenty-eight years that I'd known him, in all of our climbs and hikes, I'd never seen him visibly upset or ruffled. He'd always been steady, whether while racking up protection at the base of a climb or hunkered down in a flapping tent, waiting out a raging storm. Paul has a quiet resolve, an air of contemplative determination, which matches his solid frame. Although he can hold still for long periods, he also has a strong desire to cover ground. In his movements he is patient and deliberate, and never prone to whining. Paul and I had noticed that John Muir always played the stoic in his writings; although he must have experienced severe discomfort during his wilderness rambles, it's easy to imagine Muir describing "glorious clouds of mosquitoes" or an "invigorating" blizzard. Although we were amused by Muir's stoicism, I could not recall Paul ever complaining about the environment (flies, heat, difficult ground, rain, wind) or his companions (slow, bitchy, clumsy, verbose), other than in an occasional, elliptical and gentle way. I suspected that he sometimes was bothered more than he let on, but I had never detected much anger or frustration in him. I, too, might maintain a quiet and steady facade, but it might mask a tumult of curses and complaints, rarely voiced but acutely felt. I could play the part of a wilderness curmudgeon, but it was a role without lines. I never wanted to reveal my dissatisfaction. I had my values, and they did not permit verbal complaints, other than in the mildest form: "Tough day?" "Yeah—bad heat and bugs, but still good." The days always were "good," even when they were not.

We camped on a small granite bench, amidst scattered larch. It was a tight, uncomfortable spot—a slab of stone for a bed, far from water, with heat and flies that plagued us through the night. Our only shelter was a tarp, great for rain protection but useless against harassing insects. At one point I was simultaneously attended to by mosquitoes, black flies, small deer flies, a species that looked like a house fly, and a large, black-and-yellow hover fly, with an annoying habit that matched its name—flitting about my head, filling the air with an irritating whine, a perfect harmonic to my silent whines of complaint. Most of the flies vanished at dark, but the mosquitoes hung on in the heat. Even at midnight it was too hot for my sleeping bag; I couldn't sleep without a refuge from the mosquitoes, so I crawled into my nylon bivy sack, zipped up the netting, and sweltered. The day had exhausted me, but I lay in the claustrophobic dark, shifting from side to side, contemplating the mosquitoes, wondering if the heat would break or if we would face another nine days of it. The mapless trip seemed like folly. What was its artifice worth? Would I find the right direction? *Just where in the world was I going?* I felt my focus fraying, drawn away from the Pasayten by doubt, and by the Sirens of comfort: a hot shower, bountiful meal, and clean, mosquito-free bed. It had been years since I had been pulled from the wilderness by a thick rope of discomfort, and made less than fully present by an inability to relax. I hated this: lash me to the mast, fill my ears with wax, let me be *here*. Protect me from the seduction of desire, or the aching physics of the past, as Marilynne Robinson described in *Housekeeping*: "Memory is the sense of loss, and loss pulls us after it." Let me not drift toward another place and time.

And so, as I squirmed in my hot and fetid bed, and worried about finding my bearings, I drifted back to the previous summer, when I also had wondered about being found or lost. I had spent part of June as a member of a crew studying waterfowl on the Kuskokwim Delta of western Alaska, at the edge of the Bering Sea. The study area spanned a fifty-mile swath of coastal plain, a mosaic of meandering tidal channels, ponds, and tawny sedge meadows alive with birds. Two of us spent eleven days on the Naskonet Peninsula, a Euclidian plane of seventy square miles spread beneath a space-drenched sky. Out there, at the edge of the continent, we were 115 miles from Bethel, the nearest town of much size, and thirty miles from the main research camp. There were other research crews scattered across the study area, and some small villages and traditional summer fishing camps of the Yupik people, but we saw no one on the Naskonet. Sometimes a single-engine plane passed nearby, and there was the occasional crackle of voices on the satellite phone. But mostly we were alone with the birds and the emptiness of the coastal plain, alone and silent in a land where there was no shelter from the insistent winds, from the thick bands of ragged clouds that marched across the great arc of sky, dumping rain squalls as they ran toward the horizon. It was country that recalled a line from a Richard Hugo poem: "With land this open, wind is blowing / when there is no wind."

In our isolation and attention to our work, the outside world dissolved into the play of sun on tiny tundra ponds, the continuous light of summer solstice, the clangor of calling geese and bugling sandhill cranes, and our daily task, which was to walk the earth and search for nests in each quarter-mile by half-mile study plot—identifying them to species, noting location and status, floating eggs to see how far into incubation each clutch was. To do this well meant making patient, parallel traverses across broad patches of tundra, tracing the edges of each pond, and sloshing out to every likely looking islet that might hold a nest. My partner and I divided each plot in half, then worked alone, alive to the silence that transcended the gathered voices of the birds. We wandered through a landscape of light and space, as swirling clouds of birds rose before us: Canada geese, white-fronted geese, emperor geese, spectacled eiders, red-throated loons, arctic terns, black turnstones, semipalmated sandpipers, glaucous gulls, mew gulls, Sabine's gulls, Lapland longspurs, savannah sparrows. It was repetitious, tiring, glorious, soothing, and wonderful work, pleasing in its simplicity and satisfying in its results.

There was little to worry about on the Naskonet Peninsula, other than staying dry and finding nests. We had plenty of food, sturdy shelter, a satellite phone in case of emergency. There were no bears, polar or brown, to generate paranoia or complicate camp life, as the Kuskokwim Delta area is the one region of Alaska without either of these alpha predators. Our only concerns were to avoid getting separated from our raft by a rising tide, which could quickly turn a ten-foot-deep channel into an impassable barrier, and to stay precisely located in space as we walked to and from the nest plots, and searched their interiors. The Naskonet Peninsula is a bewildering maze of ponds and tidal sloughs, a Gordian knot of water and earth, its only relief an occasional ridge of sandy, frost-heaved soil rising a few feet above the surrounding plane. In most places the land is so low and flat that bands of wrack, deposited by winter-storm surges, wreathe ponds miles from the sea. There is no obvious pattern to the sloughs, which meander aimlessly, doubling back upon themselves, splitting off into dendritic networks of finely laced branches. The ponds vary in size from a few feet across to over a half-mile long; in many places they cover more than 50 percent of the land and form a thick chaos of intricate shorelines, tiny islands, meandering channels, and delicate, arched peninsulas. The water is all confusion, its boundary with solid ground an intricate puzzle. Little about the Naskonet Peninsula, other than the lives of the birds, with their dutiful attention to their nesting cycles, appears regular. There is no melodic line to the land; it seems atonal, as if Schoenberg had composed the score for water and earth, sedge and wind.

Seen from the air, the terrain looks like a micrograph of organ tissue—perhaps a transverse section of the intestinal wall—the channels are networks of blood vessels, the tundra a matrix of one cell-type, the water an embedded, tangled mix of glandular cells. To know our exact place in this landscape was no easy task. Topographic maps were useless for route finding; their scale was not fine enough and they lacked sufficient detail. Instead we navigated with laminated aerial photographs, each covering an area of roughly one-and-one-half by two miles. We walked with them in our hands, noting each tiny bay, the wandering thread of each slough, the lay of each narrow-waisted isthmus. The Fish and Wildlife Service had supplied us with GPS devices, but I buried mine in my pack and disdained coordinates of latitude and longitude. The numbers could not tell me where I was: there, on that tiny peninsula, kneeling before a spectacled eider nest with six olive-green eggs, the cluster cradled in a luxurious, soft bowl of dark-gray down, still blessedly warm to the touch after the incubating hen has fled, skittering across the shallow, tea-dark pond. I carefully lift an egg from the nest, avoiding the slimy stink of green feces left by the female when she flushed, quickly float it in the chilly water to determine the incubation stage, then gently return it to the clutch, which I conceal beneath a blanket of down and brown sedge blades to prevent a gull from discovering the nest. After filling out a nest card I nod toward the eggs, an acknowledegment of the female's patient tenacity amidst the milling predators and wind-driven rain. Those solid eggs, that soft nest, the delicate, acidic scent of sedge tussocks, the muttering susurrus of wind-driven chop slapping the edge of the pond, positioned me in a particular place. As I rose to resume my search, I saw the great gray-and-white bulk of Nelson Island, twenty-five miles to the southwest, rising fifteen hundred feet above the Bering Sea, its western cliffs and slopes fluted with snow, a distant but solid reference point, a spatial counterpoint to the eider nest. I understood that navigation and its necessary antecedent, location, were a matter of scale. On the Naskonet Peninsula my closest, most immediate surroundings were certain, as were the boundaries of my world, delimited by Nelson Island and the gray edge of the Bering Sea. It was the middle ground that was indistinct, and threatened to dissolve into uncertainty amidst the welter of wandering sloughs, the fractal mess of ponds and tundra—a planar, two-dimensional earth devoid of landmarks taller than my pack, which lay beside me in the thick sedge meadow, a world whose coordinates I tried to grasp with the aerial photograph that I pulled, once again, from my field vest.

The Pasayten was different. The immediate foreground was distinct (damn those pesky mosquitoes and the insistent heat), while Cathedral Peak and the Cascades crest situated me in the greater landscape. The middle ground, however, was more certain and defined than on the Naskonet Peninsula—the trails that we followed, the sharp relief of ridges and valleys, kept us anchored and induced none of the uncertainty that characterized the Alaskan coastal plain. The problem was that I had not settled into the landscape. Unlike my clearly defined work on the Naskonet Peninsula, the nature of my occupation in the Pasayten was unclear. As much as I had anticipated the trip, and contemplated my objectives, I did not know where I was going. I was four days into my hike and Mount Analogue felt more distant than ever. Perhaps it was folly, but I desired more than an opportunity to enjoy the wilderness. Rebecca Solnit writes, "the things we want are transformative, and we don't know or only think we know what is on the other side of that transformation." I yearned for metaphor, and perhaps metamorphosis, but as I lay in my rough and sweaty bed, I sensed that my desires might be too much to hang on a thirteen-day wilderness backpack trip, maps or no maps.

In the morning, groggy with lack of sleep, we rose to the press of flies and another day of heavy heat. We packed hastily, walked north for about a mile, then turned to the east as tendrils of gunmetal gray clouds streamed out of the west and the land fell away into a deep and distant glacial valley. I sank into lassitude as we descended, my body listless from lack of sleep, the humid atmosphere more like the Midwest in summer than the Pacific Northwest. In late morning we crossed the Ashnola River on a single-log bridge, then broke for water and a snack. I stripped off my sweat-soaked shirt, rinsed my face, and watched the clear rush of water across the cobbled streambed. Faint wisps of cool wind fingered the willows lining the river, and the valley bottom was mercifully free of flies. A glance at the sky, the sweet scent of rain in the air. Soon the heat would break and there would be relief . . .

We tracked the trail through thick lodgepole pine, then began climbing the steep side of the U-shaped valley trough, as great burls of storm clouds roiled above the western peaks and thunder rumbled in the distance. The trail broke into open scrub and rain began to fall, building to a steady shower. We donned rain gear and quickened our pace, hoping to reach the forest before the deluge. Unexpectedly, though, the rain tapered off—but in this hesitant interval the essence of the air shifted from hot and humid to cool and dry. I could breathe more easily, and for awhile my body claimed its rhythm. To find that space, after struggling for five days—to touch a nostalgic intimation of my twenties and thirties, when my movement was easy and quick—was wonderful. For a short while I no longer was some fifty-five-year-old geezer, plodding along beneath a battered external-frame pack, the kind that no one with any "mountain cred" would ever carry.

We switchbacked through stands of trembling aspen, their leaves a shimmer of green, with white trunks etched against a luxurious understory of thick, emerald-colored grass, in a country that felt more like the Northern Rockies than the North Cascades. Above the aspen we broke for lunch, then finished climbing and emerged onto a dry, park-like bench. As the clouds dissipated we sought a camp with water, pleasing views, and enough wind to discourage mosquitoes. After an hour of wandering we found what we were after, and there, among scrub willow and whitebark pine, where California ground squirrels complained about our presence, we took our rest. I spread out my sleeping bag, brewed some tea, sat back and let the wind and clear air wash away the heat- and fly-induced tension of the last few days. I sipped my tea, let my jaw muscles relax, and surveyed the country to the east, now as mild and gentle as a poor-will's call—close at hand, a broad valley, fully forested, the land climbing to meet subalpine parkland, and what must be Cathedral Peak and its satellite summits, a mass of grayish-tan rock rising several thousand feet above the surrounding terrain. Cathedral Peak was perhaps ten miles away, but on this journey "miles" had lost much of their relevance. Except for distances gleaned from occasional trail signs, we judged our hike, like the Inuit, in terms of time, rather than distance: this many hours walked, this many to go. And elevations, as related to the statement on USGS maps that "datum is mean sea level," were irrelevant. Instead, I thought about altitude in terms of the natural world: we have left the riparian bottomlands of the veery, climbed beyond the coniferous forest of the Swainson's thrush, and entered the timberline realm of the hermit thrush. We are descending into the lodgepole pine zone, or rising into the world of whitebark pine. We are camped among the white-crowned sparrows; tomorrow, we will sleep higher, near an alpine meadow, at an elevation of American pipits. I discarded miles and feet and understood something of where we were by the dawn chorus, the play of wildflowers in alpine meadows, the ways in which tree species gave way to one another with the rise and fall of our route, and transitions from north- to south-facing slopes.

In the morning Paul and I climbed a gentle peak southeast of our camp, to again gather a sense of where we were. We named our little mountain "Windy Peak," in honor of the breeze that kept the flies at bay. Windy Peak provided expansive views of the Pasayten, but in all that sweep of wilderness I could name only two features: to the northeast, the blocky mass of Cathedral Peak, and to the west and south, the Ashnola River. Other official names, gleaned from trail signs, lay scattered like shards of pottery along our route, but I couldn't locate them, and they formed no intact vessel to contain our journey. What surprised me about the absence of place names was that we replaced few of them with those of our choosing. We christened occasional features that held some significance for us, but mostly we were content to live in a country without names.

Traveling through a mostly nameless landscape was one of the most interesting and profound aspects of our walk. Although the lack of place names sometimes infused our hike with uncertainty, I encountered none of the angst described by Paul Shepard in *Man in the Landscape*: "An environment without place names is fearful. When men land on other planets in our solar system they will come up with place names . . . landscapes without place names are disorienting; without categorical forms, awful." Instead, the dearth of place names hid much of the Pasayten's communal history. J. B. Harley argues that this process is one way in which a dominant culture silences a subordinate one: "Naming a place anew is a widely documented act of political possession in settlement history. Equally the taking away of a name is an act of dispossession." Remove the people, then remove their names. Few Native American place names are on modern maps of the Pasayten. Ashnola, translated as "place of trading," is an exception, and I suppose that many names on trail signs were evidence of dispossession, but they were our best links to the human history of the area. Some were merely descriptive—Larch Pass and Corral Lake—but others were more evocative, such as Three Fools Pass and Peeve Pass. We did not know how Peeve Pass got its name, although I could sense one plausible past, courtesy of the pestilent dipterans at "Fly Camp," just south of the pass.

We were disinclined to name landscape features because we had not yet created our own stories. As Robert McFarlane writes in *Mountains of the Mind*, "the urge to mark places in a landscape with names—to attempt to fix a presence or an event within time and space—is a way of allowing stories to be told about that landscape. . . . Naming remains a way to place space within a wider matrix of significance: a way, essentially, to make the unknown known." The features that we did name held some personal importance, such as "Windy Peak" and "Sandy Ridge," with their dramatic and useful views; "Fly Camp"; or "Varied Thrush Camp," where the lovely, flute-like matins of the thrushes sang the meadows into night. Names help fasten us to the world and tell our stories, as with the Northern California place names invoked by Robert Hass:

> Olena
> Tamalpias Mariposa
> Mendocino Sausalito San Rafael
> Emigrant Gap
> Donner Pass
>
> Of all the laws
> that bind us to the past
> the names of the things are
> stubbornest.

Names are stubborn because they connect us, powerfully, to places through history, culture, and experience. I first learned how names grow out of an apparently unnamed landscape when I lived at Warden's Grove, a small stand of spruce along the Thelon River, deep within the Barrens, 325 miles northeast of Yellowknife. I spent eleven months there in 1977–1978, and returned during the summers of 1989–1991 to study the Harris's sparrows that bred in the area. My companions and I inhabited a land that had seen almost no residents since about 1700 C.E., when the Chipewyans retreated from the area, driven south by smallpox and economic changes that tied them to fur trading posts. Inuit and Indian groups had lived and traveled in the Thelon area since about 5000 B.C.E., but their names were lost to those who made the 1:250,000 map of the area. Instead there was only a scatter of official place names within a ten-mile radius of Warden's Grove, itself not shown on the map, and all but two connected to people: Grassy Island, Downtree Lake, Steel Lake, Dickson Canyon, Ford Falls, Helen Falls, Hanbury River, Clarke River. We used these names and added others, based upon our stories: Beddingstraw Creek, where we gathered dried grass to line shelters for our sled dogs; Cache Lake, where supplies twice were left for us by air-charter companies; Sled-dump Riffle, an open section of the Thelon River where we overturned a dogsled; Last Light Hills, sand dunes to the east of Warden's Grove that caught the last sunlight on summer nights; Home Hill, the five-hundred-foot rise overlooking Warden's Grove that guided us as we returned from expeditions into the Barrens; and Tranquility Tarn, the shallow pond near the summit of Home Hill, which in the summer warmed earlier than the river, and where we washed away the filth accumulated during weeks of fieldwork. The process by which we named features that resonated with personal history is familiar to anyone who knows a place well: it is a way to connect our story to the land. None of our names will make it onto official maps, but they hover like vivid points of light in my memory, binding me to the Thelon River and a small copse of spruce, lost within the great arctic world.

On the afternoon of our sixth day we arrived at what a sign informed us was Upper Cathedral Lake. It was a spectacular place, more alpine than anything on our hike, the lake cupped within a bowl of tan granitic rock, Cathedral Peak to the northeast, the sheer face of a subsidiary peak to the south. Massive cumulonimbus clouds reared up in the northern sky, pikas called from rock piles around the lake's margin, and from across the water came one of my favorite mountain sounds—meltwater tumbling into an alpine lake, an ebb and flow of white noise eddying on the breeze. Upper Cathedral Lake would be our "furthest out"; here, in a favored haunt of mountain goats, we would ditch our loads, rest, and explore for a few days.

The following morning Paul and I headed for Cathedral Peak, in search of another view. We had no intention of climbing the peak, because we recalled guidebook descriptions from years ago, indicating that all routes on the mountain required ropes. But we found only one or two airy moves along the way, and had no trouble reaching the summit—another case in which our expectations, based upon faulty memory, were wrong. I wanted to commemorate our trip in some small way, and so wrote in the summit register, "Chris Norment: 13-day Pasayten hike, traveling without maps." Paul's entry was laconic, and without the small, prideful note that I'd included: "Paul Willis: traveling without chewing gum."

The gumless panorama embraced an endless march of mountains and rivers, fading into a mingled atmosphere of white and blue: "This view is what one needs to love the world / when things go bad." But cutting across our view was the Canadian-American border, a few miles beyond Cathedral Peak: below timberline, a swath of downed trees tracking east-west across the Pasayten like a power-line corridor without transmission towers. The border scar slashed through the wilderness, bisecting river valleys, climbing impossibly steep slopes, knifing arêtes. Its vector accepted nothing of the Pasayten's geography or ecology; there was no logic to its path, other than a strict adherence to the forty-ninth parallel. The physical manifestation of the border demanded our attention, but we were disaffected by its arbitrary nature.

Spread open a map of the Pasayten and you are confronted with a plethora of borders: international, state, county, National Forest, National Park, wilderness area, township, and range. Stand on one side of any of these lines, and you occupy one jurisdiction and state of existence, and not the other: Canadian (universal health care) or American (health care if you can afford it), private land (stay out) or public land (welcome), Park Service (many rules about wilderness travel), Forest Service (fewer rules). But without a map our awareness of most borders vanished, a disappearing act assisted by the country itself—stay out long enough, live with the land and the absence of "current events," and political sensibilities fade. The mosquitoes, the rain and heat, the daily pattern of focused existence, the bloom of paintbrush in an alpine meadow, the song of a Townsend's warbler given out from high in a spruce, the vast panoramas and even vaster night skies: these dissolve distinctions between one jurisdiction and another, just as they erode our attention to Republican and Democratic rantings, the latest war or economic stimulus package. In the backcountry it is more difficult to be a nationalist and accept the legitimacy of human boundaries; lines inscribed on the land seem irrelevant and limiting, as Aldo Leopold recognized as he listened to the dawn chorus on his Wisconsin farm: "It's not only boundaries that disappear, but also the thought of being bounded." In the wild it is possible to become nationless.

And yet Paul and I could not avoid tracking the insistent line dividing Canada from the United States. The stark, treeless corridor reminded me of Simon Schama's description of the border between Poland and the former Soviet Union, which bisected the ancient Białowieża Forest: "a vast growling machine—Big Mower—was used to keep it [the border] clean-shaven and visible from the guard towers. For the woods had a way of invading the route-map of the police state with their undergrowth, creating botanically sheltered places of sedition." The chain saws that maintained the Canadian-American border corridor also were agents of state control, more benign than Big Mower, but still symbols of a fundamental human preoccupation with possession and nationhood. While in most societies land ownership seems necessary, the natural world, in its complexity, expanse, and otherness, insists that possession, with its borders and divisions, is artificial and carries a cost. Watersheds, geological fault lines and sedimentary deposits, climate patterns, the nesting territories and migrations of birds, the wanderings of mule deer, the distribution of lodgepole pine and pine-bark beetles, the range of alpine paintbrush: these demonstrate the limitations of political boundaries. We divide the world and ourselves into countries, states, counties, cities, and villages, insist on borders, build a fifteen-foot high, 670-mile fence between Mexico and the United States, cultivate the notion of "us" and "other," kill one another over abstract concepts symbolized by lines on maps. The Pasayten was once part of the Oregon Territory, which during the 1830s and 1840s was jointly occupied by the Americans and British. Escalating tensions over ownership of the region raised the possibility of armed conflict, hence the slogan "Fifty-four Forty or Fight," coined by Democrats during the 1844 presidential election. The 1846 Treaty of Washington defused the situation by continuing the international boundary west along the forty-ninth parallel from the Rocky Mountains; the vector north of Cathedral Peak is an artifact of this agreement. The British-American boundary dispute was settled peacefully, but the litany of human misery created by arbitrary borders is almost infinite. Take the partition of British India in 1947; the borders between the newly created Dominion of Pakistan and Union of India, both in the west (Punjab) and east (Bengal), were demarcated by boundary commissions. The boundaries were meant to separate areas with Hindu/Sikh and Muslim majorities, but it was an impossible task, particularly in the Punjab. In the months after partition, at least ten million people were displaced, as they sought the safety of a religious majority across a border. Epidemic violence, starvation, and disease associated with the partition left close to one million people dead, a legacy that lives on in the continuing conflict over Kashmir.

We have our borders and boundaries, nations and conflicts, but there is a deeper wisdom in the paths of animals and ranges of plants, one that Aldo Leopold recognized: "It is an irony that the great powers should have discovered the unity of nations at Cairo in 1943. The geese of the world have had that notion for a longer time, and each March they stake their lives on its essential truth." In the Pasayten I put aside maps and mostly ignored their boundaries, instead seeking my location in the lay of the land, the ways in which the woodpeckers flew and the spruce grew. For awhile I lived in a United States of Lodgepole Pine, a People's Democratic Republic of Black-backed Woodpeckers, a Union of Mountain Goat Socialist Republics. I dreamed that the border slash disappeared, as pines and huckleberries sprouted and overwhelmed the chain saws. I did not want the forty-ninth parallel to define nationhood. To paraphrase Charles Bowden, I did not want there to be Canadian pines or American pines, just as there aren't Canadian stars or American stars. Close up against the national border, that imaginary (never mind the scar cutting across the Pasayten) but compelling line, I held to the attitude of William Stafford in "At the Un-National Monument along the Canadian Border":

This is the field where the battle did not happen,
where the unknown soldier did not die.
This is the field where the grass joined hands,
where no monument stands,
and the only heroic thing is the sky.

After descending Cathedral Peak, we followed a trail east along the north side of a beautiful valley, beneath massive, glacier-scoured buttresses and through wildflower gardens alive with lavender and white phlox, magenta paintbrush, yellow cinquefoil, and blue lupine, against a canvas of vivid, mossy green. We crossed a pass below "Too Tired to Climb Peak," then descended into another valley until the trail curved into a short drainage, where we scrambled, self-consciously, toward Canada. In spite of our disdain for national boundaries, the notion of "Canada" still held some allure. But at the ridge we saw no sign of the border corridor—just a long, deep, and empty valley, ringed by mountain ridges. Although the wilderness to the north seemed exotic and seductive—Oh Canada!—we lacked enough ambition to descend into the trailless valley. So we halted, declared that we had attained our "furthest east," and headed back to camp.

The next day I felt weak and nauseous. I needed an easy walk, and so we hiked through small meadows and up a long, sandy slope to the crest of the ridge south of Upper Cathedral Lake. At the southern end of the ridge, on the small summit of "Nap Peak," we took our lunch; afterward I told Paul that I wanted to rest for awhile. He patiently acquiesced to my request and wandered down the ridge, while I found a sheltered, mostly fly-free alcove, and dozed for two hours—a rare behavior for me. I slept fitfully and drifted in and out of consciousness, pursued by a line from George Eliot: "The unmapped country within us." When I finally roused myself, I lay curled in my warm refuge and considered how Eliot's words related to our endeavor. Without maps, we were explorers of a sort, traveling through a mostly unknown country, our imaginations unfettered by the expectations provided by maps, and able to wander more freely. And the particularities of our experience, if not unique, were rendered uncommon by our mapless artifice. Yet the Pasayten had been explored and mapped by others—first by the Okanogan Indians, then by the Northwest Boundary Survey in 1859–1860, more recently by other surveys. In a similar way, each of us carries Eliot's "unmapped country" within, even though its uniqueness lies in the particulars created by details of our genes and experiences, and their interactions. These influences craft who we are and how we travel through the world; they grant us individuality. Yet humans are about 99.9 percent similar in their genetic makeup, and somewhere around 95 percent of the roughly twenty thousand genes in the human genome have only one allele—they are functionally invariant in terms of the proteins they produce. Others have gone before us and will go after us, people with whom we share almost all of our genetic material, and whose life experiences differ mostly in the details. Their basic concerns are similar, their joys are of the same essential substance, their hopes and fears are comparable to ours. We are more united than we sometimes recognize, or care to admit.

In one sense, Eliot was right: each person is unique and there is an unmapped country within. But in another crucial way, the country within us has been mostly mapped by others, and we had best unfold those maps and learn what we can from shared contours and coordinates of joy and suffering, cause and effect, desire and satisfaction. Paul later wrote me:

> When you were commenting on being in terrain without a map, I think that you meant that you were facing things you had never faced before. But a map might be there in that other people have faced similar circumstances, and that their experience has been shaped into a form for us in the literature they left behind. When Wendell Berry spoke at UCSB years ago, someone asked him if gardening should be taught in the schools. He replied that Homer and Shakespeare and the Bible should be taught in the schools, and that gardening should be taught after school. Then he went on to say that our stories have been lived before us, and that our literature gives us company and guidance when we think that we are alone.

Up high on Nap Peak, I lay in the warm and gentle afternoon sun, and considered these things. After some time I stood, brushed away a few flies, and called out to Paul. I felt better, and ready to hike; it was time to return to camp, and in the morning, turn to the west, and home.

It took us five more days to reach our trailhead. For the most part, we retraced our route: first the ridge northwest of Windy Peak, where the white-crowned sparrows were happy, then the long descent into the Ashnola River Valley, followed by the climb to Peeve Pass, and the undulating hike across Larch Pass and Three Fools Pass. The walking was easier than on the way into Upper Cathedral Lake; my pack was lighter and I had finally found my strength. It helped that the weather had turned cool and rainy, and the flies were mostly quiet, subdued by some magical combination of temperature, moisture, and phenology. We took our time, lingering over breakfast oatmeal and a second cup of tea, wandering off route on a long day hike, waiting out a succession of thunderstorms beneath our tarp. I read, and overcame my resistance to afternoon naps: the pleasant sound of rain against sheltering nylon, a warm sleeping bag, sleep, and then waking as the clouds dissipated and drifted eastward, the way we had come.

I felt relaxed and more comfortable with our walk, and the country. Near the end of the hike Paul observed that, without maps to guide us, our conceptual understanding of the Pasayten had developed more slowly, unfolding day by day. Without a map, we'd needed to be patient. Initially there was no overarching image, no a priori contextual framework, for understanding where we were and where we might go. Instead there was an immediacy and heightened focus to our experience. The tyranny of the future, and the anticipation of the path ahead, is one possible product of maps. But without a map, desire, which so powerfully pulls us forward through time and space, was diminished. Instead our attention was focused on the world before us, the insistent here and now of rock and meadow, fly and bird, sun and shadow. During the return from Cathedral Lake, the days began to slip away from me as I found a presence and rhythm. I felt as though I could wander for a long time — just walking and living out of a pack, without a map to guide or anchor me. On and on, north into Canada, or perhaps west across the crest of the Cascades, toward Ross Lake and the Picket Range.

And yet. Although I'd grown used to the rhythm of our hike and traveling without a map, there was in me a residual resistance to our mapless condition. I might use words like "comfort" and "relaxed" when describing my attitude, but I was not completely settled. What I missed, in a mostly subliminal way, was the security and protection that maps afford, the sense of knowing, precisely, where I was. I'd wanted to find all that I needed to know about my path in the sheer physical presence of the Pasayten, but it was not enough, not quite. I needed a map, with its definite boundaries, north arrow, and declination; I wanted to know the lay of the land, and the way in which the contour lines assemble themselves into a route. You read the map and then the country, and you understand where to travel.

On the eleventh day we climbed out of the Ashnola River Valley, waited out a rainstorm near Peeve Pass, then turned south. For the remainder of our trip we traveled against the glacial grain of the northern Pasayten, where Pleistocene ice had gouged the massive, U-shaped troughs of the Pasayten and Ashnola rivers. The rivers drained north, across the border and into Canada, while our route took us south, toward the Methow River. We walked away from the high country, away from basins holding the last remnants of winter snows, melting into meadows. Beyond Peeve Pass, Paul and I left the maintained trail, tracked a ridge, then descended a steep slope before climbing into a stunning amphitheater, perhaps a mile across, which we named "Beautiful Basin." The amphitheater was held within a deep bowl of red and tawny rock that opened toward the North Cascades, and was filled with a broad swath of rich meadow. Several streams meandered through gardens of white bog orchids, magenta paintbrush, marsh marigold, and thick pads of moss. At the west end of the meadow were stands of Engelmann spruce and larch; beyond, a series of back-lit, forested ridges and shadowed valleys, and then the main mass of the Cascades, its serrated ridges of black rock etched by gullies and basins of late-lying snow. Paul, ever the Shakespearian, quoted a line from *As You Like It*: "I like this place, and would willingly waste my time in it." We would camp here for the night, waste our time, and in the morning exit Beautiful Basin by crossing "Pulchritude Pass," south of the meadows.

After dinner we walked higher into Beautiful Basin and the quieting night. Below was our gold-and-tan tarp, the one human thing in all that space. A tumbling susurrus of meltwater drifted up from downslope, as the quarter moon sank into the western sky, and a distant quartet of hermit thrushes sang the last of the day toward darkness. In that tourmaline peace, my mind and heart were still. For the moment I felt happy and secure: I closed my eyes and put away whatever it was that made me fearful and anxious. For much of my life, I have been restless and unsettled, disinclined to appreciate what I have, disposed to yearn for what I do not have. I have reached for what the distant view suggested, rather than what the immediate ground promised. I have discovered some measure of peace and purpose in the natural world, in the deserts and mountains of this earth. I have taken much solace from these places, and from their creatures. I have found comfort and satisfaction in the physical demands of traveling through empty country, from all of the hikes, climbs, and paddles that have marked my days. The tenacity of life and the beauty of the earth have helped keep me sane. I truly do not know where I would be without wilderness and life's "tangled bank," and without the people with whom I have traveled. And so there are moments, as in Beautiful Basin, when all seems right with life, when one's history and sins fall away and you are in the presence of what I can only describe as grace. For a short while, you understand that you are holding the only the map that you will ever need, even if its details are less than certain.

You know exactly where you are. There, in the one place that you have ever wanted to be, there is no need to worry. The ice is gone, the drought not yet come. You have the best of your life; you are at peace with the world, and yourself. And even if these feelings are ephemeral and rare, you have their memory, and they are enough to bless you, always.

We went to bed beneath a clear sky, but awoke to a raw westerly wind, thick clouds, and spitting rain. We gobbled some granola and broke camp hurriedly, chased from Beautiful Basin by the sudden change in the weather. As we raced across Pulchritude Pass and descended into the marmot-filled "Whistle-pig Basin," the contrast between the numinous evening and dawn's chilly reality was jarring. Our retreat from Beautiful Basin seemed allegorical, perhaps a banishment from The Garden. Or maybe there were just those swirling clouds, the wind-driven mist condensing on my face, and the calls of marmots, echoing across the meadow. We walked until the weather improved and we encountered running water, then broke for tea. Paul talked of George Eliot and Thomas Hardy, and how they confronted the nineteenth-century religious doubt produced by, among other things, Victorian science. Eliot could not believe in God, but felt that humans could remain moral without faith in the Divine. Hardy's judgment was bleaker than Eliot's: he also did not believe in God, but had little hope that humans could behave morally without the Divine. Hardy's view was desolate and hopeless; where might we find our moral compass and compassion, if not in a belief in the nonexistent? Where, then, is our way through the world, our map into Beautiful Basin?

On the final day of the trip, Paul and I awoke to rain. We were away from camp by eight o'clock, then climbed for about two miles through broken lodgepole pine forest to the real Billy Goat Pass. And then it was down along the last few miles of easy trail to road's end, out of the Engelmann spruce and into Douglas fir and incense cedar: the Lowlands, rich with the scent of summer. Just before the trailhead, we passed the trail junction we missed on the first day. We had understood our error for some time, but the formerly invisible trail sign emphasized just how inept we'd been — to have missed the trail to Billy Goat Pass, and instead wandered off to Pseudo-Billy Goat Pass, a.k.a. Eightmile Pass. "Just call me Hopalong Perspicacity," said Paul. A final illustration of the perils of expectations and a fitting way to end the trip, which was even more anticlimactic than for most of my wilderness ventures: a few hundred yards of gentle downhill, and then a parking lot with a half dozen cars. Late in the morning of a July day, I slipped off my pack and stepped back into the world of roads, and maps. We threw our gear in the van, exchanged boots for sneakers, and began the drive that would return us to the familiar world. I had wanted an adventure, and to understand more about maps by traveling without them. I'd gotten these things, but I'd also desired some sort of powerful mapless metaphor, and this had eluded me.

Later, after showers, clean clothes, and a restaurant meal, Paul and I pulled out a map of the Pasayten and reconstructed our route. At first, I felt a surge of pleasure in tracing our passage and attaching names to the places we'd seen, and reflecting on the way in which we had traveled. But my delight was as ephemeral as the marsh marigolds that bloom below alpine snowbanks, and are quickly gone to seed. It was as though the map revealed too much of the wrong things: there were the names of rivers, mountains, and ridges; the meandering path of the trail; and the hard, insistent vector of the Canadian border, but the country itself had gone missing, in a more profound way than if we'd carried maps during our hike. Perhaps this was because the Pasayten map and my experiences were isolated from one another. This disconnect rendered the map less real; it was not the context for our travels. Three Fools Pass, Ashnola River, Cathedral Peak, "Windy Mountain," "Beautiful Basin," and "Pipit Pass," all of the named and nameless country, had been detached from the map's contours and coordinates. They were the province of a parallel dimension. I had no idea where this left me, and what message to take away from my hike. Later, though, I might understand. Or perhaps there would never be a message. Even though I was disinclined to do so, maybe I needed to leave it alone, and let the country, and my experiences, be enough.

We die containing a richness of lovers and tribes, tastes we have swallowed, bodies we have plunged into and swum up as if rivers of wisdom, characters we have climbed into as if trees, fears we have hidden in as if caves. I believe in such a cartography—to be marked by nature, not just to label ourselves on a map like the names of rich men and women on buildings. We are communal histories, communal books. We are not owned or monogamous in our taste or experience. All I desired was to walk upon an earth that had no maps.

I read this passage by Michael Ondaatje and know that my cartography has been inscribed by the ways in which I have been received and revived by the wild, a process that began in that plum orchard along the banks of Saratoga Creek. The natural world, and the love of my people, has created a profound and enduring map. I know the route, if only I can work my way through the debris of my history. And so I unfold my maps, run my eyes and mind across the intricate, imbricated network of their topologies, marvel at how time and the sensory attributes of my life (sight, sound, smell, touch, and taste) can be compressed into the printed dimensions of length and width: in my early years, the rich and sometimes sad spatials of a Saratoga orchard; the powerful seduction of those old oil-company road maps; and the magnetic pull of the *Starr's Guide* map, with its promise of adventure, beauty, and salvation. Later, the silent and empty enticement of the Demarcation Point quadrangle; the paths of the Panamint burros through the high-desert scrub, and how their maps became my maps; and the topography of the Oregon Cascades, the ways in which the rain and trees, glaciers, and cinders were written onto the maps my students made, as they learned to navigate. And, more recently, as I've moved through parenthood and into middle age: the routes to the "Lonely Train" and "Ouside," through the streets of Lawrence and the Beartooth Mountains; the stratigraphy of time, a path through the Grand Canyon, 1.5 billion years, and the first eighteen years of my daughter's life; and across the hundredth meridian, the aesthetics of a drive with my son and the manner in which I came into my home country. Of course, there are a thousand other maps out there, strewn across the landscapes of my days. I could begin again, and write narrative after narrative. But these maps will do. They flow together, mark a route through one life, a cartography of experience and dreams, love and longing.

And as I think back to the Pasayten, I understand that all of us travel, in different ways, through simultaneously mapped and mapless terrain. "All I desired was to walk upon an earth that had no maps." Well, it's there, always, in the ways that we confront each new world—one without boundaries, UTM coordinates, contour lines, names, and measured elevations. Yet at the same time we know that others have been there before us, and that they just might understand something important about finding the right direction through rough and unknown country. In spite of satellites, GPS devices, and computerized cartography, there will always be the blankness of Demarcation Point, just as there will always be the well-mapped streets of Lawrence, the 7.5-minute maps of the Santa Cruz Mountains, and the *Starr's Guide* map to the High Sierra—the symbols and images that carry us deep into the sensual world, and far into a desired country.

We go on.

Acknowledgments and Permissions

ost importantly, I would like to thank the people who have helped me draw, and follow, the maps of my life. There are too many to name here, but a few need to be mentioned. My sister, Lisa Hendricks, explored that Saratoga plum orchard with me, and together we endured the hardest years in the Santa Cruz Mountains. Her memories of our childhood were particularly important in writing the first three chapters of the book. My mother, Gwen Norment, also helped reconstruct some of my early years. Alan Beattie, Dick Penniman, and Don Summers were my first wilderness companions; together we found adventure, joy, and a sense of identity in the High Sierra and Big Sur country of California. Dr. Chuck Douglas hired me to study feral burros in Death Valley, and I'll always be grateful for the opportunity that he gave me, to roam the beautiful high-desert country of the Panamint Mountains. Many of my coworkers at Northwest (later Pacific Crest) Outward Bound—particularly Melissa Norment, Mac Bates, Bruce Jamieson, Susan Kinne, and Nancy Fitzsimmons—helped me find my way through the Three Sisters Wilderness in Oregon, and shared in the challenging, wonderful, exciting, and sometimes frustrating and exhausting work that came with teaching (and learning from) "OB" students. In the later years, my wife, Melissa, and children, Liza and Martin, have been my fellow cartographers in so many ways, and in so many places—Lawrence, Brockport, the Beartooth Mountains, the Grand Canyon, the High Plains, the Adirondacks, and Australia. (The best of times, and some pretty tough ones, too.) In particular, I'd like to thank Melissa for her steady love, patience, generosity, and determination. Finally, I'd like to doff a particularly smelly and dirty balaclava to Paul Willis, my companion on so many mountain trips, including our mapless ramble through the Pasayten Wilderness. Paul's sensitive, thoughtful, and ethical approach to the natural world also has helped my thinking about place, maps, and home.

Many people have helped directly in the writing of this book. Ralph Black, Melissa Norment, Lisa Hendricks, and Paul Hendricks read and commented on parts, or all, of the manuscript. In particular, Ralph's careful and wise reading of the early chapters helped me work out where I wanted to go with the book, and how to do it. Dr. Richard Leibe, professor emeritus of earth sciences at the College at Brockport, gave a close and valuable reading to the chapter "In the Fullness of Time"; whatever geological errors remain are entirely my own. Lisa Hendricks drew four of the maps in the book; Rhonda Hudgins drew the map that accompanies "They Always Knew Their Way," while Jim Zollweg created the map for "The Truth Shall Be Revealed." Jim Dusen and Richard Black of the College at Brockport helped transform several of the paper maps into electronic versions. Bob Gilliam, interlibrary-loan librarian at the College at Brockport, chased down many obscure references when I was collecting material for the book. Bob Kibee, map librarian at Cornell University, provided access to the university's wonderful and extensive collection, and helped me locate the Demarcation Point quadrangle described in "The Silence Was Like No Other." Joe Parsons and Carl Klaus at the University of Iowa Press believed in my project from early on, and provided the counsel, energy, and support necessary to see *In the Memory of the Map* through to publication. Others at the University of Iowa Press who have helped with this project include Karen Copp, Allison Means, and Charlotte Wright, while freelance editor Jonathan Haas did a superb job of copyediting the manuscript.

"Maps" by Robert Haas appeared in *Field Guide* by Robert Haas, published by Yale University Press, 1973. Copyright © 1973 by Robert Haas. Reprinted with permission of Robert Haas. "At the Un-National Monument Along the Canadian Border," by William Stafford, appeared in *The Way It Is: New and Selected Poems*, by William Stafford. Copyright © 1975, 1998 by William Stafford and the Estate of William Stafford. Reprinted with permission of Graywolf Press, Minneapolis, Minnesota, www.graywolfpress.org. "Native Stone" by Octavio Paz, translated by Muriel Rukeyser, from *Early Poems 1935–1955*, copyright

Source Notes

Introduction
"when we drove down that hill . . . ashamed of us": Hugo, R. 1984. "Turtle Lake," in *Making Certain It Goes On: The Collected Poems of Richard Hugo.* Norton, New York, NY, p. 239.

The Past Is Always with Me
fourth- and fifth-grade boys with bicycles: Moore, R. and D. Young. 1978. "Childhood Outdoors: Toward a Social Ecology of the Landscape," in I. Altman and J. F. Wohlwill, eds. *Children and the Environment.* Plenum Press, New York, NY, pp. 95–101.

divided themselves into competing schools: Matthews, M. H. 1984a. "Environmental Cognition of Young Children: Images of Journey to School and Home Area," *Transactions of the Institute of British Geography* 9: 89–105.

unreal transformations: Jackle, J. 1987. *The Visual Elements of Landscape.* University of Massachusetts Press, Amherst, MA, pp. 24–25.

a strict pattern of sequential development: Matthews, M. H. 1984a, p. 89.

"'Landscape' is not . . . a weakly structured space": Tuan, Y. 1974. *Topophilia.* Prentice-Hall, New York, NY, pp. 24–25.

"a prospect . . . from a specific standpoint": Ibid., p. 133.

"the external . . . subjective human experience": Quoted in Lippard, L. 1997. *The Lure of the Local: Senses of Place in a Multicultural Society.* The New Press, New York, NY, p. 7.

"scanning the land . . . panoramas and scenic overlooks": Nabhan, G. P. 1994. "A Child's Sense of Wildness," in G. P. Nabhan and S. Trimble. *The Geography of Childhood: Why Children Need Wild Places.* Beacon Press, Boston, MA, p. 5.

"by carefully . . . patterning is evident": Matthews, M. H. 1984a, p. 103.

"fairly sophisticated spatial cognition": Sandberg, E. H. and J. Huttenlocher. 2001. "Advanced Spatial Skills and Advance Planning: Components of 6-year-old's Navigational Map Use," *Journal of Cognition and Development* 2: 51–70.

"greater awareness of spatial elements": Matthews, M. H. 1984b. "Cognitive Mapping Abilities of Young Girls and Boys," *Geography* 69: 327–36.

"imagery of their immediate surroundings": Goodchild, B. 1974. "Class Differences in Environmental Perception: An Exploratory Study," *Urban Studies* 11: 157–69.

gatherers and foragers in our evolutionary past: Gaulin, S. J. and H. A. Hoffman. 1988. "Evolution and Development of Sex Differences in Spatial Ability," in Betzig, L., M. Borgerhof-Mulder and P. Turke, eds. *Human Reproductive Behavior: A Darwinian Perspective*. Cambridge University Press, New York, NY, pp. 129–52; also Silverman, I. M. Eals. 1992. "Sex Differences and Spatial Abilities: Evolutionary Theory and Data," in Barkow, J. H., L. Cosmides, and J. Tooby, eds. *The Adapted Mind*. Oxford University Press, New York, NY, pp. 533–49; Neave, N., C. Hamilton, L. Hutton, N. Tildesley, and A. T. Pickering. 2005. "Some Evidence of a Female Advantage in Object Location Memory Using Ecologically Valid Stimuli," *Human Nature* 16: 146–63.

"The Polemics of Spatial Ability": Gilmartin, P. P. and J. C. Patton. 1984. Comparing the Sexes on Spatial Abilities: Map-use Skills," *Annals of the Association of American Geographers* 74: 605.

What I Desired Most Was Escape

"took the concept . . . to magnificent heights": Yorke, D. A., Jr. and J. Margolies. 1996. *Hitting the Road: The Art of the American Road Map*. Chronicle Books, San Francisco, CA., p. 96.

"This is the . . . a world we might *know*": Wood, D. 1992. *The Power of Maps*. Guilford Press, New York, NY, p. 12.

"the locus of desire": Lippard, L. 1997. *The Lure of the Local: Senses of Place in a Multicultural Society*. The New Press, New York, NY, p. 4.

"a portion of . . . what will happen there": Ibid., p. 7.

when I was thirteen: Some of this material appeared in a different form in Norment, C. J. 2008. *Return to Warden's Grove*. University of Iowa Press, Iowa City, IA, pp. 147–48.

national credit card systems: Manning, R. D. 2000. *Credit Card Nation: The Consequences of America's Addiction to Credit*. Basic Books, New York, NY, pp. 84–85, 111, 310.

from $59 million to $400 million: Ibid., p. 85.

"the Central Valley . . . shone in all its glory": Muir, J. 1988. *The Mountains of California*. Sierra Club Books, San Francisco, CA, p. 2.

"Highways have . . . where the world could at last change": Koch, C. J. 1995. *Highways to a War*. Viking Press, New York, NY, pp. 230–31.

46,726-mile network that it is today: Federal Highway Administration. 2007. "Dwight D. Eisenhower National System of Interstate and Defense

Highways," www.fhwa.dot.gov/programadmin/interstate.cfm, [accessed May 2008].

distributed to American motorists: Yorke, D. A., Jr. and J. Margolies, p. 6.

New York City travel bureau in 1986: Ibid., p. 119.

the maturation of the Interstate Highway System: Ibid., p. 114–19.

the 1940s to 1960s era of free road maps: Ibid., pp. 114–16.

"So — when was it . . . roving the coast up and down": Quoted in Snyder, G. 1967. *The Back Country.* New Directions, New York, NY, epigraph.

"to find in motion what was lost in space": Williams, T. 1970. *The Glass Menagerie.* New Directions, New York, NY, p. 115.

It Was Impossible Not to Wonder

five primary, partly overlapping functions: Robinson, A. H. and B. B. Petchenik. 1976. *The Nature of Maps.* University of Chicago Press, Chicago, IL, p. 14.

"it is the map that precedes the territory": Quoted in Tucker, A. W., and R. Solnit. 1996. *Crimes and Splendors: The Desert Cantos of Richard Misrach.* Bullfinch Press, Little, Brown, Boston, MA, p. 40.

as Peter Turchi has observed: Turchi, P. 2004. *Maps of the Imagination: The Writer as Cartographer.* Trinity University Press, San Antonio, TX, pp. 215–20.

"Our trail follows . . . Muir Trail (8,300 — 4.0)": Starr, W. A., Jr. 1964. *Starr's Guide to the John Muir Trail and the High Sierra Region.* Sierra Club Books, San Francisco, CA, p. 63.

"Granite Basin . . . Kings River Canyon (5,035 — 9.0)": Ibid., p. 86.

"HEADS UP! . . . leave the trail and go cross-country": Morey, K. *et al.* 2006. *Sierra South: 100 Backcountry Trips in California's Sierra Nevada.* Eighth edition. Wilderness Press, Berkeley, CA, pp. 91–94.

"through *a cycle* . . . effort to comprehend and understand": Wood, D., p. 132.

travel toward the sacred fountain of Venus: Reitinger, F. 1999. "Mapping Relationships: Allegory, Gender and the Cartographical Image in Eighteenth-century France and England," *Imago Mundi* 51: 106–29.

"Map of the Island of Marriage": Ibid., pp. 119–22.

"Great Destructive Way Route": Ackerman, J. R. 2007. "Finding Our Way," in Ackerman, J. R. and R. W. Karrow, Jr., eds. *Maps: Finding Our Place in the World.* University of Chicago Press, Chicago, IL, pp. 19–63.

"We must remember . . . dance with in high school": Limerick, P. N. 1993. Dancing with the Professors: The Trouble with Academic Prose," *The New York Times Book Review*, October 31, p. 3.

Thus my desire for an identity: Some of this material appeared in a different form in Norment, C. J. 2008. *Return to Warden's Grove*. University of Iowa Press, Iowa City, IA, pp. 153–55.

"We cannot have . . . as David Brower says": Abbey, E. 1977. "Freedom and Wilderness, Wilderness and Freedom," in *The Journey Home: Some Words in Defense of the American West*. E. P. Dutton, New York, NY, pp. 227–38.

The Silence Was Like No Other

"Now when I was . . . I will go there": Conrad, J. 1971. *Heart of Darkness*. Second edition. W. W. Norton, New York, NY, p. 8.

vastness of the Brooks Range: Marshall, G. 2005. "Introduction," in Marshall, R. *Alaska Wilderness*. University of California Press, Berkeley, CA, p. xxxv.

"Conrad's delight in . . . ready for the taking": Harley, J. B. 2001. *The New Nature of Maps: Essays in the History of Cartography*. Johns Hopkins University Press, Baltimore, MD, p. 187.

legitimate title to the land: Turchi, P., pp. 28–33.

graphic and pictorial information: Cosgrove, D. 2007. "Mapping the World," in Ackerman, J. R. and R. W. Karrow, Jr., eds. *Maps: Finding Our Place in the World*. University of Chicago Press, Chicago, IL, pp. 65–115.

"I am deliberately . . . negative *blank spaces* of the older maps.": Harley, J. B., p. 86.

which nourishes us: Schafer, R. M. 1977. *The Tuning of the World*. Alfred Knopf, New York, NY, pp. 256–59.

economic, military, and political power: Harley, J. B., p. 91.

sickened residents in the 1970s: Monmonier, M. 1991. *How to Lie with Maps*. University of Chicago Press, Chicago, IL, pp. 115–21; Harley, J. B., pp. 187–89.

"No map can show . . . richness that justifies the map": Wood, D., p. 86.

"content generalization . . . the map's function or theme": Monmonier, M., p. 35.

"story contains . . . surrounded by blank spaces": Turchi, P., p. 42.

"The most accurate . . . not necessarily the best map": Ibid., p. 44.

"Oh, let me . . . ships clouted aground": Thomas, D. 1957. *The Collected Poems of Dylan Thomas*. New Directions, New York, NY, p. 192.

music of Anton Webern: Schafer, R. M., p. 252.

"The winds have died . . . penetrates each song": Hamill, S. and J. P. Seaton, eds. 2004. *The Poetry of Zen*. Shambhala, Boston, MA, p. 165.

"All that I desired . . . an earth that had no maps": Ondaatje, M. 1993. *The English Patient*. Vintage Books, New York, NY, p. 261.

"I learned not to fear . . . the white light of tomorrow": Roethke, T. 1975. "The Far Field," in *The Collected Poems of Theodore Roethke*. Anchor Books, Garden City, NY, p. 194.

"Thirty below on a windy . . . in the winds of space": Norment, C. J. 1989. *In the North of Our Lives*. Down East Books, Camden, ME, pp. 126–27.

"silence in the apophatic tradition": Lane, B. C. 1998. *The Solace of Fierce Landscapes: Exploring the Desert and Mountain Spirituality*. Oxford University Press, New York, NY, pp. 223–35.

"embrace of silence": Ibid, pp. 62–69.

"the mysteries of God's Word . . . brilliant darkness of a hidden silence": Corrigan, K. and L. M. Harrington. 2004. "Pseudo-Dionysius the Areopagite," in *The Stanford Encyclopedia of Philosophy*, http://plato.stanford.edu/entries/pseudo-dionysius-areopagite/, [accessed March 2009].

"the things that . . . save us in the end": Harvey, A. 1983. *A Journey in Ladakh*. Houghton Mifflin, New York, NY, p. 93.

"any disturbances . . . part of the signal": Schafer, R. M., p. 182.

human-perceived landscape: Ibid., pp. 3–12.

"audible acoustic energy . . . well-being of people": Kryter, K. D. 1987. *The Effects of Noise on Man*. Second edition. Academic Press, Orlando, FL, p.1.

difficulty attending to tasks: Singh, A. P. *et al.* 1982. "Effect of Chronic and Acute Exposure to Noise on Physiological Functions in Man," *International Archives of Occupational and Environmental Health* 50: 169–74; Schick, A. *et al.* 2000. "Noise Stress in Classrooms," in Schick, A. *et al.* eds. *Contributions to Psychological Acoustics: Results of the 8th Oldenburg Symposium on Psychological Acoustics*. Universität Oldenburg, Germany, pp. 533–39; Evans, G. W. *et al.* 2001. "Community Noise Exposure and Stress in Children," *Journal of the American Acoustical Society* 109: 1023–1027; Evans, G. W. *et al.* 2002. "Chronic Noise Exposure and Physiological Response: A Prospective Study of Children Living under Environmental Stress," *Psychological Science* 9: 75–77.

sensation is converted to pain: Kryter, K. D., p. 8.

pose a serious threat to hearing: Schafer, R. M., pp. 84–86, 183.

ambient noise that typifies an area: Kryter, K. D., p. 536.

to a majority of people: Ibid., pp. 8, 563–64.

30 decibels in sixty years: Schafer, R. M., p. 186.

intensity of 121–139 decibels: Flogor, B. J. and L. C. Cox. 2004. "Output Levels of Commercially Available Portable Compact Disc Players and the Potential Risk to Hearing," *Ear & Hearing* 25: 513–27.

"Every attack . . . more noise is present": Schafer, R. M., p. 129.

"Tranquility Mapping Project": Bell, S. 1999. *"Tranquility Mapping as an Aid to Forest Planning,"* Edinburgh, Scotland: Forestry Commission Information Note, http://forestry.gov.uk/pdf/fcin16.pdf.

They Always Knew Their Way

"exceed the environmental . . . possibly irreparable damage": United States National Park Service. 1976. *Management Options for Natural and Cultural Resources: Death Valley National Monument.* Death Valley National Monument, National Park Service, Department of the Interior, p. 61.

as high as anywhere in the United States: Mills, S. 1982. "The Burros in Death Valley," *Oryx* 16: 411–14.

"restor[ing] conditions . . . from nonnative plants or animals": United States National Park Service. 1976, p. 35.

in the southern Sudan, Ethiopia, and Somalia: United Nations Environment Program. 2009. "African Wild Ass — *Equus africanus,*" http://www .unep-wcmc.org/species/data/speciessheets/wildass.htm [accessed January 2009].

Panamint and Cottonwood mountains to the west: United States National Park Service. 1976, p. 34.

"wasteful foragers . . . and dropping the remains to the ground": McKnight, T. L. 1958. "The Feral Burro in the United States: Distribution and Problems," *Journal of Wildlife Management* 22:163–79.

"The bighorn is shy . . . will move to another area": Ibid., p. 171.

"Either eliminate . . . another lost American game animal": Ibid., p. 172.

"there seems to be . . . breeding by other ungulates": Ibid., p. 170.

"From time beyond . . . you can see along his back and shoulders": Weight, H. and L. Weight, quoted in Carothers, S. W. *et al.* 1976. "Feral Asses on Public Lands: An Analysis of Biotic Impact, Legal Considerations and Management Alternatives," *Transactions of the Forty-first North American Wildlife Conference* 41:396–406.

"Congress finds . . . fast disappearing from the American scene": Bureau of Land Management. 2009. "The Wild Free-Roaming Horses and Burros Act of 1971 (Public Law 92–195)," http://www.wildhorseandburro.blm. gov/92–195.htm, [accessed January 2009].

"At this stage . . . endanger other animals": Moehlman, P. D. 1972. "Getting to know the Wild Burros of Death Valley," *National Geographic* 141(4): 516–17.

"I recall the sights . . . For many years, I hope": Ibid., p. 517.

air temperatures are above 100°F: Tomkiewicz, S. 1979. *Heterothermy and Water Turnover in Feral Burros* (Equus asinus) *of the Desert Southwest.* M.S. Thesis, Arizona State University, Tempe, p. 56.

watered two or three times per day: Moehlman, P. D. 1973. *Behavior and Ecology of Feral Asses* (Equus asinus). PhD Dissertation, University of Wisconsin, Madison, p. 238.

"Close your eyes . . . not stone is light": Paz, O. 1973. "Native Stone," in *Early Poems, 1935–1955*. New Directions, New York, NY, p. 35.

body weight, much like the camel: Maloiy, G. M. O. 1970. "Water Economy of the Somali Donkey," *American Journal of Physiology* 219:1522–27.

with death following at about 18 percent loss: Schmidt-Nielsen, K. 1964. *Desert Animals: Physiological Problems in Heat and Water*. Oxford University Press, New York, NY, p. 5.

in less than five minutes: Maloiy, G. M. O., pp. 1522–27.

inhibits salivary gland function: Schmidt-Nielsen, K., p. 15.

15 percent of their body weight.: Maloiy, G. M. O., p. 1524.

that average about 3.5°F: Schmidt-Nielsen, K., p. 82.

an impressive 11.9°F: Tomkiewicz, S., p. iii.

"man is physically . . . unable to take care of himself.": Schmidt-Nielsen, K., p. 15.

Wood and Nemo Canyons: Norment, C. J. and C. D. Douglas. 1977. *Ecological Studies of Feral Burros in Death Valley*. Cooperative Park Resources Studies Unit, University of Nevada, Las Vegas, Contribution No. 17, p. 116.

which prevented burro access: Fisher, J. C. 1974. "Impact of Feral Asses on Community Structure in the *Acamptopapus-Grayia* Plant Community of the Panamint Mountains of Death Valley National Monument." Unpublished report.

at the site without burros: Carothers, S. W. *et al.*, pp. 399–403.

European discovery of North America: Leopold, A. S. *et al.* 1963. "Wildlife Management in the National Parks," *Transactions of the Twenty-fourth North American Wildlife Conference* 24:29–44.

two-and-one-half-million years ago: Oakenfull, E.A. *et al.* 2000. "A Survey of Equid Mitochondrial DNA: Implications for the Evolution, Genetic Diversity and Conservation of *Equus*," *Conservation Genetics* 1:341–55.

for at least thirteen thousand years: Weinstock, J. *et al.* 2005. "Evolution, Systematics, and Phylogeny of Pleistocene Horses in the New World: A Molecular Perspective," *PLoS Biology* 3:1–7.

"Pleistocene rewilding": Martin, P. S. 2005. *Twilight of the Mammoths: Ice Age Extinctions and the Rewilding of North America*. University of California Press, Berkeley, CA, pp. 207–13.

the dustbin of evolutionary history: Ibid., p. 29.

"alarming or intolerable,": Ibid., p. 189.

numerous other studies in the region: Abella, S. R. 2008. "A Systematic Review of Wild Burro Grazing Effects on Mojave Desert Vegetation, USA," *Environmental Management* 41:809–19.

"phylogenetic homeland . . . throttle back reintroduced equids": Martin, P. S., pp. 192–94.

"transformed by their . . . these special beings have inspired": Wild Mustang Coalition. 2009. "Peaceful Valley Donkey Rescue's Online Newsletter," http://www.wildmustangcoalition.org/id5.html, [accessed January 2009].

"The destructive aspect . . . vivid of all animal figures": Shepard, P. 1996. *The Others: How Animals Made Us Human.* Island Press, Washington, D.C., pp. 263–64.

6 percent protein and 25 percent moisture: Norment, C. J. and C. D. Douglas, p. 116.

located in the hippocampus: Burgess, N. *et al.* 2002. The Human Hippocampus and Spatial and Episodic Memory," *Neuron* 35:625–41; Harvey, C. D. *et al.* 2009. "Intracellular Dynamics of Hippocampal Place Cells During Virtual Navigation," *Nature* 461:941–46.

dissent from the majority view: Bolhuis, J. J. and E. M. Macphail. 2001. "A Critique of the Neuroecology of Learning and Memory," *Trends in Cognitive Sciences* 5: 426–33.

navigation and retrieving stored food: Burgess, N. *et al.*, p. 632.

the polygynous meadow vole: Jacobs, L. F. *et al.* 1990. "Evolution of Spatial Cognition: Sex-specific Patterns of Spatial Behavior Predict Hippocampal Size," *Proceedings of the National Academy of Sciences* 87: 6349–52.

than in other London drivers: Maguire, E. A. *et al.* 2000. "Navigation-related Structural Change in the Hippocampi of Taxi Drivers," *Proceedings of the National Academy of Sciences* 97:4398–4403.

even if they exist: Jacobs, L. F. 2003. "The Evolution of the Cognitive Map," *Brain, Behavior and Evolution* 62: 128–39; Bennett, A. T. D. 1996. "Do Animals Have Cognitive Maps?" *Journal of Experimental Biology* 199: 219–24.

"a powerful memory . . . short-cutting to occur": Bennett, A. T. D., p. 223.

"any representation of space held by an animal": Ibid., p. 219.

monkeys do possess cognitive maps: Burgess, N. *et al.*, pp. 631–32.

"hippocampal topographical maps": Burgess, N. *et al.*, pp. 631–34; Jacobs, L. F. 2003, pp. 128–32.

spatial memory in equids: Nicol, C. J. 2002. "Equine Learning: Progress and Suggestions for Future Research," *Applied Animal Behaviour Science* 78:193–208.

"the ability of horses . . . navigate over long distances": Ibid., p. 205.

"direct reduction by . . . most effective and humane method available": Norment, C. J. and C. D. Douglas, p. 125.

The Truth Shall Be Revealed

representational, configurational, and directional: Anderson, K. C. and G. Leinhardt. 2002. "Maps as Representations: Expert Novice Comparison of Projection Understanding," *Cognition and Instruction* 20: 283–321; Ishikawa, T.

and K. A. Kastens. 2005. "Why Some Students Have Trouble with Maps and Other Spatial Representations." *Journal of Geoscience Education,* 53: 184–97.

symbolization, scale, and projection: Anderson, K. C. and G. Leinhardt, p. 288.

"see through . . . to the world behind it": Anderson, K. C. and G. Leinhardt, p. 288.

recalling map information: For differing views on this issue, see Thorndyke, P. W. and C. Stasz. 1980. "Individual Differences in Procedures for Knowledge Acquisition from Maps," *Cognitive Psychology* 12: 137–75; Kulhavy, R. E. and W. A. Stock. 1996. "How Cognitive Maps Are Learned and Remembered," *Annals of the Association of American Geographers* 86: 123–45; Anderson, K. C. and G. Leinhardt, pp. 283–321.

mental rotation and related tasks: Dabbs, J. M., Jr. *et al.* 1998. "Spatial Ability, Navigation Strategy, and Geographic Knowledge among Men and Women," *Evolution and Human Behavior* 19: 89–98; Saucier, D. M. *et al.* 2002. "Are Sex Differences in Navigation Caused by Sexually Dimorphic Strategies or by Differences in the Ability to Use the Strategies?" *Behavioral Neuroscience* 116: 403–10; Ishikawa, T. and K. A. Kastens, p. 188.

relative to individual performance: Ibid.

little predictive power: Gilmartin, P. P. and J. C. Patton. 1984. "Comparing the Sexes on Spatial Abilities: Map-use Skills," *Annals of the Association of American Geographers* 74: 605–19; Prestopnik, J. L. and B. Roskos-Ewoldsen. 2000. "The Relations among Wayfinding Strategy Use, Sense of Direction, Sex, Familiarity, and Wayfinding Ability," *Journal of Environmental Psychology* 20: 177–91.

to stay on course: Sholl, M. J. *et al.* 2000. "The Relationship of Sex and Sense of Direction to Spatial Orientation in an Unfamiliar Environment," *Journal of Environmental Psychology* 20: 17–28.

"insufficiently constrained solution path": Anderson, K. C. and G. Leinhardt, p. 309.

"Pick and his coworkers": Pick, H. L. *et al.* 1995. "Topographic Map Reading," in Hancock, P. *et al.*, eds. *Local Applications of the Ecological Approach to Human-Machine Systems.* Lawrence Erlbaum Associates, Hillsdale, NY, pp. 255–84.

"In the context . . . subject to critical analysis": Bednarz, S. W. *et al.* 2006. "Maps and Map Learning in Social Studies," *Social Education* 70: 398–404.

used as propaganda, and to lie: Monmonier, M., pp. 1–4.

during the Cold War: Ibid., pp. 94–107; Harley, J. B., p. 64.

progresses toward greater accuracy: Andrews, J. H. "Meaning, Knowledge, and Power in the Map Philosophy of J. B. Harley," in Harley, J. B., pp. 1–32.

"break the assumed . . . reality and representation": Ibid., p. 152.

"borderland epistemologies": Quoted in Slingerland, E. 2008. *What Science Offers the Humanities.* University of Chicago Press, Chicago, IL, p. 87.

"The artificial reality . . . inscription devices [instrumentation]": Latour, B. and S. Woolgar. 1986. *Laboratory Life: The Construction of Scientific Facts.* Princeton University Press, Princeton, NJ, p. 64.

"do not conceive . . . artful creativity of scientists": Ibid., p. 129.

"exists as a . . . does not exist": Ibid., p. 110.

dangerously "disembodied": Slingerland, E., pp. 11–12.

"We begin to learn . . . cultural perspective": Harley, J. B., p. 153.

"Maps are never . . . themselves either true or false": Ibid., p. 53

"an intricate, controlled fiction": Muehrcke, P. C. quoted in Harley, J. B., p. 63.

"Body asking . . . do you keep up?": Snyder, G., trans. 1969. *Riprap and Cold Mountain Poems.* Four Season Foundation, San Francisco, CA, p. 37.

Fathering the Map

***Great Neighborhoods: How to Bring Them Home . . .* 1000 Friends of Wisconsin.** No date. *Great Neighborhoods: How to Bring Them Home.* Madison, Wisconsin, http://www.1kfriends.org, [accessed August 2009].

by "magnet" destinations: Ibid., p. 34.

free of adult supervision: Chabon, Michael. 2009. "Manhood for Amateurs: The Wilderness of Childhood," *The New York Review of Books* 56(12), http://www.nybooks.com/articles/archives/2009/jul/16/.

"moonlight seething on the sea": Park, R. 1993. *Fathering the Map: New and Selected Poems.* University of Chicago Press, Chicago, IL, p. 65.

In the Fullness of Time

destroyed any fossils present: Karlstrom, K. E. *et al.* 2003. "Paleoproterozoic Rocks of the Granite Gorges," in Beus, S. S. and M. Morales, eds. *Grand Canyon Geology.* Second edition. Oxford University Press, New York, NY, pp. 9–21.

for another 1.8 billion years or so: Payne, J. L. *et al.* 2009. "Two-phase Increase in the Maximum Size of Life over 3.5 Billion Years Reflects Biological Innovation and Environmental Opportunity," *Proceedings of the National Academy of Sciences* 106: 24–27.

Granite Gorge Metamorphic Suite: Karlstrom, K. E. *et al.*, p. 15.

some 1.3 billion years ago: Karlstrom, K. E. *et al.*, p. 37.

wonderfully termed "dike swarms": Karlstrom, K. E. *et al.*, p. 22.

all major, extant body types: Marshall, C. R. 2006. "Explaining the Cambrian 'Explosion' of Animals," *Annual Review of Earth and Planetary Sciences* 34: 355–84.

rise in global oxygen: Knauth, L. P. and M. J. Kennedy. 2009. "The Late Precambrian Greening of the Earth," *Nature* 460:728–36.

in the late Precambrian: Payne, J. L. *et al.*, p. 25.

"inarticulate brachiopods": Middleton, L. T. and D. K. Elliott. "Tonto Group," in Beus, S. S. and M. Morales, p. 94.

bivalves, snails, nautiloids, and fish: Beus, S. S. Redwall Limestone and Surprise Canyon Formation," in Beus, S. S. and M. Morales, pp. 120–23.

connects us to the Eternal: Rothenberg, D. 2005. *Why Birds Sing.* Basic Books, New York, NY, pp. 194–95.

limestones, conglomerates, and gypsum: Blakey, R. C. "Supai Group and Hermit Formation," in Beus, S. S. and M. Morales, p. 136.

Pennsylvanian Period to the early Permian: Beus, S. S. and M. Morales. "Introducing the Grand Canyon," in Beus, S. S. and M. Morales, p. 7.

delightfully named "hiatus problem": McKee, E. D. 1976. "Paleozoic Rocks of the Grand Canyon," in Breed, W. J. and E. Roat, eds. *Geology of the Grand Canyon.* Museum of Northern Arizona, Flagstaff, AZ, pp. 42–64.

"The tectonic layers . . . absolutely present and alive": Schlink, B. *The Reader.* Vintage, New York, NY, p. 217.

close to complete annihilation: Benton, M. J. and R. J. Twitchett. 2003. "How to Kill (Almost) All Life: The End-Permian Extinction Event," *Trends in Ecology and Evolution* 18: 358–65.

an upright, bipedal, tool-using great ape: Foley, R. A. and R. Lewin. 2004. *Principles of Human Evolution.* Blackwell Science, Malden, MA, p. 217.

"The psychology . . . that of our experiences": Fraisse, P. 1982. "The Adaptation of the Child to Time," in Friedman, W. J., ed. *The Developmental Psychology of Time.* Academic Press, New York, NY, pp. 113–40.

time, distance, and speed: Richards, D. D. "Children's Time Concepts: Going the Distance," in Friedman, W. J., pp. 13–14.

to the uncertain future: Harner, L. "Talking about the Past and the Future," in Friedman, W. J., pp. 141–69.

Patterns of order and recurrence: Friedman, W. J. "Conventional Time Concepts and Children's Structuring of Time," in Friedman, W. J., pp. 171–79.

species that ever lived are extinct: Raup, D. 1992. *Extinction: Bad Genes or Bad Luck?* W. W. Norton, New York, NY, p. 4.

"There is hardly . . . and death in adult terms": Lonetto, R. 1980. *Children's Conception of Death.* Springer, New York, NY, p. 31.

"our blood is time": Michaels, A. 2001. "Miner's Pond" in *Poems.* Alfred Knopf, New York, NY, p. 63.

move, live, and perceive the world: Solnit, R. 2003. "The Annihilation of Time and Space," *New England Review* 24(1): 5–19.

"God created . . . perished in the Flood": Vail, T. 2003. *The Grand Canyon: A Different View.* Master Books, Green Forest, AR, p. 8.

"not much happened . . . roughly 4,500-year period since": Ibid., p. 36.

"dating methods . . . what we observe today": Ibid., p. 41.

"There is . . . not restricted to children": Lonetto, R., p. 30.

around six million years ago: Powell, L. J. 2005. *Grand Canyon: Solving Earth's Grandest Puzzle.* Pearson Education, New York, NY, pp. 245—49; Pederson, J. L. 2008. "The Mystery of the Pre-Grand Canyon Colorado River — Results from the Muddy Creek Formation," *GSA Today* 18(3): 4—10.

"roughly ten to fifteen million years": Beus, S. S. and M. Morales. "Introducing the Grand Canyon," in Beus, S. S. and M. Morales, pp. 1—8.

And Then I Was Home

beginning of the twentieth century: Vogeler, I. 1995. "Dairying and Dairy Barns in the Northern Midwest," in Noble, A. G. and H. G. H. Wilhelm, eds. *Barns of the Midwest.* Ohio University Press, Athens, OH, pp. 99—124.

storage space than the gambrel roof: Ibid., p. 105.

"Wilderness is the . . . artifact called civilization": Leopold, A. 1968. *A Sand County Almanac.* Oxford University Press, New York, NY, p. 188.

east of the Missouri River: Barkley, T. M., ed. 1972. *Atlas of the Flora of the Great Plains.* Iowa State University Press, Ames, IA, p. 13.

"satisfying transcontinental dovetail": Gilfillan, M. 1998. *Chokecherry Places: Essays from the High Plains.* Johnson Books, Boulder, CO, p. 113.

agriculture without irrigation: Stegner, W. 1954. *Beyond the Hundredth Meridian: John Wesley Powell and the Second Opening of the West.* University of Nebraska Press, Lincoln, NE, pp. 212—31.

one person per square mile: U.S. Census Bureau. 2000. "Harding County Quick Facts," http://quickfacts.census.gov/qfd/states/46/46063.html, [accessed November 2009].

Homestead Act of 1862: Stegner, W., pp. 212—31.

four thousand acres: Webb, W. P. 1931. *The Great Plains.* 1971 printing. Grosset & Dunlap, New York, NY, p. 396.

under the Homestead Act failed: Stegner, W., p. 221. A lower estimate for Nebraska is in Socolofsky, H. E. 1968. "Success and Failure in Nebraska Homesteading," *Agricultural History* 42: 103—8.

"the *untransacted* destiny . . . to subdue the continent": Schnell, J. C. 1975. "William Gilpin and the Cosmopolitan Road," *Montana: Magazine of the West* 25(1): 32—41.

population increased by 19 percent: Pacific Northwest Regional Economic Analysis Project, http://www.pnreap.org/South_Dakota/, [accessed November 2009].

compared to the national rate of **12.8 percent**: U.S. Census Bureau. 2008. "Jones County Quick Facts," http://quickfacts.census.gov/qfd/ states/46/46075.html, [accessed November 2009].

two more births than deaths: South Dakota State University Department of Animal and Range Science. "County Profiles," http://ars.sdstate.edu/ SD%20County%20Profiles/Profiles.htm, [accessed November 2009].

greater than in 2000: Hobbs, F. and N. Stoops. 2002. *"Demographic Trends in the 20th Century,"* U.S. in Census Bureau: Census 2000 Special Reports Series CENSR-4., U.S. Government Printing Office, Washington, D.C.

"Beautiful my desire . . . place of my desire": Roethke, T. 1975. "The Rose," in *The Collected Poems of Theodore Roethke.* Anchor Books, Garden City, NY, pp. 196–99.

"So much space . . . and unchanging earth": Malouf, D. 1998. *The Conversations at Curlow Creek.* Vintage, New York, NY, pp. 21, 52–53.

"momentary vacuum . . . all that I love": Nabokov, V. 1989. *Speak, Memory: An Autobiography Revisited.* Vintage, New York, NY, p. 139.

33 percent during the same period: Pacific Northwest Regional Economic Analysis Project, http://www.pnreap.org/South_Dakota/, [accessed November 2009].

"on through the deep . . . the earth's held breath": Fairchild, B. H. 2003."The Blue Buick: A Narrative," in *Early Occult Memory Systems of the Lower Midwest.* W. W. Norton, New York, NY, p. 75.

Without a Map

"all maps are useless . . . and the darkness within": McGrath, C. 1999. "Campbell McGrath," in *Road Atlas: Prose & Other Poems.* Harper Collins, New York, NY, pp. 73–74.

"No exploratory adventure . . . the lands to be explored": Quoted in Lopez, B. H. 1986. *Arctic Dreams.* Scribner, New York, NY, p. 284.

"creates a false . . . enforced perspective": Richard Panek, quoted in Turchi, P., p. 226.

"if we had no . . . it's hard to tell jokes to dogs": Ibid., pp. 182–83.

"music finds its . . . into the less solid heart": Camus, A. 1979. *Selected Essays and Notebooks.* Penguin Books, New York, NY, p. 50.

"between words is . . . the unmapped and the unmappable": Solnit, R. 2006. *A Field Guide to Getting Lost.* Penguin Books, New York, NY, pp. 161–62.

"A prerequisite for . . . a place somehow unfamiliar": Turchi, P., p. 113.

"No radar . . . my best guess": Roger Clyne and the Peacemakers. 2007. "Contraband," on *No More Beautiful World*, compact disc, Emma Java Recordings.

higher-elevation forests: Williams, D. W. and A. M. Liebhold. 2002. "Climate Change and the Outbreak Ranges of Two North American Bark Beetles," *Agricultural and Forest Entomology* 4: 87–99.

"mapping is a . . . experience of the environment *shareable*": Wood, D., p. 79.

"My compass . . . with the prune pits": Daumal, R. 1960. *Mount Analogue*. Pantheon Books, New York, NY, p. 43.

"Memory is the . . . loss pulls us after it": Robinson, M. 1980. *Housekeeping*. Farrar, Straus, & Giroux, New York, NY, p. 194.

"With land this open . . . there is no wind": Hugo, R. 1984. "Camas Prairie School," in *Making Certain It Goes On: The Collected Poems of Richard Hugo*. Norton, New York, NY, p. 209.

"the things we . . . side of that transformation": Solnit, R. 2005, p. 5.

"An environment without . . . categorical forms, awful": Shepard, P. 1976. *Man in the Landscape*. Alfred Knopf, New York, NY, pp. 41–43.

"Naming a place . . . an act of dispossession": Harley, J. B., pp. 178–79.

is an exception: Washington Place Names Index, Tacoma Public Library, Tacoma, WA., http://research.tpl.wa.us/wanames, [accessed April 2009].

"the urge to mark . . . make the unknown known": McFarlane, R. 2004. *Mountains of the Mind: Adventures in Reaching the Summit*. Vintage Books, New York, NY, p. 191.

"Olena . . . the names of the things are stubbornest": Hass, R. 1973. "Maps," in *Field Guide*. Yale University Press, New Haven, CT, p. 9.

since about 5000 B.C.E.: Gordon, B. H. C. 2005, "8000 years of Caribou and Human Seasonal Migration in the Canadian Barrenlands," *Rangifer*, 16: 155–62.

"This view is what . . . things go bad" : Hugo, R. 1984. "A Good View from Flagstaff," in *Making Certain It Goes On: The Collected Poems of Richard Hugo*. W. W. Norton, New York, NY, p. 351.

"It's not only . . . thought of being bounded": Leopold, A., p. 41.

"a vast growling machine . . . sheltered places of sedition": Schama, S. 1995. *Landscape and Memory*. Alfred Knopf, New York, NY, p. 73.

artifact of this agreement: Becky, F. 2003. *Range of Glaciers: The Exploration and Survey of the Northern Cascade Range*. Oregon Historical Society Press, Portland, OR, p. 145.

one million people dead: Wolpert, S. 2000. *A New History of India*. Oxford University Press, New York, NY, pp. 346–49.

"It is an irony . . . its essential truth": Leopold, A., pp. 22–23.

Canadian stars or American stars: This is a version of a line used by Charles Bowden in "The Only Place to Go," *Harper's Magazine*, October 2008, pp. 15–16.

"This is the field . . . thing is the sky": Stafford, W. 1998. *The Way It Is: New and Selected Poems*. Graywolf Press, St. Paul, MN, p. 56.

the proteins they produce: Miller, R. D. *et al.* 2005. "High-density Single-nucleotide Polymorphism Maps of the Human Genome," *Genomics* 86: 117–26; Witherspoon, D. J. *et al.* 2007. "Genetic Similarities within and between Human Populations," *Genetics* 176: 351–59.

"We die containing . . . an earth that had no maps": Ondaatje, M., p. 261.

sightline books . . . .

The Iowa Series in Literary Nonfiction